PRAISE FOR
HOLY BORROWERS

"Most pastors see big visions; however, we also can tend to rush an important step—financing them. Too often, we treat this step as a simple formality, when in fact, it could mean the life or death of the vision. *Holy Borrowers*, written by my wonderful and gifted wife, Lisa Autry (Yes, I am partial!), consolidates over 30 years of sound commercial banking guidelines with practical Biblical wisdom. Lisa uses her extensive banking experience and actual church case studies to help us all make the "right decisions" for funding our vision.

The book is a must read for pastors, executive boards, administrators, finance committees, and capital fund-raising teams. It will bring sound equilibrium to the visionary process by addressing all the complex issues in funding. In a culture of unprecedented change, church leaders must remain on the cutting edge of financing matters. Lisa's financial knowledge has blessed our church many times over, ensuring a great legacy of ministry. In Lisa, God has given pastors a wonderful commercial banker with extraordinarily sound advice, who deeply cherishes the vision as much as we do. This is the blessing of *Holy Borrowers*—to ensure and even extend the legacy of our visions, long after we are gone."

– Dr. Terrence Autry
Lead Pastor, Christ Community

"*Holy Borrowers* is informative, instructional, and most of all, inspiring! Senior/Lead Pastors will benefit by requiring their leaders to read this book. God has ordained Lisa Autry's life to result in this thorough guide to church borrowing. Ivy League economics, UCLA MBA, career highs and lows, providing experience in major and small loans that were paid in full, others that were 'worked out,' discriminated against and honored with redemption...this book provides the detail to help churches understand if borrowing is right for them and gives insight on how to work with lenders. It also inspires confidence that He desires your best."

– Dallas Diggs
Executive Director-Administration, Oak Cliff Bible Fellowship

"I believe pastors feel the pressure to enter into financial contracts without the knowledge needed to be successful. The call to 'walk by faith' and to 'build it and they will come' does not provide churches with adequate information to walk into their God-given future. *Holy Borrowers*, by Lisa Miller Autry, enables pastors to equip both their leadership teams and their congregations in the area of church finance. *Holy Borrowers* is easy to read and not only prepares the hearts of the people of God, but also gives us insights and step-by-step directions for moving into the future, ready to conquer the land. We can't wait for the book to be in print, as we 'get ready before we are ready' to move in God's direction for our growth. Thank you for sending *Holy Borrowers* to equip the people of God!"

– **Pastor Brenda Brooks Alexander**
Lead Pastor, Campus Drive United Methodist Church

"Having known and worked closely with Lisa Autry in the banking industry for over a decade prior to her retirement, I can say there is no one better equipped to provide such insightful wisdom to the reader as she has in this work. Her expertise in formulating *Holy Borrowers* comes from both sides of the credit equation, having served as not only a banker, contemplating loans for other churches over several decades, but also possessing the direct and personal experience from the 'other side of the fence' in seeking and managing funding for the church planted by her husband, Dr. Terrence Autry, and herself. In light of that wisdom, her book reads as an exceptionally balanced piece that looks at the process from both sides of the transaction.

Should you find yourself in need of funding and know little of the proceedings involved, I consider *Holy Borrowers* a "must read" to adequately prepare you for what can be an arduous process. Personally, having been involved on the Credit side of banking for 40 years, during which time I have approved countless loans to religious and other non-profit entities, I can attest to both the completeness and accuracy of her treatise, and would unequivocally recommend her work to anyone in the non-profit field who may lack a thorough understanding of options and requirements for financing needs."

– **Peter Carey**
Senior Credit Officer

HOLY
BORROWERS

HOLY
BORROWERS

EQUIPPING CHURCH LEADERS FOR BUILDING FINANCE

LISA MILLER AUTRY

Published by reMix Publishing
P.O. Box 3143, Cedar Hill, TX 75106
475 E. FM 1382, Cedar Hill, TX 75104-9998
www.remixpublishing.com

Hardcover ISBN 978-1-7350282-00
Paperback ISBN 978-1-7350282-1-7

Library of Congress Control Number: 2020909120

Printed in the United States of America

Cover Design by Tonya Neal

DEDICATIONS

To my Heavenly Father who loved all people enough to
send His only begotten Son, Jesus the Messiah, to save our
souls and infuse our lives with His Awesome Presence.

To my father in heaven, Alfred Abram Bulkley Miller, Jr.,
who told me as a child, "Be proud, beautiful, and brilliant"—
which grounded me in ways only a daddy's love can.

To my mother in heaven, Adele Elvira Ritzberg Miller,
who modeled being proud, beautiful, and brilliant
every day of her life and twice on Sundays.

TABLE OF CONTENTS

Foreword by Dr. Frederick Douglass Haynes, III..ix

Introduction..xi

PART I. PREPARATION

Section Overview...2

Chapter 1   Should You Borrow?...3

Chapter 2   The Role of Faith..13

Chapter 3   Getting Ready Before You're Ready......................................21

Chapter 4   Common Banking Terminology...39

Chapter 5   Race, Discrimination, and the Banking Industry...............55

PART II. INSIDE THE BANK'S CREDIT PROCESS

Section Overview..72

Chapter 6   Character...75

Chapter 7   Cash Flow..83

Chapter 8   Collateral...93

Chapter 9   Capital..109

Chapter 10   Conditions...119

Chapter 11   Unique Guidelines for Churches..133

Chapter 12   The Loan Evaluation Process...143

PART III. ADVANCED LENDING TOPICS

Section Overview...158

Chapter 13   The Loan's Funded! Now What?...159

Chapter 14   Construction Loans...165

Chapter 15   Balloon Notes..177

Chapter 16   If the Loan Goes South...................................187
Chapter 17   In the Midst of COVID-19............................205

PART IV. LESSONS FROM SUCCESSFUL CHURCHES

Section Overview..220
Chapter 18   Lessons from Mt. Hebron Missionary Baptist Church........221
Chapter 19   Lessons from Friendship-West Baptist Church............233

Conclusion...253

APPENDICES

Appendix I   Sample Church Loan Application Checklist........259
Appendix II   Sample Financial Statements.....................265
Appendix III Calculation of Debt Service Coverage Ratio........269
Appendix IV   Sample Trend Analysis...........................273
Appendix V   Guidelines for Selecting an Attorney.............281

Acknowledgments...287
Bibliography..291
Index of Key Terms and Topics..299

FOREWORD
BY DR. FREDERICK DOUGLASS HAYNES, III

"If I knew then what I know now" is an old saying tinged with regret but illuminated by the insight of hindsight. After reading *Holy Borrowers* by Lisa Miller Autry, I remixed the age-old adage: "If I knew then what *Holy Borrowers* taught me now!" *Holy Borrowers* is a brilliantly written blessing to the Body of Christ that will practically help you navigate the "land minds" of loans and avoid the "loan sharks" that prey on unsuspecting church leaders who are walking by faith to fulfill God's vision. *Holy Borrowers* is a "banking GPS" that will equip and empower you with direction so that God's vision will come to fruition for your ministry.

Rev. Lisa Autry writes *Holy Borrowers* from the vantage point of being a lover of our Lord Jesus Christ and His church and as an "insider" who successfully worked in the banking industry. Lisa was lauded and applauded for her leadership and service during her auspicious tenure at one of our nation's leading banking institutions. *Holy Borrowers* is informed by the insight of an insider who knows the systems and language of banking and borrowing.

At the same time, *Holy Borrowers* comes to us from one who lives in connection with Christ and faithfully serves His Church. *Holy Borrowers* is a gift that will position you to win the game of borrowing. To illustrate, imagine playing for a sports team but your opponent plays in a different league. The rules are different. The language is unlike anything you've ever heard. The game is going to be played according to the rules your opponent plays by and on the turf of your opponent. One would need more than faith and talent to compete. You would need to know the language and the rules. It would be powerfully beneficial if your team was blessed with a bilingual coach who had starred in the other league and was passionately committed to your success. Rev. Lisa Autry is our bilingual coach who starred in banking and she's determined that churches have fruitful, God-glorifying ministries.

Holy Borrowers does not avoid the issues of race and racism in banking. Rev. Lisa Autry is a proud Christian Black woman who stands against racial injustice. Racism continues to be an organizing principle structured into systems of the "yet to be United States." An ugly history of redlining Black communities by the banking industry produced segregation in housing. Unfortunately, redlining has evolved, and racism continues to infect and inform banking practices. In *Holy Borrowers*, Lisa diagnoses "mental redlining" and the other "isms" that poison the possibilities of marginalized churches and communities. However, Rev. Autry also offers strategies for persisting through and navigating around racism in banking.

I reference Rev. Autry's tackling the issue of race in banking as one example of the fact that *Holy Borrowers* keeps it real and honestly and sagaciously deals with the issues and challenges that so many communities of faith have been hit and hurt by. It is not hyperbole to say that for some, borrowing wasn't holy but an existential and economic hell.

I write this foreword as a pastor with loan scars from the hell of borrowing. Our church was bitten by a predatory loan. However, reading *Holy Borrowers* has brought a measure of healing and fills my heart with hope that you and your ministry will be blessed by this banking GPS, and will victoriously reach the destination of fulfilling God's vision for your ministry. Read *Holy Borrowers* and you will thank God for what you know now, thanks to this gift from our anointed coach, Rev. Lisa Miller Autry.

Peace and Power,
Dr. Frederick Douglass Haynes, III
Senior Pastor
Friendship-West Baptist Church

INTRODUCTION

"Wisdom is the principal thing; therefore, get wisdom:
and with all thy getting get understanding."
— PROVERBS 4:7 KJV

"I think a lot of churches were not really prepared.
We have pastors who read the Bible and interpret
Scripture, but a lot were really not paying
attention to what was going on economically."
— AXEL ADAMS, Rainbow PUSH [1]

I n 2012, in the midst of the "Great Recession," *Reuters* released an article entitled, "Banks are Foreclosing on America's Churches in Record Numbers." The article cited the example of a 159-year old church in Georgia that had obtained an $850,000, five-year balloon note in 2005 to finance a new 300-seat sanctuary. When the loan matured in 2010, the church could not repay or refinance the balance. Their lender ultimately foreclosed on the property.

1   Craig Schneider, "Foreclosure Crisis Hitting Some Metro Churches," *Atlanta Journal-Constitution*, February 2, 2011, online: https://www.ajc.com/business/foreclosure-crisis-hitting-some-metro-churches/73kmzappmPRlavfWD41aaM/.

According to the article, the church's senior pastor shared this telling statement:

> "The bank has refused to negotiate and to this day I just don't know why."[2]

Two years earlier, *The Atlanta Journal-Constitution* had reported about this same church. In their article, an official for the governing body of that church's denomination shared a different perspective. He stated:

> "Frankly, I think the bank did everything they could to keep this from happening. No bank in the world wants to foreclose on a church."[3]

Two different viewpoints from two different people about the same church loan. In my opinion, the most noteworthy phrase in the communication above is the pastor's: "...and to this day, I just don't know why." (emphasis added). Meanwhile, the official in the church's governing body asserted that the bank had tried to work with the church, but to no avail.

In 2014, the *Fort Worth Star-Telegram* reported that a prominent church faced foreclosure after defaulting on $31.5 million in loans. Per the article, the pastor e-mailed that the church:

> "...is completely current on its mortgage payments through the end of the term of the notes and has attempted, in good faith, to meet every demand made upon it... Never in our discussions was there a mention of the possibility of [the lender] not renewing the

2   Tim Reid, "Banks are Foreclosing on America's Churches in Record Numbers," *Reuters*, March 8, 2012, online: https://www.reuters.com/article/us-usa-housing-churches/banks-foreclosing-on-churches-in-record-numbers-idUSBRE82803120120309

3   Bill Banks, "Foreclosure Threatens Survival of Longtime Lithonia Church," *Atlanta Journal-Constitution*, December 27, 2010, online: https://www.ajc.com/news/local/foreclosure-threatens-survival-longtime-lithonia-church/mrL8SRHGOG8moCr7MqdAdO/.

note and demanding the full payment at the end of the five years.
A rollover loan was the stated and expected course of action." [4]

In May 2019, Garnet Capital Advisors posted a blog headlined,
"Church Foreclosures Are on the Rise—Here's What Lenders Need to
Know." It was written as a resource for lenders, not for churches. Here's
an excerpt regarding what lenders face at the prospect of foreclosing on
a church:

> "...negative perceptions, single purpose buildings and headline
> risk. Banks often steer clear of lending to churches for this very
> reason in an effort to avoid getting stuck in a difficult position
> that doesn't usually end well for anyone involved. They simply
> don't want to be viewed as a source of objection for churches
> that comes down hard with a financial hammer and forecloses
> if the mortgage is unpaid.
>
> The problem doesn't end there, unfortunately. Even after
> foreclosure occurs, banks and lenders are often left with a large
> asset that's extremely difficult to turn around and sell to recoup
> their losses." [5]

This lack of common ground between church leaders and lenders[6]
occurs repeatedly in the United States every year. There are numerous
stories that don't make headline news, but which are no less heartbreaking for churches and their leadership teams.

---

4 Sandra Baker, "Arlington's High Point Church Faces Foreclosure on 107-Acre Property," *Fort Worth Star-Telegram*, May 20, 2014, online: https://www.star-telegram.com/news/business/article3858539.html.

5 Garnet Capital Advisors, "Church Foreclosures Are on the Rise—Here's What Lenders Need to Know," May 15, 2019, online: https://www.garnetcapital.com/news/article/Church-Foreclosures-Are-on-the-Rise----Heres-What/40062757.

6 I learned early in my career that good banks are not just "lenders;" that is, banks should do more than loan money. That said, in this context, I will use the terms *bank* and *lender* (and their derivatives) interchangeably to include banks, savings and loans institutions, credit unions, and non-bank financial institutions.

So, who's to blame?

In many instances, members of the church community hold lenders accountable for making loans to churches that are not financially sophisticated; for funding loans that never should have been approved at all. Certainly, predatory lending to churches (and to individuals) has occurred in the past and still takes place today.

"Predatory Lending" has no simple definition, but according to the Federal Deposit Insurance Corporation ("FDIC"):

> "Predatory lending involves at least one, and perhaps all three, of the following elements:
>
> › Making unaffordable loans based on the assets of the borrower rather than on the borrower's ability to repay an obligation;
> › Inducing a borrower to refinance a loan repeatedly in order to charge high points and fees each time the loan is refinanced ("loan flipping"); or,
> › Engaging in fraud or deception to conceal the true nature of the loan obligation, or ancillary products, from an unsuspecting or unsophisticated borrower."[7]

Certainly, these tactics have occurred within the church financing market. In 2008, *The New York Times* reported that in the years immediately prior to the Great Recession, specialty financing companies started bundling church mortgages to be sold to investors, and that Moody's Investors Service even rated several church mortgage securitizations just before that financial crisis.[8]

In that same article, an Executive Vice President of Bank of the West admitted the following:

---

7   Federal Deposit Insurance Corporation, "FDIC's Supervisory Policy on Predatory Lending," January 22, 2007, online: https://www.fdic.gov/news/news/financial/2007/fil07006.pdf.
8   Louise Story, "Foreclosures Don't Spare the House of God," *New York Times*, December 26, 2008, online: https://www.nytimes.com/2008/12/27/business/27church.html.

"Lenders loaned far too much, they loaned into lofty projections of future growth, and they just saddled the churches with far too much debt."[9]

I've seen numerous church loans that never should have been funded; in fact, the anguish stemming from these loans was the motivation for this book. *Holy Borrowers* closes with lessons learned from a prominent church that was severely impacted by a predatory lender. As a member of the church community, I grieve with those who have lost momentum and even buildings, particularly because of predatory lending.

As important as this issue is, however, I still have to ask the following question: Is predatory lending the full extent of the problem?

Lenders certainly would disagree, and I fully understand that perspective as well. Pastors and church leaders[10] seeking to obtain financing for church buildings frequently *drive* the process with the lender and in fact, often take lenders to task for declining their request for financing.

If there are predatory lenders who "saddle churches with too much debt," there also are church leaders who vilify non-predatory bankers who in good conscience, decline churches' requests for debt. That vilification often is shared with members of the church and sometimes, through the media to the public at large.

Moreover, church leaders who sign their loan documents state they have every intention of paying back the loan according to the terms of the agreement—including in the many cases where those terms are clearly explained.

What is the biggest issue, then? I would argue that the biggest issue in church finance is not the banks and it's not a lack of integrity or intentionality among church leaders. I believe the biggest issue that church leaders face in this area is the lack of financial knowledge on the part of pastors and church leaders who are leading their congregations in the area of finance!

---

9   Ibid.
10   It is understood that a pastor *is* a church leader; however, I make this distinction throughout *Holy Borrowers*, recognizing a senior or lead pastor's unique role within the overall church leadership structure. "Pastor" also encompasses other titles, such as Bishop, Elder, and Rector.

Let me highlight why this is an issue by asking a couple of rhetorical questions.

Would the church community expect a pastor or church leader to perform open heart surgery on a member of the choir or remove an usher's kidney stone? Pastors wear a lot of hats, but unless they've graduated from medical school and passed all the required licensing exams, the expectation is for pastors to pray before, during and after the surgery—and to stay far away from scalpels and the insides of operating rooms!

If anyone were accused of a crime, how many would choose his or her pastor as lead counsel over the legal team? Pastors make wonderful character witnesses and can provide spiritual and emotional support throughout a trial, but unless a pastor has graduated from law school and passed the bar with flying colors, pastors probably shouldn't take on the role of Johnnie Cochran or Perry Mason.

I've been married for over 30 years to a Senior Pastor, Dr. Terrence Autry, and know that many people have all kinds of unrealistic expectations of pastors. Pastors are expected to study well, preach well, teach well, pray well, blog well, lead well, and live well. They're expected to be at every member's critical life event—whether in the hospital, the funeral home, or the high school graduation—while maintaining 24/7 access on their cell phone and social media platforms.

Pastors are expected to accomplish these feats while also spending shekinah-glory personal time in the Lord's presence, maintaining a happy home, and getting their regular sabbath rest!

But even the most unrealistic congregants don't expect their pastors to take on roles that go far beyond any training received in seminary or through ministry experience. Pastors typically don't even expect that of themselves.

Then why do so many pastors and church leaders operate in the field of finance without any training whatsoever in that field?

I believe there are several reasons. First, pastors and church leaders too often underestimate the complexity of building finance. Even when I write, "complexity," there are some who may be thinking, "How complex can this be? I've borrowed money for my car, my house, my student loans, and the furniture in my house, and I'm paying them back just fine. What's the big deal?"

The big deal is that borrowing money for our personal purchases based on our personal finances is far less complex because the variables that impact our ability to repay personal loans are far fewer than they are for commercial loans—that is, loans that are made to organizations, rather than to individuals.

Second, the need—and desire—for a church building to house the ministry is one that pastors and church leaders understand very well. This need and desire, coupled with the call to walk by faith, can convince pastors and church leaders that they are called to lead the charge in building finance.

I believe the biggest reason, however, is the simplest one: There are very few, if any, resources made available for pastors and church leaders who want to better understand church finance.

LACK OF RESOURCES

Ironically, there seems to be no shortage of information for Christians when it comes to the topic of financial giving. Simply Google "Christian giving" and your hits will number in the hundreds of millions. Books, seminars, and blogs abound for helping congregants grow in their under-standing of how to be a good steward of the financial resources the Lord allows us to manage. The problem is, there are precious few written for pastors and church leaders to manage the financial resources when they are given!

Does the lack of these types of resources for church leaders surprise you? It surprised me! It is difficult to find any material on equipping these same leaders in the area of possibly the greatest single expenditure within the church—the acquisition, renovation, or construction of one or more church buildings. Further, I am hard pressed to find any material—whether in books or blogs—written by someone from within the commercial bank-ing industry where loan requests are analyzed, and loan decisions are made.

In August 2015, Vanderbloemen Search Group published an article entitled, "16 Books Every Church Leader Should Read on Their Next Sabbatical." As I perused Vanderbloemen's original list, along with numerous other added recommendations, I couldn't find one book on the topic of finance; personal, church, or otherwise. Yet, one of the most significant challenges faced by most church leaders involves the acquisition, construction, and financing of building facilities.

A seminary education is not a promised help either. *Financing American Religion,* edited by Mark Chaves & Sharon L. Miller, identifies this challenge for pastors. In the chapter entitled, "Clergy as Reluctant Stewards of Congregational Resources," contributor Daniel Conway writes:

> "Seminaries probably can do more to train prospective clergy for the administrative and practical aspects of their work. The limited training opportunities that are currently available to future church leaders in the stewardship of human, physical, and financial resources normally are not a required part of the seminary curriculum; they are not, in general, regarded as an integral part of the theological and pastoral education that church leaders receive in the seminary. As a result, future church leaders do not receive systematic, integrated preparation for the management dimensions of pastoral ministry." [11]

Janet T. Jamieson and Phillip D. Jamieson make a similar observation. They note:

> "Even the largest Protestant seminaries, such as Asbury, Fuller, Princeton, and Southwestern Baptist, offer no required or elective courses dedicated to financial ministry." [12]

---

11 Daniel Conway, "Clergy as Reluctant Stewards of Congregational Resources," in *Financing American Religion,* Editors Mark Chaves & Sharon L. Miller, 95-104 (Lanham, MD: AltaMira Press, 1999), 100-101.

12 Janet T. Jamieson and Philip D. Jamieson, *Ministry and Money: A Practical Guide for Pastors* (Louisville, KY: Westminster John Knox Press, 2009), 202.

THE PARABLE OF THE WISE STEWARD

In the parable of the wise steward, Jesus makes this telling observation:

> "...the people of this world are much more shrewd in handling their affairs than the people who belong to the light." (Luke 16:8 GNB)

This parable centers on the fact that Christians ought to apply the same type of shrewdness or "business savvy" toward righteousness that the wicked servant applied toward unrighteousness. In this context, however, I'm focusing on this takeaway: The children of light need more business savvy!

This is the purpose of *Holy Borrowers: Equipping Church Leaders for Building Finance* (*"Holy Borrowers"*). God calls pastors and church leaders to be wise and shrewd stewards of the money that people donate to the church. This wisdom includes how churches finance the buildings they build, renovate, or buy.

WHY THIS BOOK IS UNIQUE

Holy Borrowers is unique in two primary ways.

AUTHOR'S BACKGROUND

First, *Holy Borrowers* is unique because it was written by someone with in-depth experience in both finance and Christian ministry. On the one hand, I served in the commercial banking field for over 30 years. Prior to my retirement from banking in April 2019, I was the Senior Vice President and Dallas Market Manager for a $38 billion regional bank leading teams of commercial bankers in the Dallas Metroplex. These teams served organizations with up to $50 million in annual revenues with financing and diverse business services.

Over my career, I've discussed, analyzed, closed, and declined more loans than I can count. The smallest loan I ever approved and funded was for $3,000 to an entrepreneur who needed to purchase a carpet cleaning machine for his business. The largest loan I ever analyzed and got approved by a Senior Loan Committee was for $100 million to a publicly-traded corporation that simultaneously received similar-size loans from four other banks. I can tell you the positive traits these loans had in common, despite their diverse size and complexity.

I have taught commercial lending skills to recent college and business school graduates with finance and accounting degrees, and I have mentored numerous junior and senior bankers over their careers. I have an intimate understanding of the lending function within banks and how that function dovetails with the banking needs of organizations.

At the same time, I am a Christian and am intimately involved in—and passionate about—God's church. I already mentioned that I'm married to Dr. Terrence Autry. He is the Lead Pastor of Christ Community, a 22-year old church plant in Richardson, Texas, approximately 15 minutes north of downtown Dallas. I oversee the finance function of our church and serve in numerous other leadership roles. I also am a called and ordained minister of the gospel of Jesus Christ. I have served in ministry for as long as I've been a banker and have first-hand knowledge of the inner workings of God's church.

Finally, my educational background blends these two commonly-distinct fields of church and finance. I have an undergraduate degree in Economics from Brown University, an M.B.A. degree in Finance and Marketing from the Anderson School of Management at UCLA, and an M.A. degree in Cross-Cultural Ministries from Dallas Theological Seminary.

Truthfully, I didn't understand for many years what the Lord was doing in my life with these two seemingly divergent paths—but I finally have caught up with His vision! *Holy Borrowers* is made possible by the knowledge the Lord has allowed me to gain over these past 30-plus years. My father-in-law once told me, "You've paid a lot of dues to know what you know." I believe some of those dues have reaped *Holy Borrowers*.

PLAIN LANGUAGE

Second, *Holy Borrowers* is unique because it provides information about building finance in plain language that does not require a finance or accounting degree to decipher. That's important for pastors and church leaders who don't have finance or accounting degrees! My goal is to provide a resource that not only can be understood while it is read, but also can be accessed by pastors and church leaders again and again as the need arises.

BOOK LAYOUT

Holy Borrowers is divided into four parts. Part I: "Preparation" (Chapters 1 through 5) provides insights for getting ready for building finance, important considerations before applying for a building loan. Part II: "Inside the Bank's Credit Process" (Chapters 6 through 12) unveils how banks evaluate church loan requests—a mystery to many if you've not worked inside the commercial lending side of a bank.

Part III: "Advanced Lending Topics" (Chapters 13 through 17) discusses more complex lending topics, including balloon notes and construction loans. Additionally, in the context of the current coronavirus pandemic, I prayerfully added a new chapter entitled, "In the Midst of COVID-19." This chapter focuses on the economic impact on church finance and financial principles that should be applied going forward. Finally, Part IV: "Lessons from Successful Churches" (Chapters 18 and 19) provides learned lessons from two highly-successful churches that financed their large church edifices.

The Appendices at the end of *Holy Borrowers* are not considered "required reading," but will be helpful to anyone desiring to take an even deeper dive into building finance. The Appendices include: typical items included in a real estate loan application; sample financial statements for a church; trend analysis and other financial tools used by bankers; and, guidelines for choosing a good attorney specializing in commercial real estate loans.

CLOSING THOUGHTS

Nearly all of *Holy Borrowers* was written with the Great Recession as a backdrop because of its devastating impact on so many congregations and their leaders. Church leaders continued to struggle with financing decisions in the years following the economic recovery. Now, in the midst of the current COVID-19 crisis and in the years to come, the information provided here is as relevant for church leaders as it ever has been.

Moreover, although *Holy Borrowers* certainly is a resource for churches of all sizes, I have a special interest in reaching leaders of small to medium sized churches; that is, those with 300 or less in weekly attendance. Here's the reason: Many of these churches don't have members on their leadership team or in their congregation who have strong finance backgrounds. This reality places an even greater burden on the senior pastor and church leadership team who are striving to accomplish so much for the Lord, but with relatively limited resources.

The *Atlantic Journal-Constitution* shared a telling quote from a senior pastor following the foreclosure of his church building. Here's what he said:

> "I didn't have enough experience to know I was getting bad advice... How many pastors do you know who can pay the bills, run the business of the church and get out there and preach and teach and be available to the people?"[13]

Exactly.

My prayer is that *Holy Borrowers: Equipping Church Leaders for Building Finance* will begin to fill a critical knowledge gap for pastors and church leaders, to be a blessing to all those who use it as a resource. Too many pastors and church leaders have lost countless hours of sleep—and even lost their church buildings—based on what they didn't know before they obtained financing.

The bottom line? The Church is the Body of Jesus Christ and knowledge is power. Let's be equipped for the work at hand. This must include gaining a better understanding of the financing process for the largest asset most churches ever will own, for the upbuilding of God's Kingdom.

---

13   Schneider, "Foreclosure Crisis Hitting Some Metro Churches."

PART I

PREPARATION

"I'm always interested in learning something new."

– KATHERINE JOHNSON, NASA Mathematician
Presidential Medal of Freedom Recipient

SECTION OVERVIEW

Part I of *Holy Borrowers* focuses on preparation—not only preparation for those who are interested in obtaining building financing right now, but also preparation for those who are not yet interested in, or not yet qualified for, obtaining building finance. Quite transparently, some church leaders may complete this section and determine that the Lord is not leading their church to obtain bank financing. (In that case, kindly gift this book to a church leader in another congregation!)

These next five chapters cover the various costs of borrowing, the role of faith, getting prepared before you're qualified, common loan terminology, and how to navigate, if relevant, areas of race and discrimination as it pertains to bank financing. Part I focuses on your preparation as a church, before ever approaching a bank for a building loan.

CHAPTER 1

SHOULD YOU BORROW?

"The rich rules over the poor,
and the borrower is the slave of the lender."
— PROVERBS 22:7 ESV

"Debt should not be a first resort. It may be easier,
but that doesn't mean it's wiser."
— ART RAINER[14]

My church, Christ Community in Richardson, Texas, was just six years old when we obtained a 20-year building loan to purchase our 15,562 square foot church facility. We used that loan and our cash savings for the purchase. At that time, our senior pastor, my husband, only had been pastoring for that six-year period, and our non-denominational congregation included less than 300 active adults.

The timing of the bank approval could not have been better. Our lease at the public school where we held our Sunday services was about to expire and the school district had voted to preclude any religious organization from using its facilities going forward.

---

14 Art Rainer, "Should Churches God Into Debt?" LifeWay, July 13, 2018, online: https://factsandtrends.net/2018/07/13/should-churches-go-into-debt/.

At the same time, we had long outgrown the original church building we still leased for ministry purposes during the week. The sanctuary was too small to accommodate even multiple Sunday services and we had limited space for our children and youth—one room in the back to accommodate them all.

The opportunity to purchase the 15,562 square foot facility had been unveiled to us only a few months before the expiration of the school lease and it came about in a way that we only could describe as a move of the Lord. "It came to pass" that one of our members who "happened to be" a real estate agent "happened to hear" about the building being put on the market before it went on the market.

As a result, our church was able to place the building under contract before one "For Sale" sign went up. We also received an additional blessing: The appraised value of the building was well above our agreed-upon purchase price. In other words, we got a great deal!

Christ Community purchased that property in 2005 and it continues as our church home today. We've never come close to missing a payment on our loan since we moved in; in fact, we obtained additional financing in 2015 to fund needed updates to our sanctuary and facility. In sum, we ultimately obtained two separate loans: our original loan to purchase the facility in 2005 and our "renovation" loan 10 years later to make needed updates.

Our church has paid the balance of the first loan according to schedule, with the exception of a sizeable extra principal payment we chose to make in 2015. Moreover, we paid the second "renovation" loan well ahead of the bank's 20-year repayment schedule, reducing the balance by more than half in just two years!

This sounds wonderful, doesn't it? We purchased our church building below market when our church only was six years old. We were able to house our ministry just as our lease at the public school was expiring and we had nowhere else to go. We not only have never come close to missing any loan payment, we even reduced our debt well ahead of schedule!

If you believe this is a great testimony, you would be correct. However, you also would miss that our testimony—and that of every church that borrows money—comes with costs and sacrifices. These costs and sacrifices must be evaluated by church leaders before making the decision to borrow. We will review some key costs and sacrifices in the remainder of this chapter.

INTEREST EXPENSE

The first cost that needs to be assessed is interest expense that every borrower must pay to the lender for the use of the lender's money. It might surprise many to know how costly this expense is!

I'll underscore this point with a hypothetical example of a church that obtains a $1.5 million loan to purchase a building. Here are my assumptions:

- Original Loan Amount (also called "Principal Balance"): $1,500,000
- Repayment Period: 20 years
- Repayment Schedule: Monthly payments of principal and interest expense over 20 years
- Fixed Interest Rate: 6.0% per year for the entire 20-year repayment period[15]
- Monthly Payment Amount: Approximately $10,800, including principal and interest[16]

In my example, this church obtains a $1,500,000 building loan that it must pay back over a 20-year period. Payments are due monthly and include principal—where some portion of the loan balance is reduced—and interest expense.

---

15 The interest rate in this example was chosen for discussion purposes only and is not in any way indicative of what an interest rate might be on an actual church loan.

16 The calculation of the loan payment was derived using a financial calculator, plugging in the original loan balance, the assumed interest rate, and the number of months of payments. It is not an intuitive calculation for most people without a financial calculator or computer software program.

Let's take a closer look at the interest expense. If this church made every payment on time, at the end of 10 years—halfway through the repayment period—this church would have paid the lender a total of $1,296,000. That's $10,800 per month, all year, every year.[17]

Remember that the original loan balance in this example was $1,500,000. If the church paid $1,296,000 in payments over 10 years, what would you guess their new loan balance would be halfway through their loan repayment?

Would you guess $204,000, which equals the $1,500,000 original balance minus $1,296,000 in total payments? Would you guess the new balance would be $750,000, which is half of the original $1,500,000 balance because they're halfway through the scheduled repayment period? Neither of those guesses would be correct.

Would it surprise you to know that after $1,296,000 in loan payments, this church's loan balance only has been reduced from $1,500,000 to approximately $960,000[18]? That balance only is $540,000 below the original loan amount of $1,500,000. That means that the total payments to principal equaled $540,000 in this example. [19]

Where did the rest of the payments go? Interest expense! Remember, we said at the outset that these loan payments included principal *and* *interest*! How much was their interest expense?

What were the church's total payments over the 10-year period? They were $1,296,000 that, as we said, equates to $10,800 in principal and interest expense paid every month over 10 years. If we take the difference between the $1,296,000 in total payments and the $540,000 in principal payments, we'll arrive at the interest expense paid over these 10 years. That figure is $756,000.[20]

---

17   $10,800 x 12 x 10 = $1,296,000.
18   This balance also was calculated using a financial calculator.
19   $1,500,000 - $960,000 = $540,000. The $540,000 equals the total "principal payments" made on this loan.
20   Total payments of $1,296,000 less total principal payments of $540,000 = $756,000 total interest expense paid the first 10 years.

In other words, the cost to borrow the $1,500,000 for the first 10 years was $756,000! Moreover, in this example, the church still has $960,000 in principal remaining on its loan, which means there is more interest expense to be paid!

Does this cause you to think twice about borrowing money? It should! Furthermore, the amount of interest expense that borrowers pay rises with an increase in any of the following factors, all other things equal: the loan amount, the length of the repayment period, the interest rate, and the length of an "interest-only" period in which principal is not required to be paid.

On the consumer lending side for personal loans, many individuals get themselves into a financial hole when borrowing money to buy a car because they only consider whether or not they can afford the monthly payment. They don't think about the interest rate charged. Some interest rates are as high as 20% or more per year, compared with 0% to 3% that is the norm for many. They don't think about how long they'll be paying the car note. Why not? Because they want the car, literally at any cost. The problem is that the amount they're paying in interest expense can be exorbitant.

The same holds true for a great number of borrowers on the commercial lending side. Too many borrowers desire what they're purchasing or constructing so badly that they don't focus enough on the interest rate they're charged, the interest expense they're paying, or how long it will take to pay back the loan.

Let me share observations made in 1938 by J. Reuben Clark, Jr. who at that time, held the title of President (First Counselor in the First Presidency) within the Mormon Church. Clark's statement made then still holds true for any borrower today:

> "May I say something about interest? Interest never sleeps nor sickens nor dies; it never goes to the hospital; it works on Sundays and holidays; it never takes a vacation; it never visits nor travels... Once in debt, interest is your companion every minute of the day

and night; you cannot shun it or slip away from it... and whenever you get in its way or cross its course or fail to meet its demands, it crushes you... Whoever borrows should understand what interest is; it is with them every minute of the day and night."[21]

Interest expense is the most obvious cost stemming from the decision to obtain a building loan. There are other costs, however, that while less obvious, are no less important.

OPPORTUNITY COSTS

When my church obtained our original building loan in 2005, we celebrated God's grace toward us. We remain grateful for all that the Lord did (and is doing!) on our behalf. In addition to the interest expense that we continue to pay our lender, however, there have been other costs. The most notable costs have been the cost of what we've had to sacrifice elsewhere in our ministry to repay our loans. The term for this sacrifice is "opportunity cost."

"Opportunity cost" is not a common term outside of economics and business, but it is one that every church leader should consider. Opportunity cost is defined as, "the value of the next best alternative choice you could have made instead of the actual choice you made."[22]

Translation? What else you could have done with the money if you had not borrowed and paid interest on the funds you borrowed. For example, what missions could have been funded with that money? What ministry to youth and children could have been supported? What staff could have been hired? What services could have been extended to the community?

I previously mentioned that my undergraduate degree was in Economics. I honestly have forgotten far more theories than I learned, but one definition remains firmly entrenched in my mind: "Economics

21 J. Reuben Clark, Jr., *Conference Reports of The Church of Jesus Christ of Latter-day Saints* (Salt Lake City; The Church of Jesus Christ of Latter-day Saints, 1938), online: https://archive.org/details/conferencereport1938a/page/n103/mode/2up.

22 Opportunity cost. 2019. *Learn.stashinvest.com*, online: https://learn.stashinvest.com/definition-opportunity-cost-economics-finance.

is the allocation of scarce resources." That means when we don't have unlimited resources, we have to prioritize and make difficult choices. How and what we prioritize speak to what we value most.

I am not criticizing building purchases or building construction. I am saying there is a real cost to doing so that needs to be understood, evaluated, and prayed about before investing funds in a building.

IS BORROWING BIBLICAL?

Of course, this question is the most important consideration. Larry Burkett dedicated several chapters to this question in his book, *Using Your Money Wisely: Biblical Principles Under Scrutiny*. He states:

> "Borrowing is not prohibited in Scripture. It is discouraged. There are no positive references to borrowing, and in fact, there are explicit warnings to avoid. 'The rich rules over the poor, and the borrower becomes the lender's slave' (Proverbs 22:7 NASB). Thus, the Word indicates that an unnecessary authority is created by borrowing."[23]

Burkett cites other Scriptures that can be referenced by church leaders studying this issue, including: Proverbs 17:18, Luke 6:38, Deuteronomy 28:12, Exodus 25:1-2, 1 Chronicles 29:16, 1 Kings 6, and 2 Kings 12.[24]

Art Rainer provides additional insights in his article entitled, "Should Churches Go into Debt?" He writes:

> "DEBT IS NOT A SIN, BUT THE BIBLE ISN'T EXACTLY A FAN OF DEBT... Some treat taking on debt as sinful. It's not, at least on its own. Psalm 112:5 [CSB] tells us, 'Good will come to the one who lends generously and conducts his business fairly.'

23 Larry Burkett, *Using Your Money Wisely: Biblical Principles Under Scrutiny* (Chicago, IL: Moody Publishers, 1985), 78.
24 Ibid., 79.

God would not reward someone (the lender) who is knowingly participating in the sin of another (the debtor)." [25]

Rainer then provides four useful questions:

- Is the debt for a ministry need or want?
- Can we pay off the debt quickly?
- What is the budgetary impact?
- What are our other options? [26]

These questions are excellent and should be discussed at length before entering into a borrowing relationship. I will add three more:

- What is the current economy and what is the economic forecast?
- What is the financial health of your congregation? (Are they overwhelmed with personal debt?)
- Has your leadership team considered using 100% cash to finance the building? Many churches have done so and can serve as great examples for other congregations.

CLOSING THOUGHTS

There are times when debt does serve a purpose. While some say, "Wait," there are times when waiting is not an option if a church is to survive. This certainly was the case for my church in 2005 when we were faced with an expiring lease and no other available property to lease. I continue to believe that the building we acquired was God-sent, and the loan we used to pay for it was God-sent as well. I believe our building and the means we used to acquire it were both God's answers to our prayers and His will for Christ Community.

That said, I have tried to communicate that there are significant costs to debt financing—even when every payment is made on time or even

25 Rainer, "Should Churches God Into Debt?"
26 Ibid.

ahead of time. Certainly, the costs are even greater when churches are not able to make their payments, or they struggle to do so. The Bible does tell us that the borrower is the slave of the lender and this proverb has proven to be true for too many.

For those who prayerfully proceed with debt financing or who already have obtained building loans, I leave you with this principle: Remain in a position to manage your debt or it will manage you. This applies to individuals and families, and it certainly applies to church leaders and congregations.

There is one additional topic that needs to be addressed as it relates to the decision regarding whether or not to borrow. For Christians, our decisions are rightly influenced—and even driven by—what we believe the Lord can and will do, in spite of what may seem logical or factual. The critical topic of faith is addressed in the next chapter.

CHAPTER 2

THE ROLE OF FAITH

"Now faith is the assurance of things hoped for,
the conviction of things not seen."
— HEBREWS 11:1 ESV

"Religious organizations may be subject to
the laws of God, but they are also subject
to the laws of economics."
— CHRIS MACKE, senior real-estate strategist at CoStar[27]

P astor Dumars closed the church meeting by quoting this passage by heart:

"Have faith in God. Truly, I say to you, whoever says to this moun-
tain, 'Be taken up and thrown in the sea,' and does not doubt in
his heart, but believes that what he says will come to pass, it will
be done for him. Therefore, I tell you, whatever you ask in prayer,
believe that you have received it, and it will be yours."[28]

27 Shelly Banjo, "Churches Find End Is Nigh," *Wall Street Journal,* January 25, 2011, online:
    https://www.wsj.com/articles/SB10001424052748704115404576096151214141820.
28 Mark 11:22b—24 ESV.

Pastor Dumars spoke with sincere, heartfelt passion: "We've done a lot of talking and praying over the past six months about the pros and cons of going into the building project, and I appreciate the time, work and prayer that you all have put in. We've talked about the real need in our church and in our community for this new facility. We've also talked about the estimated cost of the building and the challenges in getting this done. But now as your pastor, I must tell you that this ultimately comes down to one word and that word is: 'faith.'"

Pastor Dumars continued. "The passage I quoted was from Mark 11:22 to 24 where Jesus tells us that *whatever* we ask in prayer will be received *if* we believe. I don't know about you, but I'm going to believe what Jesus says, regardless of what the numbers on a page might say and regardless of the challenges we may face along the way! Let's have faith in God and watch what He will do for a people who trust in Him and His Holy Word!"

Sound familiar? It should. Numerous pastors and church leaders, when faced with the unfamiliar territory of financial statements, capital campaigns, and loan documents, shut those conversations down by moving into familiar territory: a call for their congregations to "Have faith."

Church leaders are sincere in this type of charge to their congregations. When confronted with revenues, expenses, and budgets, their first instinct many times is to lift those numbers before the Lord in prayer and faith. "The prayer of a righteous person has great power as it is working" (James 5:16b ESV).

I'm not in any way minimizing the role of faith nor the power of prayer. The Bible teaches us otherwise. I personally have seen the Lord work in my own life and in the lives of others too many times to question Him or His Word. More importantly, the Lord and His Word are true whether I question them or not!

What I am saying is that it is a false contrast to place faith on one side of the spectrum and sound financial principles on the other. Counting costs and financial analysis do not automatically point to a lack of faith, nor does declining a building project because funds are insufficient. Rather, sound financial analysis and decision-making can show wisdom—also a cherished value for decisions led by the Spirit of God.

Look at the following passage that Jesus shared with His disciples:

> "For which of you, desiring to build a tower, does not first sit down and count the cost, whether he has enough to complete it? Otherwise, when he has laid a foundation and is not able to finish, all who see it begin to mock him, saying, 'This man began to build and was not able to finish.'
>
> Or what king, going out to encounter another king in war, will not sit down first and deliberate whether he is able with ten thousand to meet him who comes against him with twenty thousand? And if not, while the other is yet a great way off, he sends a delegation and asks for terms of peace." (Luke 14:28-32 ESV)

To be sure, Jesus' primary focus in this passage is for His followers to understand the great cost and sacrifice of being His disciple, of bearing our own cross. The key application of this parable is for Christians to focus on the cost of following Him, not lessons about constructing buildings or going to war against another regime.

So why am I using this Scripture here? Because in citing these examples, Jesus assumes the underlying premise of these illustrations to be true. Therefore, we can infer that Jesus finds it unwise to build a building without first factoring in the costs, or to go into battle without first counting the number of troops on both sides. In the illustration about the king, Jesus even underscores the wisdom of saying "no" when the king realizes he does not have enough resources at that time to win the war!

Are there cases in which congregations and even church leaders don't move forward in potential building projects based on a lack of faith? Absolutely. Is every instance of not moving forward in a potential building project an indication of a lack of faith? Absolutely not.

Is faith a necessity in pleasing the Lord? Let's read this passage from Hebrews to immediately answer that question in the affirmative:

"And without faith it is impossible to please Him, for whoever would draw near to God must believe that He exists and that He rewards those who seek Him." (Hebrews 11:6 ESV)

Does abundant faith mean that everything I ask for will come to pass? Clearly not. When the White Star Line was informed that its world class ship, the RMS *Titanic*, was foundering, it is reported that its Vice President, P.A.S. Franklin announced, "We place absolute confidence in the *Titanic*. We believe the boat is unsinkable."[29] At the time Franklin reportedly spoke those words, *Titanic* already was lying at the bottom of the ocean.

The fact of the matter is faith can be used to override sound analysis. Eric Knowles is the former CEO of Church Brokers, a San Diego firm that specializes in church real estate and financing. He shared the following in 2009, one year after the Great Recession began:

"There's that faith, you know, that often we think that the Lord is directing us to go do something. Well, how do you refute that when I deal with a pastor that says that the Lord is calling me to buy this building? And I have many situations where it will not pencil... But then the pastors continue to say, 'Well, I believe God is directing me for this... I understand by earthly standards this will not work, but God has called me to do it.' And that's the trump card. What do you do? You're just kind of like, 'okay.'"[30]

---

29 Historic UK: The History and Heritage Accommodation Guide, "The Sinking of RMS Titanic," online: https://www.historic-uk.com/HistoryUK/HistoryofBritain/RMS-Titanic-the-unsinkable-ship/.

30 Fred de Sam Lazaro, "Churches in Financial Distress," *Religion & Ethics News Weekly*, June 19, 2009, online: https://www.pbs.org/wnet/religionandethics/2009/06/19/june-19-2009-churches-in-financial-distress/3281/

In understanding how we are to walk in faith in this context, we might be better served looking to the posture of the three Hebrew boys, Shadrach, Meshach, and Abednego. When ordered by King Nebuchadnezzar to worship his golden image following his arrogant declaration:

> "...what god is there who can deliver you from my power?" (Daniel 3:15 ISV),

the three men responded:

> "Your majesty, if it be His will, our God whom we serve can deliver us from the blazing fire furnace, and He will deliver us from you. But if not, rest assured, your majesty, that we won't serve your gods, and we won't worship the golden statue that you have set up." (Daniel 3:17-18 ISV)

That's faith! The Hebrew boys' faith was demonstrated in their assurance that our God was able to deliver them from the fiery furnace and from Nebuchadnezzar himself. Their faith was demonstrated in their refusal to bow down to false gods, even at peril to their own lives. Their faith was demonstrated in their sole allegiance to the one, true, living God.

They did not, however, confuse faith with God's *having to* provide them what they needed in that moment: deliverance from the furnace and from Nebuchadnezzar.

This account is a lesson for us all. Faith means knowing that our God is *able* to provide financing for building projects from whatever source He deems fit. God is *able* to provide financing through a generous donor or a greedy business owner. God is *able* to provide financing through a lending institution or several family members. God is *able* to create money from scratch and deposit it into our bank account or onto our doorstep! Faith knows that God *is* and that God *is able*!

Faith does not, however, assume that our will is God's will. Our prayers and ultimate decisions should be littered with, "Lord, if it be Your will..."

This does not make us unfaithful. This makes us Biblical. This makes us like Jesus. Remember His prayer in the Garden of Gethsemane when He was facing upcoming torture at the hand of soldiers and the shame and brutality of the cross?

> "And going a little farther, He fell on the ground and prayed that, if it were possible, the hour might pass from Him. And He said, 'Abba, Father, all things are possible for You. Remove this cup from Me. Yet not what I will, but what You will.'" (Mark 14:35–36 ESV)

Jesus certainly knew God the Father was able and would raise Him from the dead. Still, in His humanity, Jesus asked for His Father's will. It would be an impossibility to believe this is a lack of faith on the part of our Savior. Rather, the posture of truly seeking the Lord's will—and not always receiving the answer we desire—is a hallmark of faith. Saying "no" to what we desire or think is right goes hand in hand with faith. It's not the opposite of faith.

I read an article entitled, "Churches in Financial Distress," published in 2009.[31] While the article was both interesting and heartbreaking overall, what stood out most was a comment posted as a follow-on to that article, by someone named Jackie. Here's what she said:

> "[Our Pastor] wanted to build a million-dollar addition to the church when the church had twenty checks to bounce in one month. Most of our members are old and retired. The new ones that join are having a hard time and he keeps on repeating, 'GOD WILL MAKE A WAY.' No bank would finance the project. THANK GOD!!!!!"

---

31   "Churches in Financial Distress," *Religion & Ethics Newsweekly*, June 19, 2009, online: https://www.pbs.org/wnet/religionandethics/2009/06/19/june-19-2009-churches-in-financial-distress/3281/

Here is a case in which the pastor's perspective on faith was trying to override sound judgment and even the best interest of his congregation. Not being able to move forward can be a reason to thank God in faith.

CLOSING THOUGHTS

As we move forward in *Holy Borrowers*, please be assured that I in no way diminish the role of faith in the all-powerful, all-loving, faithful God whom I serve. I also do not want to be disrespectful to any pastor or church leader who has focused predominantly on faith in God over finances, budgets and costs. My prayer is that we all walk in a place of prudent financial evaluation and decision-making within our walk of faith, not in contrast to our walk of faith. The call is for both, not one or the other. It's good for us all to keep this truth in mind as we proceed.

If you've read this far and borrowing funds is still an option for you, then it's time to discuss steps that need to be taken before you borrow. This is the subject of the next chapter: "Getting Ready Before You're Ready."

CHAPTER 3

GETTING READY BEFORE YOU'RE READY

"Give me six hours to chop down a tree and
I will spend the first four sharpening the axe."
— ABRAHAM LINCOLN

"There are no shortcuts to the top of the palm tree."
— CAMEROONIAN PROVERB

When we planted Christ Community in 1998, we were in no way positioned to—or interested in—taking on debt. Yes, we obtained a building loan in 2005, but when we founded the church in 1998, there was no discussion of a loan.

It's a good thing we weren't interested in a church loan when we first started. Why? Because we could not have qualified for a church loan if we had wanted one! In 1998, we were a brand-new church with a brand-new pastor and three adult members, including my husband and myself.

We didn't need a church loan. We couldn't have qualified for a church loan. We were not discussing a church loan. But as a commercial banker, even then, I knew we had to prepare for a church loan.

As I reflect back on our thought process then, there was an overriding principle that greatly influenced our thinking. It was a principle that my husband and I consistently shared with our two sons when they were growing up. The principle is this: You always want to have options. You may not need to use them, but you always want to have them.

This was the same principle we had in mind for our church. We didn't know we would need or even want to obtain a church loan, but we wanted to retain the option of obtaining a church loan if we needed or wanted one at some point in our future.

On that basis, it was extremely advantageous to us that as a commercial banker, I already knew what banks would require when it came time for us to evaluate building finance. Regrettably, without this information, too many churches are not positioned for church loans when they desire church financing.

This is the goal of this chapter: to provide church leaders that same information before they're ready to evaluate financing options. These steps are even important if you don't ever obtain bank financing. Donors in your own congregation and in the community always respond well to churches that model financial excellence for the sake of excellence. For that reason, I believe this chapter is applicable to all church leaders.

Let me reiterate that the steps discussed in this chapter were taken when we had just three adult members, and nearly one year before we held our first public worship service. Church leaders may not choose to begin that early in your process, but it underscores the point that it never is too early to get started!

FINANCIAL STATEMENTS

I can tell you how much money our church had in its bank account on December 31, 1998, our first year of existence. That date was two weeks before we had our first worship service. The reason I know this information is that our church started maintaining financial records from the moment our three founding members paid our first tithes and offerings.

There were two primary reasons we were this meticulous. First and foremost, we wanted this financial information for ourselves. Accurate financial records are needed for church leaders and the entire congregation to understand the financial health of the church. Accurate financial records also communicate the importance of accountability and transparency by leadership to the members of the church.

In fact, one of our long-term members joined the church at a business meeting a few years after we started. She told her daughter that if our church's leadership team could tell her how much we spent on postage, this was a church leadership team she could trust!

The second reason we kept meticulous financial records relates to church financing. Based on my experience, I knew that the first item that most lenders request when evaluating a commercial loan request is the organization's historical financial statements.

Moreover, I knew that commercial bankers don't just request financial statements for the most recent year. Rather, commercial bankers request financial statements for at least the past three years *and* financial statements for the current year that are dated within the last 90 to 120 days.

For example, if a church is applying for a loan sometime in August 2020, lenders will request that church leaders provide the church's annual financial statements for the years ending December 31, 2019, December 31, 2018, and December 31, 2017, the most recent three years. Lenders also will require the church's more recent "interim"[32] financial statements; for example, financial statements for the six months ending June 30, 2020.

That's not all. Many lenders also request the church's corresponding prior year interim financial statement; in this example, for the six months ending June 30, 2019. Why? Because comparing the church's financial performance for the first six months of 2020 to the church's financial performance for the first six months of 2019 provides an "apples-to-apples"

---

32 An "interim" financial statement is one that covers the "interim" or "in-between" periods between an organization's year-end statements. The other term bankers use is "year-to-date" financial statements.

comparison. This is particularly important for churches that receive a good portion of their donations in the fourth quarter of the year.

Here's the point: If lenders have a preference for three years of annual statements and the most current interim statement, then at whatever point we approached a lender about a loan, I knew we would need to provide three years of annual statements and the most current interim statement!

I emphasize this because I have met numerous churches that approach the bank with no financial statements whatsoever and they try to build their financial history at the time of the request. At that point it's too late!

What are the specific financial statements that lenders use in evaluating an organization's financial performance? There are three primary financial statements that are described below. Examples of these financial statements also are provided in Appendix II.

"BALANCE SHEET" OR "STATEMENT OF FINANCIAL POSITION"

The Balance Sheet presents a snapshot at a specific point of time of an organization's assets, liabilities, and equity (also called "net worth"). Balance Sheets typically are prepared at the end of a month, quarter, or year.

In very general terms, assets are resources that an individual or organization owns that can provide future economic benefit. Examples of assets include: cash in bank accounts (or under a mattress), equipment, buildings, land, and inventory.

Liabilities represent an individual or organization's obligations—either money that must be paid or services that must be performed. If a church purchases a building and finances that building with debt, the building becomes an asset and the debt becomes a liability.

Finally, equity or net worth refers to the portion of resources that has been contributed by owners or has been earned and retained by owners. Many homeowners are familiar with this term when referring to the "equity" in their residence; that is, the difference between the value of their home and the balance of their mortgage note.

For churches and other non-profit organizations, the terminology changes, but the concepts are the same. The Balance Sheet often is called a "Statement of Financial Position" and "Equity" is referred to as "Net Assets," given that there is no owner.[33]

Regardless of terminology, with proper accounting, the following equation holds true:

$$\text{Assets} = \text{Liabilities} + \text{Equity}$$
$$\text{or}$$
$$\text{Assets} = \text{Liabilities} + \text{Net Assets.}$$

"INCOME STATEMENT" OR "STATEMENT OF ACTIVITIES"

An Income Statement provides a measure of an organization's operating performance over a period of time—say a month, a quarter, or a year. An Income Statement lists the total revenues and total expenses that were generated during that time period.

As is the case of the Balance Sheet, the terminology changes in describing the "Income Statement" for churches and other non-profit organizations. For these types of organizations, the Income Statement often is called a "Statement of Activities" and "Net Income" is called "Change in Net Assets."

With proper accounting:

$$\text{Net Income} = \text{Revenues} + \text{Gains} - \text{Expenses} - \text{Losses}$$
$$\text{or}$$
$$\text{Change in Net Assets} = \text{Revenues} + \text{Gains} - \text{Expenses} - \text{Losses.}$$

"CASH FLOW STATEMENT" OR "STATEMENT OF CASH FLOWS"

A Cash Flow Statement or Statement of Cash Flows is a financial statement that provides the cash generated and spent during a specific period. This statement incorporates information from both the Balance Sheet/

---

33   We will use terms common to non-profit and for-profit organizations interchangeably in *Holy Borrowers*.

Statement of Financial Position and the Income Statement/Statement of Activities. Unlike the Balance Sheet and the Income Statement that are provided by borrowers to the bank, lenders typically create the Statement of Cash Flows themselves using internal financial programs. The three sections of a Cash Flow Statement are:

- Cash Flow from Operations: cash flow that is generated and spent through the primary activities of the organization.
- Cash Flow from Investing: cash flow from acquiring or disposing of long-term assets, such as buildings or equipment. (The term, "investing" in this context is different from the type of investing done in the stock market.)
- Cash Flow from Financing: cash flow from debt and equity inflows (for example, new loans) or outflows (for example, extra principal payments on a loan).

When I first learned about the Cash Flow Statement, I was taught a shortcut for each section that still serves me well today:

- Cash Flow from Operations: how they made it.
- Cash Flow from Investing: how they spent it.
- Cash Flow from Financing: how they financed the difference.

Lenders use information from these three financial statements to analyze an organization's financial capacity and can produce numerous analytical ratios and financial models from these statements. More detail regarding how lenders evaluate loans is provided in Part II of *Holy Borrowers*. At this point, suffice it to say that one of the most important components of a lender's loan decision is the existence and quality of the church's financial reporting. Lenders need to determine if the church makes enough money after expenses to pay back its loan or loans on time.

QUALITY OF FINANCIAL STATEMENTS

I used the term "proper accounting" above and did so for a reason. One of the most significant mistakes churches make is not entering their financial information into a good accounting software program at all; or, not having someone with an understanding of basic accounting enter that information. As a result, when the church requests financing from a lender and the lender asks for three years of financial statements, the information either is unavailable or is incorrect. Software programs like Quick Books and Wave can help, but they cannot replace a sound understanding of how financial data should be entered.

With this understanding, even though I have an accounting background, our church hired a CPA firm our first year, even when we had just three members. This may have been overkill, but I can tell you that it served us well in being able to produce proper financial statements for our entire church history from 1998 to 2004 when we requested our first building loan in 2005.

There are different levels of "quality" in financial statements and the higher the "quality," the higher the price. "CPA Audited" financial statements typically are used by the largest churches and they are the most expensive—but they also provide lenders the most comfort for larger loans. Many lenders require CPA Audited financial statements for loans over a certain amount in size; say, $5 million.

Other levels of CPA financial quality are "CPA Reviewed" financial statements (typically required for loan requests ranging from $2.5 million to $5 million) and "CPA Compiled" financial statements. Our church obtained CPA Compiled financial statements our first year. These essentially converted our internal financial data into an acceptable presentation expected by lenders.

Whether a church uses an external CPA or an online accounting program—or both, all financial statements need to adhere to what's called, "Generally Accepted Accounting Principles" or "GAAP" (pronounced "Gap"). At a basic level, GAAP dictates what constitutes, for example, an asset and what does not; and how an asset is valued. GAAP dictates when revenue should be included on an Income Statement and provides direction regarding where expenses should be categorized.

There is a language to financial statements that individuals in the financial field expect to see. If a lender cannot trust the church's financial statements, it is difficult to impossible for the lender to properly evaluate or approve a commercial loan request. Churches need to have their financial statements in order if they're to be relied upon by any outside party.

FUND ACCOUNTING

"Fund accounting" is used by many large churches and non-profit organizations. Fund accounting should be used by all organizations, regardless of size, that have a significant portion of donations that are "restricted" in terms of use. Restricted donations refer to funds that only can be used for specific purposes that are established by the donor. In contrast, "unrestricted funds" can be used for any reason that the church leaders or general congregation establish. Tithes and offerings typically are considered unrestricted funds.

The purpose of fund accounting is to provide transparency and accountability for the donors and the organization to show clearly that restricted donations only are being used in accordance with the restriction the donor or donors placed on them.

Four types of funds are common to churches that use fund accounting:

- General Fund (also called the Operating Fund or Undesignated Fund): This fund is for normal day-to-day ministry and expenses.
- Special Projects Fund: This fund is for donations with a specific, typically time-bound purpose, such as funds raised for a specific Missionary Trip.
- Endowment or Trust Fund: This fund is used when a donor specifies that the principal of a donation is to be preserved and only the interest or investment income earned on that principal can be used.
- Plant or Property Fund: This fund is used for all capital assets, such as funds for land, buildings, and equipment.

I'm not an accountant and cannot advise any church regarding if and when it is appropriate to use fund accounting. Rather, my two primary points are:

- It is *critical* that churches be able to accurately monitor and report on all restricted donations. If a church does not wish to accept the restriction placed by the donor, then the church must return that donation. If the donation is accepted with a restriction, the restriction must be honored.
- Did I mention that I'm not an accountant? Church leaders should consult with a strong external accountant to set up a tracking system that is suitable to their church, and/or use someone internally that has strong accounting skills.

BANK STATEMENTS

In addition to the financial statements listed above, lenders typically request the most recent three months of bank statements for each account owned by the church and any church affiliate (such as a school). The lender is looking for several things with this request: confirmation of average deposit balances; the types of deposits and withdrawals (for example, credit card deposits versus check deposits); and, any negative indicators such as insufficient funds throughout the month and check or ACH return fees.

PAYROLL TAXES AND 1099 FORMS

If your church has employees, the church is required to withhold and pay payroll taxes by the established deadlines. Christ Community relied on our CPA to file our payroll taxes for the first few years and then switched to Automatic Data Processing, Inc. ("ADP"). ADP handles not only all of our payroll tax filings, but also our required year-end W-2 reporting for church employees, as well as the preparation of required 1099 forms for our contractors. We also use this firm to provide direct deposit services for our employees.

There are other reputable processors besides ADP. I would encourage church leaders to consider using these types of services, particularly if you are a small to medium church and do not have individuals with a solid financial background on staff or serving in the ministry.

LEGAL FORMATION

The original name of my church was "Eirene ("Eh-ray-nay") Christian Fellowship." Eirene is the Greek word that is translated as "peace" in the English New Testament, and overall. Our slogan was: "Where Jesus is our Peace."

The vision the Lord gave my husband is that "Eirene" would be a conversation starter, which it certainly was in those days. When people asked about the meaning of the word we would tell them... and then share that Jesus is indeed our Peace!

We did not limit ourselves, however, to sharing the name of our church. We took the legal step of incorporating Eirene Christian Fellowship. This involved taking the time to create corporate bylaws and Articles of Incorporation. With that in hand, Eirene Christian Fellowship was incorporated in the Office of the Secretary of State of Texas on February 2, 1998, nearly one year before our first public worship service.

Years later, Terrence felt led of the Lord to change our name. We had grown too much to be able to personally communicate with all potential members and guests what the name "Eirene" meant. On that basis, we changed our name to Christ Community. Here again, however, we did not just change the name on our church sign, church stationery, and website! We went back to the Secretary of State of Texas and filed a Certificate of Amendment to legally change our name. That Amendment was approved by the Secretary of State on December 29, 2011.

Why is this important? It's important because organizations are meant to operate as legal entities in the same way that individuals operate as legal entities. Whatever the form of organization, the legal entity must be on record with a recognized authority, such as a Secretary of State or a County.

One of the errors I've seen many churches make is not forming a legal entity, and keeping that legal entity separate from, say, the legal identity of the pastor. Pastors that co-mingle the church's funds with their own personal funds in one bank account are a red flag for every lender.

The red flag does not automatically mean that the pastor must be embezzling church funds or is dishonest in some way. Rather, the red flag is raised because it communicates to the lender and others that the pastor and church leaders don't understand sound business principles. An organization that does not operate under sound business principles is not an organization with which lenders want to do business.

I already stated that I'm not an accountant. I'm not an attorney either. Therefore, I can't give advice about what type of legal entity to form. The important point is that the existence of your church and any legal affiliates—such as a 501(c)(3) non-profit—needs to be legally established with a recognized governing authority or authorities.

LEGAL COUNSEL

Speaking of... One of the most important relationships a church should have is with a reputable attorney that represents the church. Regrettably, church leaders who rely on reading their own loan documents and real estate contracts without expert advice too often end up paying the price when they are surprised by loan requirements or stipulations they didn't notice or fully understand.

My church is blessed to have one of the top attorneys in Dallas, Sharon K. Simmons, as a long-term friend and now church member. We have not signed a single contract without her prior review and she guided us diligently in the purchase of our current building. In my opinion, good legal counsel is not an option for any organization that will enter into legal contracts.

In Appendix V of *Holy Borrowers*, Ms. Simmons provides guidance for evaluating and selecting a good attorney that is equipped to provide legal counsel in the specific area of commercial real estate financing.

FACILITY READINESS

Would you agree that for many pastors and church leaders in this generation, a key component of "American Christianity" has been owning a large church facility; or in more recent years, operating in multi-site locations? This trend can place undue pressure on pastors and church leaders to move their ministries into larger spaces without the proper preparation for occupying those spaces.

What types of preparation? I recommend that church leaders ask themselves several questions to evaluate their "facility readiness."

CAPACITY

First, I would ask: Are you currently at or near capacity in your existing location? I've heard counsel that when a congregation reaches 80% capacity in its existing location, then it's time to look for a new space. I don't necessarily agree with that premise, at least without better defining "capacity."

For some, "capacity" means you're at one service and 80% of the room is full. I wouldn't define that as capacity. If, on the other hand, "capacity" means you're running three to four services and you're still turning away people, then perhaps it is time to move to another building. Even in that case, however, I would ask these additional questions:

- Should you plant a completely independent church out of your congregation, rather than move the entire congregation to a larger facility?
- Can you increase the number of services in your existing location?
- What impact will the purchase or construction of a larger building have on your ministry and mission dollars?

Joe Dillard, III is the Director of Project Management for Friendship-West Baptist Church in Dallas, Texas. Friendship-West's worship facility and conference center is nearly 174,000 square feet. Joe mentors other church leaders who are seeking larger facilities.

When these church leaders share that their church is ready to purchase or build a larger facility, Joe asks them, "Do you have the people now?" If they say, "No," Joe responds, "Well, if you don't have the people now, you're not ready!" Joe has stopped many projects because of this. He advises church leaders to wait until they have overflow, stating that the "If you build it, they will come" mentality only is for the movies!

HIGHER EXPENSES

Church leaders also should ask themselves if they are prepared to take on higher utility expenses, repairs, and maintenance associated with a larger space. Does the church have sufficient furniture? What about a budget for new landscaping expenses?

By way of example, Mt. Hebron Missionary Baptist Church (highlighted in Chapter 18), posted its 2020 budget on the church's website. Mt. Hebron owns and operates two building facilities: one that is 77,102 square feet and a second that is 16,528 square feet.

According to Mt. Hebron's posted information, the budgeted expense for electricity alone in their smaller facility is $22,000 for the year. Their budgeted expense for electricity alone for the larger facility is $92,000 for the year. These costs do not include costs for telecom, gas, and importantly, building maintenance. Church leaders must factor in the many additional costs of owning larger facilities, above and beyond the costs of financing those facilities.

An additional note: Good bankers certainly will ask these questions about facility readiness, and will factor higher expenses into their evaluation of any church loan request. The banker's goal is to have as realistic an analysis as possible to reduce the likelihood of the church and the bank being caught by surprise after the congregation moves into a larger space.

ASSET UTILIZATION

Here's another question: Are you prepared to maximize the use of a new facility, or will it be a situation in which you and your congregation purchase an asset that the church only uses on Sundays and sits empty

Monday through Saturday? The business terminology for this concept is "asset utilization."

Successful businesses understand the concept of asset utilization; unfortunately, too few church leaders do. If we're going to spend that much money on an asset such as a building, proper stewardship of funds demands that our church building be used as much as possible for effective ministry and effective use of funds. Further, with the significant increase in social media platforms to stream services into one's own home, the challenge of effective asset utilization for buildings is increasing all the more.

COMMITMENT

My final question in this section is this: Is your congregation fully committed to *your ministry*, or are they just committed to the glamour and excitement surrounding a new building? I ask this question because if they're only committed to the building, when another church erects a newer, larger, prettier building two years after you move into yours, are your "members" going to head for greener pastures?

There is a term in banking called "hot money." Hot money represents deposits or investments that are volatile because the deposit holder will move the money between banks, or between countries, at the first sign of a higher interest rate or investment return. These are not stable deposits.

Do you have "hot members"? Will they move at the drop of a hat? Part of your preparedness is evaluating your membership's commitment to your ministry before making that investment in a building.

CONGREGATIONAL READINESS

This leads to my next question: How prepared is your congregation for a building loan? For example, do your members have a lot of personal debt? Is your congregation struggling financially?

In our earliest years, one of our members testified about how the Lord blessed her and her husband to pay off all their debt. She referred us to the gentleman who had coached them. He was the former Vice President of

Financial Services of a Fortune 500 company and a member of the Board of Trustees of a local seminary.

This gentleman walked our entire congregation through the steps to personal debt reduction and personal debt elimination in two consecutive annual seminars. He did so at no cost to our church. Our congregation learned about the perils of consumerism, of living beyond our means, of not planning financially for retirement, and of course, of not giving financially to the church and God's Kingdom overall.

Importantly, we did not bring in this expert so our congregation could give more to a building fund! At the time, we didn't even have a building loan envisioned and even if we had, that would have been the wrong motive.

I encourage church leaders to help their church members walk in personal financial health. Again, the goal is not to make them better givers. The goal is to be a blessing to them through the power of Godly financial stewardship. The overflow will come, but the blessing is for them first.

Is your congregation financially healthy? Would a building loan put more on them than God wants them to bear? These are questions that should be asked.

RELATIONSHIPS WITH BANKERS

There is a common saying that is not flattering to bankers that goes like this: "Never go to a bank when you need a loan. Go to a bank before you need a loan." The main point of this saying is that banks won't give you money when you need it, so you're better off getting the money when you don't—and depositing the funds in a "rainy day" fund.

I respect that this perception is real because I've heard this saying too many times to think otherwise! While I don't agree with the underlying premise shared above, I wholeheartedly agree that it's a great idea to establish relationships with commercial bankers at various lending institutions in your city or town.

I say commercial bankers—those who focus on organizations— because too many churches mistakenly limit their banking relationships to branch personnel. While I know and have worked with many phenomenal branch bankers, I need to point out that their focus is on consumer banking; that is, providing services to individuals. Most banks moved lending decisions for commercial loans out of the branches decades ago.

For this reason, I strongly recommend that church leaders meet their commercial banker now. Ask them in advance if they're open to church lending. Some banks are not. Ask them what kind of guidelines they have for building loans to churches. Ask them about their interest rates. Ask if they offer promotions on building loans.

See if you like them and if they like you! There are too many banks in town to do business with anyone with whom you're uncomfortable, and that you don't believe works hard to earn your business. Further, see if they respect you.

PRAYER

Of course, the best preparation is prayer. Prayer honors God and brings Him into the process as nothing else does. On a pragmatic level, we also pray because as the Scriptures state:

> "There is a way that seems right to a man, but its end is the way to death." (Proverbs 14:12, 16:25 ESV)

In other words, going with our feelings can be a terrible strategy!

Asking the Lord for direction is not enough. Many individuals pray, but I always ask, "What did the Lord say? Further, what outside confirmation do you have?" We can follow Mother Teresa in this as she said:

> "God speaks in the silence of the heart. Listening is the beginning of prayer."

Many Christians get a little prickly when I ask about outside confirmation. They respond, "I know what the Lord told me!" Well, here's another Scripture I try my best to keep at the forefront, written by the Apostle Paul:

> "For now we see in a mirror dimly, but then face to face. Now I know in part; then I shall know fully, even as I have been fully known." (1 Corinthians 13:12 ESV)

If the Apostle Paul who wrote nearly 30% of the New Testament and was caught up to the third heaven says he saw dimly and says he knew in part, then I think all of us need to have a lot of humility in recognizing that we may feel something is right, but it actually is wrong. We may feel we know what the Lord is saying, but we need to recognize it may not be the Lord's voice at all! Outside confirmation is not meant to be insulting, it's meant to be instructive.

CLOSING THOUGHTS

The primary goal of this chapter has been to help church leaders position themselves for a building loan well before there is a need—or even if there never is a need. Remember, church leaders should have options at your disposal as you continue to lead your church.

Of course, one of the best ways to get ready before you're ready is to familiarize yourself with financial concepts. The next chapter, "Common Banking Terminology," is designed to do just that.

CHAPTER 4

COMMON BANKING TERMINOLOGY

"Let the wise hear and increase in learning,
and the one who understands obtain guidance..."
— PROVERBS 1:5 ESV

"I am always doing that which I cannot do,
in order that I may learn how to do it."
— PABLO PICASSO

I grew up in the Lutheran church. Among other distinctions, Lutherans believe that infants can and should be baptized in saving faith as Christians, with the prayer that they will confirm their faith in Christ individually when they are old enough to articulate their understanding of salvation for themselves.

On that basis, I was baptized on Christmas Day when I was two months old. I attended Sunday School until eighth grade and then "Confirmation Class" in the ninth grade where the senior pastor spent much of that year undermining what I had learned about Christianity to that point.

It was not until many years later, after college and business school, that I accepted Jesus Christ as my Lord and Savior. My husband, Terrence, played an instrumental role in discussing the faith with me, along with my father-in-law and two dear friends in my business school class. (It is rumored that my husband was motivated by his desire to date me, but I'm sure his reasoning was much purer!)

A key turning point in this process was learning that *all* have sinned and fall short of the glory of God. This was in contrast to what had been told me on the streets of Los Angeles: "*You* have sinned and fall short of the glory of God!" I always wondered how they knew I had sinned if they didn't even know me!

When I was about 27 years old, in the midst of this process, I began visiting a Baptist church in Los Angeles. The pastor was dynamic and I would sit crying through his sermons Sunday after Sunday, realizing that despite my degrees and a newly-established career in banking, my heart and life felt empty. I could feel the Lord drawing me to Himself.

Finally, I decided to join that church. My only problem was that I didn't understand how to join! In the Lutheran church that my family joined when I was four years old, my parents had done all the work. Somewhere along the line they had filled out a card and given it to the right person, and just like that, we were members! I had never joined any church on my own.

Unfortunately, I received no clue from the pastor. After preaching, he would extend his arms wide and say, "The door of the church is now open!" And I thought, "What does *that* mean?"

I was too embarrassed to tell anyone I didn't know how to join that church, so I sat in the pew Sunday after Sunday trying to figure it out on my own. I finally put together three options the church was offering, based on the individuals who went down the aisle:

- Option #1: I could go forward for prayer;
- Option #2: I could go forward to be baptized;
- Option #3: I could go forward on something called "Christian experience."

After several more Sundays, I was sure I had it down and was ready to walk the aisle after the sermon.

I thought, "I don't have any prayer requests and I've already been baptized (remember Christmas Day?), so that leaves Option #3." The third option really made sense to me because after all, I had a lot of Christian experience growing up in the Lutheran Church! And down the aisle I went one Sunday, letting them know I was joining the church on Christian experience. The pastor shook my hand, which seemed to confirm that I'd made the correct choice!

Thankfully, the wonderful sister who met with me afterward quickly figured out that I wasn't saved and I wasn't a member of anyone's church. She graciously confirmed my salvation and told me that I should have come forward for baptism, as an indication that I needed salvation and a church home.

I've since learned that the phrase, "Christian experience," does not denote an experience with Christians as I had surmised, but was code for individuals who already were Christians, who were changing their church membership. I was baptized by water immersion a few weeks later, recognizing that I had no clear understanding of salvation either when I was an infant or in the years that followed.

A few years later, after Terrence and I married and relocated from Los Angeles to Dallas, we heard the late, great Dr. E.K. Bailey preach at Concord Baptist Church. He preached a powerful sermon and then extended the invitation. It was the clearest invitation I ever had heard in my life.

Dr. Bailey never once said, "The door of the church is now open." Instead his invitation discussed three clear options: Option #1 was for those who had never trusted Jesus Christ as Lord and Savior. He explained what that meant and what a person needed to do. Option #2 was for those who weren't sure they were saved. He explained how they could be sure. Finally, Option #3 was for those who already had trusted Jesus for salvation and wanted to join Concord.

It was clear as day and I told my husband, if that invitation had been provided to me years before in Los Angeles, I would have joined that church the first Sunday I attended.

KEY TERMS

I did not recount this story to be disrespectful in any way toward the invitation that is used by many pastors, or toward the pastors who extend it! That fact of the matter is that thousands of individuals respond to that invitation Sunday after Sunday. My point is the invitation was confusing to me.

Why? Because at that time, I was an outsider trying to understand what I call, "insider code words" such as: "The door of the church is now open" and "You can come on Christian experience." Such insider code words are easily understandable only to those who already have understanding! For the rest of the population, not so much!

In similar fashion, there are many insider code words that are used by bankers and others in the finance industry that are easily understandable to everyone...within the banking and finance industries! For the rest of the population, not so much! This same type of language can be overwhelming to church leaders who are on the outside of the banking industry, even though they are crystal clear to those on the inside.

For this reason, my next task will be defining some key terms that are foundational to understanding building finance. We will repeat these terms throughout *Holy Borrowers* so that they will become increasingly familiar to church leaders. The hope is that one day, using these terms will be as familiar as saying, "The door of the church is now open."

FINANCE OR FINANCING

Let's start with the related words, "finance" and "financing." Each can be used as a noun or as a verb. As a noun, one of the definitions provided by Merriam-Webster is: "the science or study of the management of funds."[34]

---

34 Finance. 2019. In *Merriam-Webster.com*, online: https://www.merriam-webster.com/dictionary/finance.

Let's not make it too complicated: That's money, honey. Finance involves how we handle money (or the lack thereof); something all of us deal with every day. When either "finance" or "financing" is used as a verb, the term simply means to provide funding.

Please note that this funding does not necessarily have to come from a lender. Many individuals mistakenly use the terms "finance" or "financing" to mean bank loans, but in its broadest sense, the word "finance" in all its various forms relates to funds or money obtained from any source.

With that in mind, we now can break "finance" into two main categories, discussed below.

Equity Financing

I shared in the previous chapter when we discussed the equity section of the Balance Sheet that equity denotes ownership. Similarly, equity financing refers to funds that are provided by an individual owner or organization, rather than funds that are borrowed. The phrase "down payment" when purchasing a building (or any other asset) describes the equity portion of the financing that comes out of an organization's or an individual's own resources. If a church purchases a building with 100% cash from its savings accounts, that denotes 100% equity financing.

The alternative to 100% equity financing is described by the far more prevalent phrase, "debt financing." This, of course, is the primary focus of *Holy Borrowers* and is discussed next.

Debt Financing

Debt financing refers to money that is borrowed. The more familiar word to describe debt financing is "loan." A loan describes something that does not belong to the borrower; rather, it belongs to the lender. I understand this seems obvious, but in my 32 years in the finance industry, there have been times I've had to remind borrowers that it's actually the lender's money that is sitting in their bank accounts or that was used to finance their assets!

PRINCIPAL BALANCE

As previously mentioned, the principal balance refers to the amount of the loan that is outstanding at a specific point of time. If a church obtains a loan for $1,000,000 and the loan is fully funded at closing, the outstanding principal balance at closing is $1,000,000. The principal balance typically is reduced over time through loan payments.

PRINCIPAL PAYMENT

The principal payment refers to the amount of money that a borrower pays to the lender to reduce the principal balance of a loan. For example, if the principal balance of the $1,000,000 loan referenced above is reduced to $975,000, we can infer that a principal payment of $25,000 was applied to that loan.[35]

PROMISSORY NOTE

The promissory note refers to the document the borrower signs that obligates the borrower to repay a loan. The promissory note is basically a written "I.O.U." A promissory note also is called a "note" for short.

ORIGINATION DATE

The origination date refers to the date that the loan is "effective," as stated in the promissory note. The origination date will be on or near the date that the loan closes. The origination date also is referred to as the date of the promissory note.

MATURITY DATE

The maturity date refers to the date the entire principal balance is obligated to be paid in full, unless a lender agrees to renew or refinance the outstanding principal balance on or before the stated maturity date. *The maturity date trumps any verbal assurance or side agreement that lenders may provide regarding what they might do in the future.* The maturity date of the

---

35 $1,000,000 - $975,000 = $25,000.

loan, as listed in the promissory note, is the date 100% of the principal (and outstanding interest) is due in full.

TERM OF THE LOAN

The term of the loan, also called the loan term, refers to the time period between the origination date and the maturity date. For example, if the stated origination date on the promissory note is December 1, 2020 and the stated maturity date is December 1, 2030, then the term of the loan is 10 years. This means the church has 10 years to either repay the loan in full or to refinance the outstanding balance when it matures, subject to a new bank approval.

AMORTIZATION SCHEDULE

The amortization schedule communicates when principal payments and interest payments must be paid to the lender, as documented in the promissory note. The word, "amortize," in this context means to reduce or pay on a debt with regular payments. Payments can be set to be paid annually or quarterly; however, most notes require monthly payments. The amortization schedule also is referred to as a repayment schedule.

Some amortization schedules are structured with "interest only" payments for some period of time, possibly over the entire term of the loan. This means that no principal payments are required during that "interest only" period. (This structure is what I meant above when I referenced paying "on" a note.) Most amortization schedules for commercial loans require that some portion of principal be paid before the maturity date.

TYPES OF PROMISSORY NOTES

FULLY-AMORTIZING NOTE

A fully-amortizing note is one in which the payments are calculated in the amortization schedule so that the loan balance is paid off in full—that is, "fully amortized"—by the maturity date. An example of a fully-amortizing note is a car loan in which the original loan balance is reduced to zero by the time the loan matures, if all payments are made on time.

BALLOON NOTE

A balloon note is a short-term loan that usually is due and payable within five to 10 years; meaning, the loan term is five to 10 years. The loan payments are calculated in the amortization schedule, however, as though the loan is not due and payable for a longer period—say 15 years or 20 years. A lender would say, in this example, that the loan is amortizing over 15 years or 20 years.

A balloon note is the opposite of a fully-amortizing note in that with a balloon note, the principal balance, intentionally, will not be paid off in full by the maturity date. The benefit of a balloon note is that the monthly payments will be much lower than they would be if the borrower were required to make payments that would pay off the loan in full in five years or 10 years.

On the other hand, a significant downside of this repayment arrangement is that because the loan will not be paid off in full by the maturity date, there will be a lump-sum payment that is due when the loan matures. That payment will equal the unpaid principal balance plus interest that is due. The term used to describe that outstanding balance that is due is "balloon balance."

Another disadvantage of a balloon note is that a borrower pays more interest expense on a balloon note than on an amortizing note, all else equal. This is because the principal balance of a balloon note typically remains higher than the principal balance of an amortizing note.

The topic of balloon loans is one of the least understood concepts in building finance. It is so important that an entire chapter is devoted to the topic in Part III: "Advanced Lending Topics," and is showcased as an issue in Part IV: "Lessons from Successful Churches." It also is noted that every foreclosure discussed in the "Introduction" to *Holy Borrowers* involved a balloon note.

INTEREST RATE

The interest rate refers to the rate that a lender charges on the principal balance over a certain time period. Interest rates are expressed as a percentage; for example, 5.50% per year. Rates either can be "floating" or "fixed," as further discussed below.

FLOATING INTEREST RATES

Floating interest rates also are referred to as "variable" and "adjustable" rates. The interest rate can fluctuate up or down over the entire term of the note, or over some portion of time within the term of the note. The level of fluctuation is a function of some index, such as "Wall Street Journal Prime Rate," the "London Interbank Offered Rate" ("LIBOR"), or a "Swap Rate." Most of these indexes are published daily or throughout the day on financial databases and websites.

Floating rates can be very advantageous when overall market rates are low and/or declining. Of course, floating rates have the opposite effect in times of rising interest rates—particularly if a loan no longer is affordable for a borrower at a higher interest rate. Residential mortgage loans that contained an adjustable rate structure after five or seven years were one of the primary causes of the Great Recession, as loan payments increased with the higher interest rates.

FIXED INTEREST RATES

Fixed interest rates do not fluctuate over the entire term of the loan or after some portion of time within the term of the loan. Rather, the interest rate remains constant. The primary advantages of a fixed interest rate are the removal of the uncertainty associated with floating interest rates and being able to "lock in" a relatively low interest rate when other interest rates are increasing in the overall market.

INTEREST REVENUE & INTEREST EXPENSE

Interest revenue is the revenue that is earned by the lender on the money the lender has loaned to the borrower. Interest revenue comes from the interest payments that the borrower makes and is based on: (1) the interest rate on the loan and (2) how much principal is outstanding on the loan over a specific period of time. As previously discussed, interest payments are paid in addition to any principal payments that are due.

Of course, what is considered interest revenue to the lender is interest expense to the borrower! Interest expense is the expense that borrowers incur for borrowing the lender's money and is included on an organization's Income Statement or Statement of Activities.

PREPAYMENT PENALTY

A prepayment penalty is a fee that the borrower must pay if they pay off all, or a portion, of the principal balance of a loan prior to a mutually agreed-upon repayment schedule. If they exist, prepayment penalties are imbedded in the promissory note and should have the borrower's prior agreement. If applicable, prepayment penalties are paid in addition to any principal and interest that is due.

When they are in place, prepayment penalties protect the lender from the risk of losing interest revenue if a borrower pays off a relatively high-interest rate loan ahead of schedule and interest rates have dropped. When this occurs, lenders have to redeploy loan funds at a lower interest rate. Prepayment penalties also protect lenders from losing loans to competitors that might offer the borrower a lower interest rate than the existing interest rate on the loan.

Why in the world would a borrower ever agree to a prepayment penalty? One primary reason: to obtain a lower interest rate than they would obtain on the same loan with no prepayment penalty. It's similar to the concept of "buying down" your mortgage rate with a higher fee, although in this case, the borrower only has to pay this fee if they repay the principal ahead of schedule.

In sum, prepayment penalties amount to a compromise: The borrower receives a lower rate than they otherwise would have received, and the lender is better able to lock in interest revenue over a set time period. It is noted that some lenders will waive the prepayment penalty entirely if the loan is refinanced with that same lender, and not with a competitor bank. Some lenders also will waive the fee if unforeseen circumstances arise.

It should be noted, however, that in many cases, lenders cannot waive prepayment penalties because the penalty that the borrower is paying the bank is offsetting the penalty that the lender must pay on funds that they secured at a certain rate[36] to loan to the borrower.

Prepayment penalties can be in place for the entire term of the loan, or they can be in place for just a portion of the loan term. For example, a borrower may obtain a prepayment penalty that is in place for the first two years of a five-year loan, but then is eliminated entirely for the remaining three years of that loan.

This structure may be advantageous to a borrower who does not have the financial capacity to pay down principal ahead of schedule during the first few years of that loan but believes they might have the capacity in later years. All else equal, loans with prepayment penalties in place for a portion of the loan term have a higher interest rate than loans with a prepayment penalty in place during the entire term of the loan; but, a lower interest rate than loans with no prepayment penalty whatsoever.

COMMITMENT FEE OR ORIGINATION FEE

Much like a fee on a residential mortgage, a commitment fee or origination fee is paid to the lender as a percentage of the original loan amount. Most commitment or origination fees are paid to the lender when the loan closes. For example, if a lender charges a 1.0% commitment fee on a $1,000,000 loan, the borrower will pay the lender $10,000 at closing.[37]

---

36 The interest rate for funds that a lender obtains to loan to a borrower is referred to as the lender's "cost of funds." The lender adds a profit margin or "spread" to the cost of funds to arrive at the interest rate charged the borrower.

37 $1,000,000 x 0.01 (the equivalent of 1.0%) equals $10,000.

PRICING NEGOTIATION

The combination of the interest rate, a prepayment penalty requirement, and commitment fee dictates the overall pricing for a loan. All of these items are negotiable, individually and collectively.

For example, a lender may not charge a church an upfront commitment fee but may charge a higher interest rate than another bank charges. One bank may have higher prepayment penalties than another—or none at all. These considerations all should be taken into account when comparing offers between different lenders, or even when negotiating with one lender.

TYPES OF COMMERCIAL LOANS

It's a good idea to have a general understanding of the types of commercial loans that lenders typically extend. The first set of commercial loans listed below differs by loan term; that is, the number of years between the origination date and the maturity date.

SHORT-TERM LOANS

Short-term loans mature in one year or less, and sometimes in as little as three to six months. Some short-term loans are called "bridge loans" because they are designed to "bridge" the time span between an immediate need for funds and an expected receipt of funds within a short time frame. The financing request also may occur because of a seasonal need. Other short-term loans include revolving lines of credit that typically mature in 12 months.

INTERMEDIATE/LONG-TERM LOANS:

Intermediate and long-term loans typically mature in two to five years (intermediate) or longer (long-term). These loans also are referred to as intermediate or long-term debt.

The focus of *Holy Borrowers* is on intermediate and long-term real estate loans in which the borrowed funds are used to purchase and/or renovate an existing building or to construct a brand-new building from the "ground up." Long-term debt also is referred to as "permanent" financing, but make no mistake: This financing is not meant to be permanent!

In terms of inside code words, commercial bankers typically lump any debt that has a term exceeding one year into the "long-term debt" bucket. "Intermediate loan" is not a phrase that's commonly used. The common acronym for long-term debt is "LTD."

CURRENT PORTION OF LONG-TERM DEBT

"Current Portion of Long-Term Debt" refers to that portion of long-term debt that is due within the next 12 months. Current portion of long-term debt often is abbreviated as "CPLTD" or "CP-Long-Term Debt."

The next types of commercial loans that we'll discuss all fall within the category of real estate loans. These loans may be short-term or long-term.

REAL ESTATE LOANS

- Construction/ Ground-up Construction Loans: loans to finance the costs of constructing a building or buildings from scratch, where no previous building exists at all. Construction loans are discussed in more detail in Part III: "Advanced Lending Topics."
- Renovation Loans: loans to finance the costs of making physical improvements to an existing building. Renovation loans have similar requirements to ground-up construction loans and therefore are incorporated into the same chapter as ground-up construction loans.
- Owner-Occupied Real Estate Loans: loans to finance a building or buildings in which the borrower occupies 51.0% or more of the available space. *Holy Borrowers* focuses primarily on owner-occupied real estate loans.
- Investment Real Estate Loans: loans to finance a building or buildings in which the borrower occupies less than 51.0% of the available space. In this case, the space that is not occupied by the borrower—up to 100% of the total space—typically is leased to one or more tenants.

DEED OF TRUST OR MORTGAGE DOCUMENTS

The use of a "Deed of Trust" or "Mortgage" document differs by state in the United States, but both serve the same overall purpose. These documents allow the lender to place a lien (pronounced "leen") on the specific real estate that is identified in the document, thereby pledging that real estate as collateral for a specific loan or loans. Deeds of Trust and Mortgages permit lenders to foreclose on the real estate property strictly under the conditions outlined in those documents. The documents typically are filed or "recorded" as public records in the county where the real estate is located.

Typically, Deeds of Trust or Mortgages also contain "Assignment of Rents" clauses, unless the lender chooses to make the Assignment of Rents a separate document. An Assignment of Rents clause or document gives the lender a lien on any rental or lease income that may be generated on that real estate property.

"NO ORAL AGREEMENTS" CLAUSE

Finally, lenders include a clause and often, a standalone document, that states there are no verbal agreements between the lender and the borrower that supersede the written documents themselves. This clause is commonly called the "No Oral Agreements" clause. A sample of this clause is provided below:

> "NO ORAL AGREEMENTS. THE LOAN DOCUMENTS EMBODY THE ENTIRE AGREEMENT AND UNDERSTANDING BETWEEN THE PARTIES AND SUPERSEDE ALL OTHER AGREEMENTS AND UNDERSTANDINGS BETWEEN SUCH PARTIES RELATING TO THE SUBJECT MATTER HEREOF AND THEREOF. THE LOAN DOCUMENTS REPRESENT THE FINAL AGREEMENT BETWEEN THE PARTIES AND MAY NOT BE CONTRADICTED BY EVIDENCE OF PRIOR, CONTEMPORANEOUS OR SUBSEQUENT ORAL AGREEMENTS OF THE PARTIES. THERE ARE NO UNWRITTEN ORAL AGREEMENTS BETWEEN THE PARTIES."

For church leaders, this means that no matter what a banker may promise verbally, no matter what assurances he or she may provide, if those promises and assurances are not incorporated in writing into the loan documents themselves, they are not enforceable with a bank or court of law.

This clause is so important that most loan documents not only capitalize all the words of this section as shown, but also print this clause in bold font. Therefore, when borrowers sign the loan documents, they agree to this bold, capitalized statement that there are **NO** side agreements between the bank—or any bankers—and themselves.

CLOSING THOUGHTS

At this point, you might be feeling a bit overwhelmed, but don't worry! You don't need to memorize these terms and there's no quiz in the morning. The hope is that you will earmark these pages and refer to them as the need arises. Of course, I'll also use these terms in the pages ahead.

We're almost ready to move to Part II: "Inside the Bank's Credit Process." There is one more topic I want to cover, however, in "getting ready." Our next chapter will deal with the topic of race, discrimination and the banking industry. This topic is particularly relevant for church leaders and congregations who are members of historically underserved communities.

CHAPTER 5

RACE, DISCRIMINATION, AND THE BANKING INDUSTRY

"A false balance is an abomination to the LORD,
but a just weight is His delight."
— PROVERBS 11:1 ESV

"Let me just say that to imagine that racism does not
exist is imagination. And to imagine that it does not
create its own set of problems is true imagination."
— PHYLICIA RASHAD

The *New York Times* published the following excerpt from a memorandum that reportedly was written by Jamie Dimon, Chairman & Chief Executive Officer of JPMorgan Chase ("Chase"). Chase currently is the largest banking institution in the United States as measured by total assets.[38]

"I am disgusted by racism and hate in any form. Any such behavior—explicit or veiled, deliberate or unconscious—is unacceptable

---

38 Alicia Phaneuf, "Here is a List of the Largest Banks in the United States by Assets in 2020," *Business Insider*, August 26, 2019, online: https://www.businessinsider.com/largest-banks-us-list.

and does not reflect who we are as a company and how we serve our clients and communities every day."[39]

Jamie Dimon reportedly e-mailed the memorandum to all Chase employees following the publication of a *New York Times* article a few days prior. That article had reported that an African-American Chase client experienced racial discrimination at Chase branches in the Phoenix, Arizona area and had made audio recordings as proof. The client also was a nine-year veteran of the National Football League who reportedly had earned $13 million over his NFL career. [40]

According to the *New York Times*, when this client attempted to become a "private client" at Chase—an elite designation reserved for the wealthiest individual clients—he was declined. At that time, the client already had transferred $800,000 in deposits to the bank, which reportedly was well above the $250,000 minimum for private client status.[41]

Moreover, the *New York Times* article reported that an African-American Chase employee offered the following "explanation" to the client, which the client recorded and provided to the newspaper:

> "You're bigger than the average person, period. And you're also an African-American. We're in Arizona. I don't have to tell you about what the demographics are in Arizona. They don't see people like you a lot."[42]

These reported events did not occur in 1863 or in 1963. They occurred in 2019 when most people would hope that these types of occurrences

39 Hugh Son, "Jamie Dimon Says He's 'Disgusted by Racism' and Progress is Needed at JPMorgan After Report," *New York Times*, December 13, 2019, online: https://www.cnbc.com/2019/12/13/jamie-dimon-says-hes-disgusted-by-racism-and-progress-is-needed-at-jp-morgan-after-report.html.

40 Emily Flitter, "This is What Racism Sounds Like in the Banking Industry," *New York Times*, December 11, 2019, online: https://www.nytimes.com/2019/12/11/business/jpmorgan-banking-racism.html?smid=nytcore-ios-share.

41 Ibid.

42 Ibid.

would be behind us. Unfortunately, this is not the case. Moreover, racial discrimination in the United States has not been limited to bigotry between individuals, but continues to be systemic.

One definition for the adjective, "systemic," is the following: "relating to a system, especially as opposed to a particular part."[43] In this context, systemic racism extends far beyond prejudice and bigotry, as evil as those mindsets and actions are. Systemic racism is institutionalized because it transcends individual biases and hatred and encapsulates entire societal and legal structures that oppress people based on race.

Examples include federal, state, and local laws precluding the right to vote, where you can or can't live, which fountain you can or can't drink from, where you can and can't attend school, and of course, legalized slavery and the negation of citizenship. It also includes which communities and which ethnicities receive loans and services when credit qualifications are otherwise equal.

The banking industry has been a complicit partner in systemic racism. In his book, *The Color of Law*, Richard Rothstein describes racially explicit policies of federal, state, and local governments that incorporated overt discriminatory lending practices in the mid-twentieth century. Rothstein submits the following:

"At the time, the Federal Housing Administration and Veterans Administration not only refused to insure mortgages for African Americans in designated white neighborhoods like Ladera; they also would not insure mortgages for whites in a neighborhood where African Americans were present. So once East Palo Alto was integrated, whites wanting to move into the area could no longer obtain government-insured mortgages... State insurance regulators had no objection to this stance. The Bank of America

43 Google Dictionary, online: https://www.google.com/search?sxsrf=ACYBGNR8O9yJvjhoi
H9WWNMlEVN46yKoyA:1580832056257&q=Dictionary&stick=H4sIAAAAAAAAONQe
sSoyi3w8sc9YSmZSWtOXmMU4-LzLojNc8lMLsnMzossqrRiUWJKzeNZxMqFEAMA7_
QXqzcAAAA&zx=1580832197823#dobs=systemic.

and other leading California banks had similar policies, also with the consent of federal banking regulators."[44]

These actions were part of a deeply-imbedded racial profiling system that subsequently was called "redlining." As defined by the Federal Housing Administration ("FHA") themselves:

"Redlining is the practice of denying a creditworthy applicant a loan for housing in a certain neighborhood even though the applicant may otherwise be eligible for the loan. The term refers to the presumed practice of mortgage lenders of drawing red lines around portions of a map to indicate areas or neighborhoods in which they do not want to make loans."[45]

While the FHA's definition cites "presumed practice" of redlining, there is abundant historical documentation that demonstrates that this practice was not just presumed, but was codified into federal and banking policies and consistently implemented.

Why am I including this history in a book on building finance for churches? Because the JPMorgan disclosure about current day racial discrimination in banking is not an isolated one. Racism still is imbedded in the banking industry today.

We can look at the following excerpt from an article in the *Chicago Tribune* written by Aaron Glantz and Emmanuel Martinez:

"Fifty years after the federal Fair Housing Act banned racial discrimination in lending, modern-day redlining persisted in 61 metro areas even when controlling for applicants' income, loan amount and neighborhood, according to millions of Home

---

44 Richard Rothstein, *The Color of Law: A Forgotten History of How Our Government Segregated America* (New York: Liveright Publishing Corporation, 2017), 13.

45 Federal Fair Lending Regulations and Statutes, "Fair Housing Act," online: https://www.federalreserve.gov/boarddocs/supmanual/cch/fair_lend_fhact.pdf.

Mortgage Disclosure Act records analyzed by Reveal from The Center for Investigative Reporting.

The analysis—independently reviewed and confirmed by The Associated Press—showed black applicants were declined at significantly higher rates than whites in 48 cities, Latinos in 25, Asians in nine and Native Americans in three."[46]

"MENTAL REDLINING"

The bottom line is that although structural redlining is now against the law, what I will call "mental redlining" is alive. Mental redlining exists when any banker and/or decision-maker mentally determine who he or she won't do business with, for reasons that are not within the lender's credit or corporate policy. It also exists when that same banker and/or decision-maker are less comfortable with a certain individual or community and therefore give disparate treatment and outcomes. Banks only are as good as their bankers and human beings still carry racial prejudices and mindsets that result in mental redlining.

This may be an uncomfortable subject for some, but it is a reality that can't be ignored. African-Americans, Latinos, and other marginalized communities do not need *The New York Times*, *Chicago Tribune*, or an e-mail from the Chief Executive Officer of the largest bank in the United States to tell them that racism exists and persists in today's society in general, and in this context, in the banking world.

Just like the "old gray mare who ain't what she used to be," racism may not look as it looked in the past, but it is "sheer imagination" to not only pretend it doesn't exist today, but also to believe that it doesn't continue to unlevel the economic playing field for many clients and prospective clients of color.

It also is noted that the perpetuation of racism is not limited to any particular race or gender. Black, Latino, and other minority bankers

---

46 Aaron Glantz and Emmanuel Martinez, "Modern-day Redlining: How Banks Block People of Color From Homeownership," *Chicago Tribune*, February 17, 2018, online: https://www.chicagotribune.com/business/ct-biz-modern-day-redlining-20180215-story.html.

are not automatically excluded from playing a role in perpetuating racism within the banking industry. As a case in point, it is noted that in the *New York Times* article, the Chase employee that was "advising" the African-American client also was an African-American. Although that Chase employee did not appear to be the decision-maker regarding private wealth status, he showed no evidence of directly confronting the racism that he observed, nor recognizing the negative racial stereotyping he communicated. As a result, he also was part of the problem.

OTHER "ISMS"

Sexual assault and sexual harassment against women, physical assault and murders of individuals who consider themselves part of the LGBTQ community, hiring and firing decisions based on age, and many other atrocities, make it clear that racism is not the only type of unlawful discrimination that occurs in society. Therefore, racism is not the only mental redlining that potential borrowers may face today.

Sexism, for example, can take on many forms for potential borrowers. I have met numerous business owners who are women, who shared stories of being denied financing because their husband was not involved in the business, because their husband was formerly involved but had passed away, or because they never had or wanted a husband! Too many women have been marginalized by bankers who don't believe women are equipped to make "the hard decisions" that it takes to lead a company successfully.

As it pertains to discrimination against church leaders, female pastors and elders may not be viewed by some bankers as being "legitimate." Theological views regarding women in ministry have no place in a credit decision made by bankers. I state the same for borrowers who face discrimination from banks because of their religious affiliation, sexual orientation, gender identification, or national origin. Decisions about loans and other banking services must be approached with parity in the criteria used, without prejudice.

Given these historical and current realities of systemic racism, sexism, and mental redlining overall, how should you proceed as a borrower if you are part of a marginalized community? I am going to offer several recommendations to those church leaders—and to all church leaders for their own awareness.

KNOW YOUR CHURCH'S FINANCIAL CAPACITY

The first step in seeking a banking relationship in general, and financing in particular, is to do exactly what you're doing right now: Educate yourself to better understand how banks evaluate loans and make credit decisions. One of the best ways to be empowered is to be equipped. If you have no idea what a lender's metrics are then you leave yourself more vulnerable to being unfairly declined.

On the flip side, without understanding your church's financial capacity, church leaders may be more likely to incorrectly believe their loan request was declined because of racism, sexism, or some other prejudice. This leads to my second point.

RECOGNIZE THAT IT'S NOT ALWAYS RACISM, SEXISM OR OTHER DISCRIMINATION

Those who never have spent time as an ethnic and/or gender minority in a classroom, social group, church, or business organization, don't comprehend the mental and emotional calisthenics associated with having to ask oneself: "Is there prejudice within this group?" "Will I be treated equitably?" This is particularly the case when entering new business environments.[47]

As an African-American woman, I also can tell you this is not a victim mentality, as some have opined. Rather, it is required strategic thinking as minorities also have to plan how we will manage ourselves and the situation if the answer to the first question above is "yes" and the answer to the second is "no."

---

47 I recognize there are questions that also must be asked pertaining to threats of murder, sexual assault, bodily injury, and other issues. The current discussion that specifically focuses on navigating discrimination within the banking industry is not meant to minimize that reality.

Phrases that advise "Don't think about race" or "Don't think about gender" are naïve and ignorant at best, and insensitive and cruel at worst. Individuals would *love* to work, learn, and play in a society that judges preeminently on the content of one's character. Unfortunately, there are daily reminders that this dream has not yet been realized. That is the reality.

That said, it also is the reality that there are numerous bankers that do not operate through a lens of racism, sexism, or other "isms" when making loans or seeking new business. I personally have experienced significant support and career opportunities from bankers and leaders who are Caucasian. At the risk of sounding as though I'm invoking that tired cliché, "Some of my best friends are _____," I will share that I count many male and female bankers who are white as respected colleagues, and some as friends and/or mentors.

I would not have used the word, "many" 30 or even 20 years ago, but I can use it now. Why now?

First, commercial bankers not only are paid to make loans, but also are promoted for making loans. They even can be fired for not making loans! Bankers need qualified borrowers as much as qualified borrowers need bankers! I can't speak to what's in someone's heart nor to conversations that may occur in the privacy of someone's home. I can say, however, that the people I have worked with over the last decade came to work to do business.

Second, the United States has become increasingly diverse—by ethnicity, gender, nationality, sexual orientation, and age. This diversity is displayed in the business community, among business leaders, and within lending institutions. While this obviously does not mean borrowers won't face "isms" or that systemic racism has been eradicated, it does make a tangible difference.

I remember one business lunch I set up a few years ago with a potential client and several banking colleagues that demonstrates the changing landscape of diversity in today's business environment. Here's who attended the lunch:

Representing the Potential Client's Organization:

- A woman who is a first generation Japanese-American, born and raised in New York in an English and Japanese speaking household. Her father, the majority owner, was born and raised in Japan. She served in a "Chief Operating Officer" type of capacity. Although her father was the final decision-maker, she clearly had significant influence over the banking decision;
- A man who was born and raised in Mexico who served as the company's Operations Manager. He speaks English fluently with a Spanish accent.

Representing my Bank:

- Me, an African-American woman born and raised in New York in an English-speaking household. My title was Senior Vice President and Dallas Market Manager;
- A woman who was born and raised in Mainland China, who speaks English fluently with a Chinese accent. Her title was Senior Vice President;
- A man who was born and raised in Guatemala in Central America who speaks English fluently with a Spanish accent—but a different Spanish accent from that of the Director of Operations who was born and raised in Mexico. His title was Vice President;
- A man who is Caucasian, born and raised in Dallas, Texas in an English-speaking household. His title was Vice President.

My banking colleague who was Caucasian was the ethnic "minority" that day. There were an equal number of men and women at the table and the women at the table held the highest corporate ranks, respectively, for both the bank and the prospective client.

Again, this example is not making a statement that entire power structures have shifted because of this type of diversity, and it certainly is recognized that many communities still do not enjoy this level of diversity. My point is that this type of diversity is becoming increasingly common. As a result, if there is any type of on-the-job racism, sexism, or prejudice on display by bankers, it is increasingly likely in more and more business settings, that they will not be successful.

Here's another key issue. If a borrower mistakenly assumes that a decline is because of race or gender, then they may miss the opportunity to work with a banker who wants to be a "trusted advisor," seeking to provide the best guidance possible to that borrower.

Dr. Frederick Douglass Haynes, III, Senior Pastor of Friendship-West Baptist Church, states that this is what occurred when Friendship-West was applying for a large construction loan. Dr. Haynes is a national leader, senior pastor and social activist who is committed to fighting for justice and empowerment for African-Americans and other underserved communities.

I interviewed Dr. Haynes for Part IV of *Holy Borrowers*: "Lessons from Successful Churches." During that interview, Dr. Haynes shared information that I believe is pertinent to this chapter. Dr. Haynes recounted that when Friendship-West was seeking financing to construct their current 174,000 square foot facility, Bank of America approved a lower loan amount than the loan amount the church ultimately obtained through a bond company.

In retrospect, Dr. Haynes shares that they should have gone with Bank of America ("BofA"). Here's what he said:

> "We were banking with BofA at the time. They said based on your budget, you can do a loan for $19 million. Our general contractor came back and played the race card beautifully. He used my passion for justice, my passion for black people, and my passion for standing up against racism in all forms against me. If we had gone with BofA, we'd have paid off that loan by now.
>
> I'm a Black man pastoring a Black church, so I look for institutional racism. And that was used against me. BofA told me this

is how the industry works. They just gave me the bare facts. I was looking for the racial aspect and didn't believe them. That's how we moved our money from a bank that was letting me know what the deal was to a bank that gave us a 'church payday loan.'"

Veta Holt, Friendship-West's Chief Operating Officer, echoed Dr. Haynes' statements. She recounted how Friendship-West chose $25 million in bond financing plus $5 million for audio-visual equipment over Bank of America's $19 million offer.[48] She stated:

"One bank offered Friendship-West a loan, but the representative at the bond company said, 'Oh, you can get much more than that.' He black-balled the bank and everyone thought, 'Oh, the bank is horrible.' Everyone started thinking maybe the bank didn't have the best interest in a minority church. In the end, the bank was right. The bank was right."

There is a similar caution in trying to identify unlawful discrimination based on age. For example, if bankers are concerned because a 67-year old senior pastor is requesting a 20-year building loan, is that necessarily unlawful discrimination based on age? No, it's not. An additional requirement in this example of, say, "Key Person" life insurance, can be a prudent decision for both the bank and the church.

With Key Person life insurance, the bank's loan would be paid off in full if, hypothetically speaking, the 67-year old senior pastor went home to Glory. This requirement may not be imposed if the senior pastor were 40-years of age because in this example, when the loan matured in 20 years, that pastor would be 60 years old, not 87 years old.

The reality is that racism, sexism, and other "ism's" that create an unlevel playing field exist and it is one that must be navigated. Part of that navigation is exposing and fighting against them in Jesus' Name whenever

---

48 This financing, as well as its negative impact on Friendship-West, is discussed in Part IV: "Lessons from Successful Churches."

and wherever they raise their ugly heads. We all must be careful, however, to not assume it exists, including when we receive feedback that we consider negative.

EXERCISE YOUR RIGHTS: GO TO MORE THAN ONE BANK

For minorities, do you detect any discomfort or outright prejudice because of your ethnicity? For foreign nationals, does the banker appear irritated by your cultural dress or "accent" that is different from theirs? If your church is located in a predominantly African-American or Latino community, do you perceive a reluctance to do business with you or obvious discomfort visiting your neighborhood? Do you connect with your banker on a personal level?

The banking world is too competitive to deal with anyone who for any reason does not treat you with the respect and dignity you deserve. If you find a banker or bank that does not uphold your dignity, report them and move on to a worthy competitor who wants to serve you and fight to earn your business.

CLOSING THOUGHTS

Discrimination in general and racism in particular continue to be sensitive discussion topics for many. I'm quite confident there are many readers who don't believe this type of chapter belongs in *Holy Borrowers*. I'm equally confident there are others who read this chapter and don't believe I went far enough in the discussion.

While I respect the right to both viewpoints, I will continue to stand by my opinions shared in this chapter. These opinions also have been shaped by my own experiences in the banking industry.

As an African-American woman who has thrived in and benefited from the banking industry, I also include myself as someone who does not need to read a media article to know that racism and sexism in the banking industry didn't vanish with formal redlining.

My husband and I relocated from Los Angeles to Dallas in 1990 for him to attend seminary. My bank at that time was headquartered in Los

Angeles, but had just purchased a bank in Texas. My original plan was to transfer to the Dallas office at my then-current rank, as an Assistant Vice President in Corporate Banking. At that time, Corporate Banking focused on companies with $50 million to $1 billion in annual revenues.

Despite an Ivy League degree in Economics, an M.B.A. in Finance and Marketing, the completion of a highly competitive corporate banking training program, early success in my career, and very strong recommendations from executive management in Los Angeles, I was declined a banking position in five different areas in the Dallas affiliate. These employment rejections occurred despite being assured before I arrived that I would have my choice of those positions. That assurance disappeared when I arrived in person and could be seen in the flesh.

After relocating to Dallas without a job, I ultimately accepted a position with that bank in the "Workout Loan" Department. The manager hired me into a position that paid half the salary I had received in Los Angeles and which was expected to be eliminated within the year.

One year later, one of the Executive Vice Presidents from the Los Angeles headquarters transferred to the bank in Dallas. He had been one of the executives who had provided a recommendation for me when I moved to Dallas. He met with me soon after his arrival and told me this: "Dallas is not ready for an African-American female working as an Assistant Vice President in Corporate Banking." The Executive Vice President told me he could force them to hire me, but that in his opinion, until hearts and minds changed, it would be virtually impossible for me to succeed in that role.

He asked me if I would be willing instead to run the bank's Credit Training Program for North Texas, using my credit skills to teach new college and business school graduates how to analyze credit requests—teaching them how to become corporate bankers. This Credit division reported to him and supported the Corporate Banking group. The executive shared that as unfair as it was, this strategy would give the officers in Corporate Banking an opportunity to "get used to working with a Black person."

I accepted that position running the Credit Training program for that bank, as insulting and demeaning as the offer was. Why? Because it was already 1991 and I thought, "If not me, who? If not now, when?" I knew I stood on the shoulders of countless African-American women and men who had opened doors for me and others. I truly believed the Lord was telling me to do the same as a Christian; as a highly-qualified, African-American woman. My call was to open doors in Corporate Banking that were closed at that time and place to African-Americans.

I worked through those years at the bank and developed great relationships. Indeed, corporate bankers "got used to working with a Black person." I trained individuals for positions that I was not yet hired for. I was called names. I was minimized. I was told that it was not the bank itself that wouldn't accept me in Corporate Banking, it was the customers of the bank.

Was every day terrible? Not at all. But every day was an assignment in which I had to represent not only myself, but also those who would come after me. In fact, I hired the first African-American person into that bank's Corporate Banking Training Program in Dallas, a highly-qualified African-American man who reported to me.

I'd love to tell you that it all just worked itself out from there. That is not the case. For full disclosure, after years of praying, trying, waiting, and enduring, I ultimately had to sue the bank. Their initial response was to offer me a suddenly-created position in which my job would have been to call on corporate clients and prospective clients with minority ownership; or, on organizations located in underserved communities. I declined that offer!

The Lord persevered. I dropped the lawsuit when I finally was offered the position of Vice President in Dallas Corporate Banking with the ability to call on the same types of companies in the same locations as all the other bankers on that Corporate Banking team. There was no legal settlement, no payout of any kind. I merely was allowed to resume my career as a Corporate Banker at a salary that was competitive with that of my peers, after seven years of fighting for that right.

In so doing, I became the first African-American and first minority Vice President in Dallas/Fort Worth Corporate Banking for that banking institution. One customer asked to be reassigned when he met me (which he was); but overall, I resumed a highly-successful banking career in the Corporate Banking arena.

I worked for five more years in that office and did extremely well. I developed excellent working relationships and a few friendships that endure to this day. When I left that bank in 2002, I did so having developed a mutually respectful relationship with the leaders and staff, and later receiving strong recommendations from those leaders in subsequent employment assignments. As important, other minorities followed me into similar positions in that office and throughout the Dallas/Fort Worth Metroplex.

I also will tell you that I learned a lot about myself—particularly in the areas of character, dignity, endurance, and faith. While the trajectory of my banking career was forever altered, as promised, God caused it all to work together for my good.

Is the banking industry perfect today? Absolutely not. It is a microcosm of the world overall and we don't seem to be able to "all get along." If prejudice is in the heart and mind, legislation at best produces tolerance, not acceptance, and certainly not celebration. Given that every human being has been created by God in the image of God, the dignity of every person—of every client and prospective client—must be upheld and championed.

This subject and chapter bring Part I: "Preparation" to a close. It now is time to get a more in-depth understanding of how lenders evaluate commercial loan requests and make credit decisions. This information is provided in Part II: "Inside the Bank's Credit Process."

PART II

INSIDE THE BANK'S CREDIT PROCESS

"Knowledge is a process of piling up facts;
wisdom lies in their simplification."

– REV. DR. MARTIN LUTHER KING, JR.

SECTION OVERVIEW

"I don't know where to start." "We never know what the banks are looking for!" "I was declined." Sound familiar?

These are a few of the typical statements made by business owners, budding entrepreneurs, and yes, church leaders, as they seek bank financing. The goal of the next several chapters of *Holy Borrowers* is to provide pastors and church leaders a better understanding of how banks view loans to organizations in general, and to churches in particular.

BANK LENDING GUIDELINES

One of the best places to start in understanding how lenders evaluate loan requests is understanding what lenders refer to as, "The Five C's of Credit," or the "Five C's." Having a better understanding of these concepts will enable church leaders not only to better interface with banks, but also to better evaluate their own loan package before approaching banks!

So, what are the Five C's of Credit? The Five C's of Credit are: character, cash flow, collateral, capital, and conditions. Collectively, they represent a framework that commercial lenders use in their credit decisions. This framework is not written in cement. Many have rightly surmised that loan underwriting[49] is both an art and a science. Different lenders may place more weight on certain attributes than others or may even have a different assessment of each of these factors. Yet, the Five C's of Credit serves as the main grid through which commercial loan requests are evaluated.

As a case in point, I previously mentioned that the largest business loan I ever had a part in evaluating was for $100 million, and that the smallest business loan I ever approved was for $3,000. Yet, despite the

---

49 In the context of commercial lending, "loan underwriting" or "underwriting" refers to the process that a lender uses to evaluate the creditworthiness and risks associated with a loan request.

significant difference in size between these two loan amounts, there was not a difference in applying the Five C's of Credit to each loan decision.

It also is important to understand that *all five* of the "C's" must be adequately addressed for a commercial loan request to be approved. Many organizations and individuals mistakenly believe that if they have some of the Five C's or even most of the Five C's then they should qualify for the loan request. This is not true. Unlike a grade of 80% that is considered good enough to pass in most universities and high schools, having four of the Five C's often warrants a decline. This fact alone may be one of the widest areas of misunderstanding between potential borrowers and lenders.

In the coming chapters, we'll take a closer look at each of the Five C's. A better understanding of how each of these characteristics contributes to the credit decision will go a long way in helping church leaders evaluate their own loan requests.

This section also contains two chapters which will prove useful to church leaders: a chapter which focuses on unique lending criteria for churches, and a chapter which provides an overview of the lending process.

Now let's begin with the most important of the Five C's of Credit: character.

CHAPTER 6

CHARACTER

"This is what the LORD has commanded. When a man
makes a vow to the LORD, or swears an oath—an obligation
that is binding to himself—he is not to break his word. Instead,
he is to fulfill whatever promise came out of his mouth."
– NUMBERS 30:1b–2 ISV

"Character is like pregnancy; it can't be hidden
forever."
– AFRICAN PROVERB

One of my earliest memories in banking was being taught that the perceived lack of character is a deal killer, right from the start. At the banks where I worked, perceived lack of character was an automatic decline for the wealthiest individuals who had millions in their savings accounts and it was a deal killer for those with far less funds.

Why? Because regardless of all the other strengths of a financial package, if the individuals within a business—or a church—do not have good character, the risks are very high that the loan will not be repaid under its original terms, or repaid at all. And make no mistake about it—loans are meant to be repaid.

Let's say you have an Uncle Bob whom you've known all your life and as part of that knowledge, you know that Uncle Bob never follows through on any promise he's ever made, no matter how large or small. In short, you know that Uncle Bob has low character through your personal interactions with him.

What if you loaned Uncle Bob money five different times and he was late in paying you the first three times, he only paid you back half of what you had loaned him the fourth time, and the fifth time, he didn't pay you back a dime. How would you feel?

I'm not done. What if Uncle Bob got angry *with you* when you reminded him about the agreed-upon payment deadlines *and* said you didn't even need the money anyway? What if Uncle Bob then told the rest of the family how hardhearted you were after he told you he was trying his best to come up with the funds? Would you be excited about loaning Uncle Bob money for a sixth time? Not likely.

Lenders don't have that "Uncle Bob" type of personal experience with new potential borrowers. Most individuals whom bankers meet are absolute strangers before the bankers receive their loan requests. In some cases, borrowers are referred by someone whom the banker knows—perhaps a mutual acquaintance that is a co-worker, an outside attorney, or an insurance agent. Even in those cases, however, lenders still don't know their new acquaintance well.

How, then, can a bank assess that potential borrower's character? One of the first places to start is that potential borrower's credit report. A credit report provides lenders an individual or an organization's past payment history on loans. The credit report is meant to indicate how well borrowers do what they said they would do as it pertains to repaying a loan under the original terms, or at all. In sum, the credit report signals not only the ability to repay debts on time, but also the willingness to repay debts on time.

Character is the primary issue for lenders because they are in the business of extending loans that must be repaid over time, on time, every time. It's not enough for the lender to be repaid eventually. Therefore, what's called a "slow pay" on a credit report alerts a banker that even though a borrower agreed to pay the creditor on the first of the month, it might be the 15th of the month before that money was received... or maybe the 15th of the following month! This was not the original agreement. Although borrowers may think they're fine as long as they eventually repay the money, it's not fine. Paying almost on time is not the same as paying on time!

Just as none of us wants to chase "Uncle Bob" for money we loan him, banks don't want to chase borrowers for money they loan them. Banks don't want to hire collection agencies, they don't want to charge off a loan as unpaid, and they certainly don't want to foreclose on a church building or any other asset.

It's also not good character for a borrower to dismiss the bank's concern about the late payments with the words, "They have enough money, they don't need mine." Lenders are trying to assess character and will use credit reports to do so.

There are at least two types of credit reports that lenders access. The first type of credit report is a credit report on individuals. This is the same type of report that is pulled when individuals apply for car loans, mortgage loans, apartments, and credit cards. One or more of the following three credit bureaus are used by most lenders: Experian, Equifax, and TransUnion.

Why do lenders pull individual credit reports for a loan to an organization? The answer is that organizations don't repay loans; individuals who work for those organizations do! Therefore, the reports that may be accessed could be for the pastor, for the church treasurer, or for any other person who is responsible for ensuring that loan payments are made on time.

The second type of credit report that lenders typically access provides historical payment information for the organization itself. These types of business credit reports include *Dun & Bradstreet* reports that reflect how the organization pays its suppliers and vendors. Lenders also access reports from various online databases in search of past bankruptcies, defaults on government debt, income tax liens, and even criminal records.

If you know any credit report contains incorrect information, or there is, in your opinion, a viable reason for a poor report, then bring that to the lender's attention immediately. There is no guarantee that the lender will overlook that information, but it's important for individuals to make the effort if they believe the information listed doesn't accurately reflect either their character or that of their organization.

Not all negative issues on credit reports are automatic deal killers and different lenders have different levels of tolerance for past bankruptcies. All past bankruptcies require explanation, but some lenders view a bankruptcy that occurred more than three years ago as something that can be mitigated by an excellent current payment history. Other lenders believe seven or more years of payment history are needed to mitigate a bankruptcy.

In my experience, no lender will move forward when credit reports reveal an existing tax lien because the Internal Revenue Service can claim priority over the organization's assets. Additionally, many lenders will not loan money to an organization in which any bank experienced a loan loss with that borrower.

Even as I'm writing this chapter, I can hear church leaders raising the issues of Wall Street corruption and evil business dealings throughout our country and around the world. I even know that it wouldn't take anyone too long to Google specific examples of how those of high character were walked over, and those of low character seemed to win the day.

In fact, this cry is not new, is it? Throughout Scripture, God's people cried out to Him about the victories of those who were corrupt; those who practiced ungodly character.

Remember how Habakkuk questioned God?

"...the Law has become paralyzed, and justice never comes about. Because criminals outnumber the righteous, whenever judgments are issued, they come out crooked."[50]

---

50 Habakkuk 1:4 ISV.

What was God's response?

"For the revelation pertains to an appointed time—it speaks truthfully about the end. Though it delays, wait for it, because it will surely come about—it will not be late! Notice their arrogance—they have no inward uprightness—but the righteous will live by their faith."[51]

The prophet Malachi communicated this to God's people:

"You have wearied the LORD with your words. You ask, 'How have we wearied You?' By your saying, 'All who do evil are good in the eyes of the LORD and He's pleased with them,' or 'Where is the God of justice?'"[52]

God's answer?

"'They'll be Mine,' says the LORD of the Heavenly Armies, 'in the day when I prepare My treasured possession. I'll spare them, just as a man spares his own son who serves him. When you return, you will see the difference between the righteous and the wicked, between the one who serves God and the one who does not.'"[53]

Christian character means we don't get a pass when we see evil seeming to win the day. Therefore, phrases such as these are not acceptable if we're looking at the Word of God and the God of the Word:

"Wall Street does this all the time."
"I didn't know what I was signing, so I don't care what it says."
"God showed me that it's okay to walk away."

---

51 Habakkuk 2:4–5, ISV.
52 Malachi 2:17, ISV.
53 Malachi 3:17–18, ISV.

Character asks, "Are we trustworthy?" Let me modify that. Character asks, "Are we trustworthy even when our backs are against the wall?" Character shows up in pressure, not just in the absence of pressure. Character shows up when we do what we say we're going to do. This is what banks seek—borrowers with character.

CLOSING THOUGHTS

In 2006, I was privileged to contribute as a devotional writer to *Aspire: The New Women of Color Study Bible*. My devotional topic was about character. Here's what I wrote:

> "As leaders, we are always watched, often critiqued. Whether we agree with or approve of others assessing us, this is a fact we must accept in our leadership roles. It is our character—our actions, thoughts, motives—that people are evaluating. Are we above reproach? Of all the things that the Lord counts as precious, our character leads the list (see 1 Peter 3:4)[54]. This truth alone should inspire us to emulate the character of Christ. In fact, our character is so precious to the Lord that when it pleases Him, He showcases it. Remember Job (see Job 1:8, 2:3 ESV)[55]?
>
> In His teaching, Jesus clearly underscored the importance of character. For instance, in Matthew 5:11 we are told that we are blessed when people insult us and falsely say all kinds of evil against us because of Christ. Why are we blessed in this situation? Because if we are falsely accused, it means that despite their best attempts, our accusers—including the devil—cannot find anything against us that we have done or that we have not already confessed in true repentance. We have to guard our character,

---

54 "Rather it should be that of your inner self, the unfading beauty of a gentle and quiet spirit, which is of great worth in God's sight." (1 Peter 3:4, NIV).

55 "And the LORD said to Satan, 'Have you considered my servant Job, that there is none like him on the earth, a blameless and upright man, who fears God and turns away from evil?'" (Job 1:8, 2:3 ESV).

paying attention to our actions and words so that this is always the case.

Character does not mean perfection, but it does mean striving for perfection by the power of the Holy Spirit. It has often been said that character is defined by who we are when no one is looking. For us as Christian leaders, character is better defined by who we are because we know the Lord is always looking!"[56]

---

56 Katara A. Washington, ed., *Aspire: The New Women of Color Study Bible*, (Grand Rapids, MI, Zondervan, 2006), 1473.

CHAPTER 7

CASH FLOW

"Entrepreneurs believe that profit is what
matters most in a new enterprise. But profit is
secondary. Cash flow matters most."

– PETER DRUCKER

"The three most dreaded words in the English
language are 'negative cash flow.'"

– DAVID TANG

Al Johnson was excited about the capital campaign he and his team
were planning to introduce to the congregation on Sunday. He was
the leader of their new capital campaign team and he had invested a lot of
time and energy in his role. The biggest challenge his team had faced was
selecting the firm to lead their capital campaign—there were so many!
After several months and more presentations than he could remember,
his team finally selected a highly recommended firm and was prepared to
move forward.

This capital campaign was critical to raising funds for their church's
upcoming building expansion. These would be funds that were above and
beyond their normal tithes and offerings.

It was an exciting time, but just between him and the stained-glass windows, Al had to admit to himself that he was nervous about relying on campaign pledges to repay their new church loan. But then, as before, he reassured himself with the firm's long track record of helping churches cast a compelling vision for raising capital campaign funds. Plus, their bank had even approved the financing! It might be a stretch, but Al was sure they'd be able pay their new loan and still conduct powerful ministry.

Al shook off the nervous feeling and said out loud: "It's going to be fine. No...It's going to be phenomenal."

What Do We Mean by "Cash Flow"?

Capital campaign pledges, tithes and offerings, ministry expenses, and loan payments that Al was thinking about all fall under the umbrella that covers the second of the Five C's: cash flow. Cash flow measures an organization's ability to make all required loan payments after paying for normal operating expenses and any other costs. Cash *flow* is not the same as cash *equity* or cash *down payment*, which we will discuss in Chapter 9.

Cash flow is the most important factor for a bank after character and it should be just as important to church leaders. Why is cash flow so important to lenders? The answer is that it's the lender's "plan A": how the lender believes the loan will be repaid if all goes as expected.

The first C, character, assesses if a borrower will pay back a loan. This second C, cash flow, assesses if a borrower can pay back a loan.

We understand this concept when Aunt Jeanne (Uncle Bob's twin sister) asks us for a $500 loan. We ask profound questions like, "How am I going to get my money back?" Aunt Jeanne might respond, "I have a new job and I'd like to pay you $50 a month from each paycheck for five months." If Aunt Jeanne gets paid twice a month, that's $100 a month, and there's your $500 after five months.

After evaluating Aunt Jeanne's character, you're now relying on her new job to provide her enough funds to pay you back. That's cash flow!

And, if you take the time to figure out what other bills Aunt Jeanne has in addition to your loan payment—such as taxes that will be deducted from her paycheck—that's the beginning of cash flow analysis!

Yet, this is the challenge, isn't it? In this scenario, Aunt Jeanne's salary hasn't yet materialized, so what you're actually relying on is projected cash flow, not proven historical cash flow. This distinction between projected cash flow and historical cash flow is one that is frequently missed by potential borrowers. Misunderstanding this distinction also causes significant repayment problems.

Historical cash flow is just that: cash flow that an organization has generated in the past. In contrast, projected cash flow is cash flow that an organization tries, hopes, and prays to generate in the future.

Now let's go back to the capital campaign planned by Al Johnson's church. No matter how wonderful the capital campaign firm that is hired, no matter how excited the leadership team and even congregation, every campaign pledge only represents future cash flow—and future cash flow can't pay current bills!

You could rightly state that no cash flow is guaranteed and you would be correct. The next tithe collected always is part of future cash flow. Here's the difference. You can reasonably rely on cash flow that's been taken up week after week, month after month, year after year in your congregation. It certainly is not guaranteed. Members move to new towns and to new churches, and they lose jobs. At least, however, you have a reasonable historical trend.

In contrast, when we look to future cash flow levels that are well above historical trends, we have entered into a higher level of risk than we might be willing to take with Aunt Jeanne if we're not quite sure when her new job will start. We certainly have entered a higher level of risk than banks typically take. We understand this view when it comes to Aunt Jeanne. Many church leaders don't fully appreciate this view when they apply for church loans.

Why don't banks like to rely on projected cash flow? The primary reason is that projected cash flow is far more unreliable than proven, historical cash flow. By analysis and experience, banks have learned that projected cash flow never pays a bill—only cash in hand does.

I'll share an inside secret. After all my years in banking, I've learned that if the first thing an organization's leaders show me are their projected financial statements it means there's something in the recent past that's gone wrong! This belief has proven true repeatedly when the leaders eventually unveil historical financial statements that show losses and negative cash flow.

Now let me ask an equally important question: Why shouldn't church leaders rely on projected cash flow? The answer is that church leaders should not rely on what could be rather than what actually is.

How many capital campaigns were the basis of a leadership team's decision to move forward in building a new sanctuary, only to learn the hard way that promised capital campaign contributions don't pay a present day loan? In fact, promised campaign funds don't pay anything!

Too many pastors have learned with perfect 20/20 hindsight that individuals can pledge, not pay, and not lose one wink of sleep over that decision! In contrast, how many pastors have lost sleep and even their health because their projected cash flow never materialized?

I'll take it one step farther. There is a cliché that all pastors care about is... okay, you've heard it too! All pastors care about is money! In actuality, I have found that's not the case. Why, then, do so many pastors preach about finances every week? I believe the answer lies in this very issue: These pastors and church leaders relied on projected cash flow that hasn't come in.

Whether that shortfall in capital campaign receipts is because church members have relocated, there is a bad economy, or they simply changed their mind, too many pastors are put in the position of practically begging for money week after week because they have to, not because they want to. The church needs the funds that were projected and promised.

But there is a better way. The lesson that banks have learned, that church leaders can emulate, is to rely primarily on an organization's historical cash flow, instead of projected cash flow.

ANALYZING HISTORICAL CASH FLOW

Ever get a car loan? The finance company always asks about your salary and other sources of income because they want to know your revenues. That's inflow. They also ask about your household expenses because they want to know your outflow. If the difference between your inflow and your outflow is positive, that's a surplus and you may be approved for the loan. If the difference is negative, however, that's a deficit and you'll likely be declined—or asked to locate a co-signer with positive cash flow.

How do lenders obtain this income and expense information for churches, not-for-profits, and businesses? The answer is that organization's financial statements. As discussed in Chapter 3, lenders require several years of historical financial statements to assess the entity's cash flow over time, along with a recent year-to-date financial statement. Lenders are seeking to evaluate the historical trend.

In addition, as discussed in Chapter 2: "The Role of Faith," God calls us to have faith, but He doesn't call us to take a bet. A careful analysis of your church's cash flow capacity will enable the leadership team to exercise greater wisdom in evaluating outside debt to purchase, build, or expand a building.

There certainly still is a risk that something could change to negatively impact that historical cash flow. An organization's cash flow is not guaranteed, even from week to week. The risk of historical cash flow disappearing, however, is far lower than the risk associated with unproven, pie-in-the-sky, projected cash flow.

BIG PICTURE

If you open an introductory book about finance, you'll find different "models" for calculating cash flow and then evaluating how well that calculated figure covers expected loan payments. There are individuals who are paid substantial salaries for creating and running those models. These are individuals with strong accounting and finance backgrounds or people who can create computer models that produce those calculations for you.

My goal is not to transform pastors and church leaders into financial gurus or computer geniuses if that's not already their skill set. My primary goal is to underscore two points: First, the church's historical cash flow must be measured and evaluated. Second, the church's excess cash flow—that is, the cash flow that remains after paying for normal church expenses—must cover their expected loan payments. The term that bankers use is "Debt Service Coverage" that measures how well the organization's excess cash flow covers all required loan payments.

Moreover, bankers don't want that excess cash flow to barely cover the expected loan payments or to cover it by just a hair. Bankers look for historical excess cash flow to cover the expected loan payments by a comfortable cushion, to protect against unexpected decreases in giving and/or increases in expenses.

The Cash Flow Statement was previously discussed in Chapter 3 and an example is provided in Appendix II. Debt Service Coverage will be discussed in greater detail in Chapter 11 and in Appendix III.

OTHER CONSIDERATIONS

POTENTIAL PITFALLS OF CAPITAL CAMPAIGNS

My fictious story about Al Johnson at the beginning of this chapter notwithstanding, one of the most common—and successful—means of raising funds for a building project is a capital campaign. Many churches hire professional capital campaign managers to run their capital campaign. Christ Community did not use a capital campaign when we purchased our existing building, but we did use one when we renovated our facility several years ago. The advantages are many, including buy-in of your congregation into the project and reduced need for debt financing.

Capital campaigns can have several drawbacks, however, that relate to cash flow. First, capital campaigns always should be above and beyond your normal tithes and offerings. If capital campaign dollars go up, but tithes and offerings go down, the church is sacrificing funds for on-going ministry and general operations for cash that will be tied up in a building.

The second drawback is that capital campaigns can artificially inflate giving when applying for a building loan. If a church has an inexperienced banker or one that is more interested in closing a loan than they are in what's best for the church, the banker will use the higher revenue figures to justify a larger loan than the church will be able to afford on an on-going basis.

Let me be more specific. Most capital campaigns are set for one, two or three years. Congregations are asked to give above and beyond their normal tithes and offerings over that period and many of them do. The problem? If the loan repayment is based on those temporary capital campaign contributions, what will happen when the capital campaign ends? That's right. There will be insufficient cash flow to pay the debt.

I believe this is one of the reasons many church leaders extend existing capital campaigns, launch new capital campaigns, or just constantly preach to their congregation about giving!

It gets even worse when we layer in the last drawback of capital campaigns: Campaign pledges are not the same as cold, hard cash. Anyone can write what they're going to give to the campaign on a pledge card or on-line. Some people are just scribbling something to blend in with the others and have no intention of honoring a pledge.

In my experience, however, most members do intend to honor their pledge, but then something unexpected occurs. These unexpected occurrences include the loss of a job, relocation to another state, health issues, the loss of a college scholarship that previously covered their child's tuition, or an economic downturn.

In my experience, some members work to honor their pledge even in these circumstances, but many won't or can't. For these reasons, reliance on capital campaigns should be conservative. Many banks won't fund a loan that involves a capital campaign until at least 50% of the capital campaign pledges has been received in cash. Some banks won't rely on capital campaign pledges at all.

I'm not a fan of including capital campaign contributions in cash flow to evaluate debt service coverage. Rather, I believe the best practice is for church leaders to rely on historical cash flow from tithes and offerings when establishing your loan amount, and even there, to use about 75% to 80% of tithes and offerings to leave the church a cushion.

In my opinion, capital campaign contributions certainly can be used to raise cash for the down payment. They are not, however, an on-going source of revenue for the church and should not be viewed as such.

Tenant Income

Quite frequently, borrowers who have or expect to own real estate property incorporate rental income from a tenant in their cash flow revenue. This tenant may be an organization or individual that is leasing a portion of the borrower's property full-time. Alternatively, it may be another organization—often a church—that is leasing the property part-time. For example, another congregation may use your facility on Saturday mornings or Sunday afternoons. Finally, a church may own investment real estate that is 100% leased to tenants.

Whatever the source of this tenant income, church leaders should realize that most lenders will exclude any tenant income from their cash flow analysis; meaning, lenders will not give churches credit for this income. This may seem overly conservative, but the reason is sound. Tenant income has proven to be unreliable over the years, particularly in an economic downturn.

If reliance is made, what will happen if the tenant moves out? What will happen if the tenant goes out of business? What will happen if the tenants are late with *their* rent? These are not just hypothetical considerations. These events occur quite frequently.

For a lender to rely on a tenant's income to repay the borrower's loan, the lender would have to do one or more of the following:

- Obtain the tenant's financial statements and evaluate their financial strength and capacity in the same way the lender is evaluating the borrower's financial strength and capacity;

- Require that the minimum term of the lease agreement between the borrower and the tenant equal the term of the loan;
- Require the tenant to be a co-borrower or guarantor on the loan.

Of course, most tenants would not be willing to proceed on this basis because they have no vested interest in doing so.

For all these reasons, tenant income certainly can provide an added cushion for borrowers, but it should never be relied on by the borrower or the bank for loan repayment. On this basis, banks do not give credit to tenant income when evaluating loans.[57]

WE CAN AFFORD IT

The last consideration is this: Just because the church can cash flow a loan, doesn't mean it should take on the loan. This concept is similar to the recommendation I would give anyone when going to purchase a car or a house: Beware of salespeople who only want you to focus on the question, "How much can you afford?"

As discussed in Chapter 1, the "how-much-can-you-afford" model of financing typically results in borrowers who don't focus on the interest rate they'll be paying or how long they'll be paying the loan. These borrowers may pay for what they're purchasing two to three times over because their sole focus is on whether or not they can afford the note!

This is the same premise when it comes to building finance. I've heard too many pastors focus on the so-called "affordable" payment and miss the significant opportunity costs they are bearing and the interest expense they are paying.

---

57 This assumes that we're looking at owner-occupied real estate wherein the borrower occupies at least 51% of the real estate property. Investment real estate loans necessarily rely on tenant income and therefore are more risky, requiring more specialized lenders who focus on those types of loans.

CLOSING THOUGHTS

So, what's the big picture? The big picture is the purpose of cash flow calculations and analysis is to see if the church, or any organization, receives enough cash revenue over a specific period to pay all required expenses—and then have more than enough to make the loan payments over that same period. The shorter version? Does the church consistently receive enough money to pay all its bills, including the loan payment, with cash flow left over in case something unexpected happens.

That's the concept and it's a critical one: Understand that the second "C" of cash flow is a lender's Plan A; that is, how the lender expects to be repaid if all goes as planned. In the next chapter, we'll discuss the third C of Credit: collateral.

CHAPTER 8

COLLATERAL

"I could never convince the financiers that Disneyland
was feasible, because dreams offer too little collateral."
— WALT DISNEY

"On the one blind date I went on, I had a backup. If I texted
you the code word, you call and say my dogs are sick."
— BRITT ROBERTSON

My church uses Quicken software to record our financial transactions. Every so often, we receive a message asking if we would like to "back up" our data. The idea, of course, is that if something happens to our primary Quicken file—for example, if the data are corrupted—then we can access the back-up file. This back-up file might be on a zip drive or more likely these days, "in the Cloud."

Is a back-up file worth it? If you've ever lost data, you know that the answer to that question is a resounding, "Yes!" While the back-up file may not allow us to recapture 100% of the data, it keeps us from losing 100% of our data! Quicken gives its users a back-up plan.

In similar fashion, prudent lenders have a back-up plan for every loan they make. Lenders perform in-depth analysis regarding how they think they're going to be repaid. We called that "Plan A" in the previous chapter. Plan A typically is the second C of Credit: cash flow.

Although it's every lender's hope that Plan A works, prudent lenders do not rely on Plan A alone. They have at least one back-up plan, which we'll call, "Plan B." Why do lenders have a Plan B back-up plan? The answer is simple. Just as with Quicken, the purpose of the back-up plan is to keep from losing everything if something goes wrong with Plan A.

Let's say a bank makes a $500,000 building loan and expects to earn approximately $27,000 in interest revenue in the first year of that loan. This equates to a 5.4% average rate of return in Year 1.[58]

Now let's further speculate that the borrower committed outright fraud and did not pay the bank one thin dime on the loan. As a result, the bank has to write off the entire $500,000 for nonpayment. In this example, rather than earning $27,000, the bank loses $500,000—and loses out on the $27,000 it didn't receive.

This still may not seem significant to some, especially if you're thinking about how many millions or billions of dollars that banks are worth. So, let's add a zero and assume instead that the bank made a $5,000,000 building loan, rather than a $500,000 building loan. Assuming the same 5.4% average rate of return, the expected interest revenue to the bank in the first year would be approximately $270,000—not bad![59]

Now let's assume that the bank had to write off the $5,000,000 in its entirety for nonpayment. Rather than receiving $270,000 the first year, the bank now has to write off the entire $5,000,000—and loses out on the $270,000 in interest revenue it didn't receive. I don't know too many organizations that won't blink at $5,000,000, do you? And certainly, $500,000, or even $50,000 write-offs aren't treated lightly either.

For this reason, lenders need a back-up plan. Lenders don't want to write off that amount of money at a loss. Further, if a lender has too many losses, they can't afford to remain in business. Banks have, in fact, gone out of business for just this reason.

---

58 $27,000 ÷ $500,000 = 5.4%.

59 $5,000,000 x 0.054 (the equivalent of 5.4%) = $270,000.

So, what is the lender's back-up plan or Plan B? The third C of Credit: collateral. Most of us are familiar with this concept without even realizing it. Ever get a loan to purchase a car? What is one of the first documents you sign when getting that car loan? The pink slip giving the creditor a lien on that car you're purchasing. Collateral.

Ever get a loan to purchase a home? What is one of the first documents you sign when getting that home loan? A deed of trust or mortgage document giving the creditor a lien on that home you're purchasing. Collateral.

If you were to search the Internet for a definition of the word "collateral," you might find these definitions on various sites:

- Something pledged as security for repayment of a loan, to be forfeited in the event of a default;[60]
- Something provided to a lender as a guarantee of repayment;[61]
- Valuable property owned by someone who wants to borrow money that they agree will become the property of the company or person who lends the money if the debt is not paid back.[62]

Creditors certainly extend unsecured loans to companies and even to individuals. For example, credit card debt and student loans are unsecured. Those loans, however, have higher associated risk and only the largest creditors can afford the write-offs that come when those loans are not paid. For this reason, lenders almost always require some type of collateral on commercial loans and larger consumer loans—such as your home mortgage or car note.

Collateral provides lenders alternatives to taking a total charge-off for unpaid loans. Why? Because the asset that serves the lender best is one that they can sell in the event of payment default. The collateral actually is assigned to the lender for that very reason.

---

60 Due, "Need a Secured Loan? Here's a Guide to Understanding Collateral," October 24, 2017, online: https://due.com/blog/guide-to-understanding-collateral/.
61 Merriam-Webster, online: https://www.merriam-webster.com/dictionary/collateral.
62 Cambridge Dictionary, online: https://dictionary.cambridge.org/us/dictionary/english/collateral.

What is the collateral when church leaders borrow money to purchase land and an existing building, or obtain financing to construct a new building? The collateral is that land and building.

This is critical for pastors and leaders to understand: The bank has a lien on your real estate property. Your. Church. Building. Could. Be. Lost. Of course, there are accompanying ramifications for the church: poor witness, wasted energy, diverted focus, and a discouraged or even grief-stricken congregation.

One of the largest misunderstandings that church leaders have is not realizing that banks have a responsibility to minimize losses and will take every measure to do so. The notion that a bank will not foreclose upon a church for public relations reasons is not accurate. While it certainly is true that banks are highly sensitive to foreclosing on churches, it is equally true that banks have changed that practice in recent years.

While banks certainly are aware of the impact of negative public opinion, banks certainly are foreclosing on church buildings! Further, because many banks can sell the foreclosed property to another church waiting in line, it is not clear that this is even the public relations nightmare that it may have been in the past. The days when lenders do not foreclose on church buildings are over.

I also will tell you that, in my opinion, this type of thinking on the part of church leaders is flawed. Let's look at two directives that the Lord gave to the nation of Israel. The first occurred immediately following God's deliverance of His people from 400 years of Egyptian slavery. The second occured 40 years later when the next generation was poised to enter the Promised Land.

> "If you loan money to My people, to the poor among you, don't be like a creditor to them and don't impose interest on them. If you take your neighbor's coat as collateral, you are to return it to him by sunset, for it's his only covering; it's his outer garment, for what else can he sleep in? And when he cries out to Me, I'll hear him, for I am gracious." (Exodus 22:25-27 ISV)

"When you loan something to your neighbor, don't enter his house to seize what he offered as collateral. Stay outside and let the man to whom you made the loan bring it out to you. If he is a poor man, don't go to sleep with his collateral in your possession. Be sure to return his garment to him at sunset so that he may sleep with it, and he will bless you. It will be a righteous deed in the presence of the LORD your God." (Deuteronomy 24:10-13 ISV)

In both passages, the Lord spoke very clearly through Moses that the people of Israel were not to act like creditors, either in charging interest or in foreclosing on collateral. In today's language, the Lord tells Israel not to be like a bank!

Here's the problem: The Lord's directive was given to the people of God for their interpersonal transactions. It was not given to a business community. It's incorrect to confuse a for-profit bank that operates in the business world with a people or even an organization that seeks to operate under Biblical precepts. And, by the way, even in the referenced passages above, the Lord only discusses returning collateral to those individuals who are poor!

Creditors are not tasked with being lenient and absorbing losses that hurt their business because the loan is to a church. Collateral is a lender's back-up plan to prevent or reduce losses, including losses that can put them out of business. While lenders will seek to work with churches, church leaders should recognize that banks have the right to exercise their options in ways they consider best for their own interests.

LOAN-TO-VALUE

The term that lenders use to reflect what proportion or percentage the requested loan makes up of the total collateral value is "Loan-to-Value" or "LTV" for short. A typical LTV for a church building ranges from 50% to 75%, although 80% has become increasingly common for very strong churches. Even an 85% LTV is not unheard of for some lenders.

Let's look at an example showing how LTV is calculated. Let's assume the following:

- Approved Loan Amount: $ 750,000
- Value of the Church Building: $1,000,000

The Loan-to-Value or LTV is calculated as $750,000 (the loan) divided by $1,000,000 (the value), which equals 75.0%, expressed as a percentage.

If there is more than one loan secured by the same collateral, then the combined loan amounts are compared to the value of that collateral. Let's assume the following:

- Existing Loan Amount: $ 350,000
- New Loan Amount: $ 550,000
- Value of the Church Building: $1,000,000

In this case, the LTV is calculated as $900,000 (the combined loans) divided by $1,000,000 (the value), which equals 90.0%.

I never have seen an LTV of 90% or higher for a church. This is the case for two reasons. First, lenders want to leave themselves a "cushion" if they foreclose and sell the property. Everyone knows that most people expect some type of discount when purchasing an asset from a bank's foreclosure department. Lenders incorporate that knowledge when they set the maximum LTV on a loan. Think about it: When is the last time you paid top dollar at a liquidation sale?

Second, and perhaps more important, lenders want the borrower to inject some cash equity in the deal, rather than provide the borrower 100% financing. This topic will be covered in greater depth in the next chapter when we cover the fourth C of Credit: capital.

HOW DOES A BANK ESTABLISH THE VALUE OF COLLATERAL?

Knowing that lenders almost always require collateral as their Plan B, church leaders should ask themselves two questions about that collateral: "What's it worth?" and "Who says so?" These questions are answered in the next section.

APPRAISALS

When lenders approve a loan, they typically do so on condition of receiving an acceptable "appraised value" that provides a professional opinion regarding how much the real estate collateral is worth. When lenders consider the collateral that serves as a back-up plan on their loan, they want to ensure that the value of that collateral exceeds the amount of the loan.

A real estate appraisal provides a qualified opinion as to the "appraised value" of the real estate property that will be pledged as collateral. It is important to note that most lenders must conform to federal guidelines when obtaining appraisals; more specifically, to the Federal Institutions Reform, Recovery, and Enforcement Act of 1989 commonly known by its acronym, "FIRREA" (pronounced Fy-ree-uh).

FIRREA stipulates that all federally regulated lenders must obtain an appraisal by a state certified appraiser; and, follow their primary regulator's FIRREA requirements for real estate appraisals for commercial loans exceeding $500,000 that are secured by commercial real property.[63] These appraisals are required to comply with the "Uniform Standards of Professional Appraisal Practice" that are the generally recognized ethical and performance standards for the appraisal profession in the United States.[64]

---

63 Federal Deposit Insurance Corporation, "FDIC Law, Regulations, Related Acts, Part 323 - Appraisals," online: https://www.fdic.gov/regulations/laws/rules/2000-4300.html.
64 The Appraisal Foundation, online: https://www.appraisalfoundation.org/imis/TAF/Standards/ Appraisal_Standards/Uniform_Standards_of_Professional_Appraisal_Practice/TAF/USPAP. aspx?hkey=a6420a67-dbfa-41b3-9878-fac35923d2af.

Among its many requirements, FIRREA stipulates that an appraisal must be ordered by a bank. This means that borrowers cannot order their own appraisals and expect the bank to use that appraisal in their credit decision. Moreover, if it's learned that a borrower directly ordered an appraisal from a specific appraiser in the past, the bank will not use that same appraiser to evaluate the same property. In fact, not even individual bankers are allowed to directly order appraisals at most lending institutions.

Why are most banks precluded from using appraisals that were ordered directly by borrowers or by individual bankers? The bank is reducing the risk of an appraisal not being completed on an "arms-length" basis. "Arms-length" describes a service or transaction between two parties that have no prior relationship, and who have negotiated a fair price and outcome through normal market forces. To put it in plain language, arms-length means there's no "hook-up" or side deal.

In this context, borrowers and individual bankers cannot order their own appraisal to reduce the risk that the appraiser that was used was the individual banker's first cousin once removed or the head of the deacon board who happens to own an appraisal firm!

This requirement is critical because if church leaders order their own appraisal and attempt to submit it to the bank, that appraisal will be rejected and another appraisal will be ordered by the bank in its place. As a result, the church would have to pay for two appraisals, not just one.

On this basis, to help ensure an arms-length appraisal that meets FIRREA requirements, the entire appraisal process is managed by a separate appraisal department within most banks. The individuals in these departments have the expertise to evaluate appraisers and appraisals, and even maintain a list of pre-qualified appraisers with whom they work.

The appraisal department also manages a bidding process when it's time to order an appraisal. The appraisal department invites three appraisal firms from its pre-qualified list to submit competitive bids to appraise the real estate property. Once those bids are received, the appraisal department invites the borrower to select one of those firms on a "blind" basis. "Blind" means that the identity of the appraisal firm is not disclosed during the selection process.

The only information the borrower typically sees at that point is each appraiser's proposed fee and estimated time for completing the appraisal. I strongly recommend that church leaders request to see one more criterion before selecting the appraisal firm: the appraiser's experience in appraising church buildings. Church leaders do not want their appraisal to be the first church property that firm ever has appraised!

Once the appraiser is selected, the identity of that appraisal firm is revealed to the borrower. At that point, the appraiser will reach out to the borrower's designated contact person. The entire appraisal process typically takes two to four weeks. This timeframe includes up to one week for the bank's appraisal department to review the appraisal report when it is completed, to ensure that it complies with FIRREA requirements.

Cost of Appraisal

The cost of the appraisal depends on the size, type, and complexity of the real estate property and how quickly the appraisal is needed. Typical church appraisals range in price from $3,000 to $7,000 for a normal four-week turnaround time. If the appraisal is needed more quickly—for example, if there is a very short deadline to close the loan—then the appraiser will charge a premium. In my experience, this premium typically ranges from $500 to $2,000, but can be higher.

Appraising Existing Buildings and New Construction/Renovation

There are two types of value that coincide with valuing existing buildings or valuing new construction or renovations, respectively. The most common appraised value is what's called an "as-is" appraised value. This value is appropriate for an existing real estate property. "As-is" means valuing the land and the improvements just as they are right now, with no changes or improvements.

The second type of value is pertinent to construction loans or loans for renovating an existing building or buildings. In this case, the lender starts with the "as-is" valuation, based upon the value of the property before construction or renovations have occurred.

Then, because at least some portion of the property has not yet been constructed or renovated, the lender also needs a value that extends beyond the "as-is" value. An additional component is needed that will be an assessment of what the property will be worth once the construction or renovation is completed. This additional value is referred to as an "as-complete" value.

This "as-complete" valuation is understandably harder to determine because it doesn't yet exist! The appraiser must rely on a detailed construction budget from a reputable general contractor, which in turn is based on detailed plans and specifications ("plans and specs") from a reputable architect.

In this case, the appraiser will provide two valuations in the appraisal report: an "as-is" value and an "as-complete" value. In turn, the lender will extend a certain amount of financing based on the "as-is" value and additional construction or renovation financing based on the "as-complete" value.

"UNDER-VALUATION"

Someone just read this section and asked a great question: "What happens if the appraised value is less than anticipated?" From the lender's perspective, if the appraised value is lower than anticipated, this means that the actual loan-to-value is higher.

Remember the example that was given earlier in the chapter?

- Approved Loan Amount: $ 750,000
- Value of Church Building: $1,000,000

As discussed, this scenario resulted in an LTV of 75.0%, calculated by dividing $750,000 by $1,000,000.

But now, let's say that the church building only appraised for $850,000 instead of $1,000,000. What happens to the LTV?

- Approved Loan Amount: $ 750,000
- Value of Church Building: $ 850,000

In this example, the LTV increases to 88.2%.[65] Why is this an issue? Because if the lender approved the $750,000 loan on condition that the LTV would not exceed 75.0%, then the higher LTV of 88.2% means that the lender no longer has enough "cushion" in its collateral.

As a result, the lender likely will not move forward in the financing without one or more remedies. What are some of the possible remedies?

- The lender may lower the approved loan amount to reduce the LTV to an acceptable level. In this example, the loan would have to be reduced to $637,500, which is a $112,500 reduction.[66] Where would that additional $112,500 shortfall come from? Most likely, it would have to come from the church's cash balances, if available;
- If the building finance is for a construction loan, the project itself may have to be scaled back;
- The borrower could pledge additional collateral acceptable to the lender, such as a certificate of deposit ("CD") or additional real estate. It is highly likely that any non-cash collateral also would need to be valued;
- The lender could agree to increase their acceptable loan-to-value (LTV). This option is not realistic in this example, however, because the calculated LTV of 88.2% already is not considered prudent from a lender's perspective.

Regrettably, under-valuations occur quite frequently and can be a significant issue for churches that are unaware of this lender requirement.

65 $750,000 ÷ $850,000 = 88.2% (rounded).
66 $850,000 x 0.75 (equivalent to 75.0%) = $637,500. To confirm, $637,500 ÷ $850,000 = 75.0%.

During the Great Recession, this very issue kept many churches from being able to renew their loans that matured during the recession when property values declined below the appraised value that was in place when the loan originated—for many, just five years before. This issue occurs in every economic downturn.

Additionally, most church buildings are more susceptible to short-falls in appraised values because they are considered "special purpose" properties. Special purpose properties are those that have a unique physical design, special construction materials, and/or a layout that restricts its use to the specific purpose for which it was built. The properties are designed specifically for that one use and if they were put up for sale, the only purchasers typically would be those interested in that same use.

Even church buildings that don't have a steeple and formal sanctuary (stained glass windows, pulpit, balcony) are considered special purpose properties because they are much more difficult to sell than, say, a traditional office building or warehouse that have multiple uses. Other examples of special purpose properties include bowling alleys, car washes, gas stations, and hotels.

I recognize that churches have been turned into night clubs—such as The Limelight in Manhattan in the early 1980s—but that is not the standard![67] The point is that the sale of special purposes properties is more challenging than the sale of "multi-purpose" facilities that can more easily accommodate many different types of occupants.

Churches also may be more difficult to appraise simply because there are fewer sales providing good comparison figures and because the appraiser may not be as familiar with the sales market for churches. This is the reason I strongly advise church leaders to ask the lender to include "prior church appraisal experience" as one of the required qualifications for any appraisal firm valuing their collateral.

---

67 I went to The Limelight once in my early 20s. It was not a comfortable experience!

RAW LAND

The term "raw land" denotes land that has no building or other improvements. It's just...land. Many congregations that plan to construct a new building or buildings seek to finance that type of project in stages. They start with the purchase of raw land as "Phase 1" and at a later date, continue with the building construction phase as "Phase 2."

Financing raw land is a challenge for most commercial lenders, however, because most raw land is not considered good collateral. The reason? It is more difficult for the lender to sell raw land after foreclosure because they have to find a purchaser that not only is willing to pay a reasonable market price to purchase that land, but also is capable of developing that land for a profitable return.

As a result, even if the bank were to finance the purchase of raw land, the maximum LTV likely will be much lower than it would be for financing land with improvements or land with an immediate construction plan. The LTV for raw land typically would be 50% at most. This means that the church would have to use its own cash to pay the remaining 50% of the purchase price.

ENVIRONMENTAL RISKS

Dry cleaners, gas stations, auto repair facilities, and other businesses that may use or store significant quantities of hazardous chemicals can cause significant environmental risk for property owners and for lenders that finance that property. From the lender's perspective, the risks of environmental contamination include: remediation costs that could negatively impact the borrower's ability to repay the loan and/or continue to operate; reduced value and marketability of the real estate; and, potential liability for the lender.

For these reasons, lenders take measures to assess the potential environmental risks of a real estate property that will serve as collateral. This environmental assessment takes place before the loan is closed and typically must be approved by a designated environmental specialist within the bank.

The specific environmental risks associated with a particular real estate transaction vary greatly depending on the property in question and the type of transaction. Generally speaking, every property should be evaluated for potential soil and groundwater contamination, both onsite and on surrounding properties. Historical records, regulatory files, and possible use restrictions may also be studied.

What does all of this have to do with a church building? The answer is that potential environmental risk is not limited to a church building that is being purchased or constructed; it also can pertain to properties in close proximity to the church property. "Close proximity" may include a property far down the street, but which is uphill from your property. The risk here is that hazardous material may flow down to your property.

The level of assessment needed typically starts with questionnaires that the bank requires both the existing property owner and a commercial bank officer to complete. Those questionnaires are typically based on "To the best of your knowledge" type of responses. If there are no known risks, if the loan does not involve new construction, and if the requested loan is relatively small ($500,000 or less), the responses on these questionnaires often are sufficient for the lender.

On the other hand, if it is deemed that a property has had environmental risk, if the loan is for new construction, or if it's a relatively large real estate loan, then many lenders require what's called a "Phase I Environmental Site Assessment" ("Phase I"). In my experience, Phase I Assessments range in price from $2,500 to $7,500, depending upon the size and complexity of the property.

The cost of the Phase I Assessment is typically paid by the borrower unless the seller agrees to pay for it as part of the purchase-sale negotiation. Of course, in a property purchase, the seller may already have a Phase I that may be acceptable, if it's deemed current and there are no prior identified environmental risks.

If environmental risks are identified in a Phase I, then remediation is required and that remediation must be documented and deemed satisfactory by the bank's environmental officer. As is the case of the Phase I, the responsibility for getting this done and paying for the work is negotiable between the current owner and purchaser.

PERSONAL GUARANTIES

When lenders make loans to for-profit, privately owned businesses, the lenders almost always require another element to their back-up plan: a personal guaranty or personal guaranties from every individual or affiliate owning 20% or more of the borrowing entity. By so doing, the individual owning and profiting from the business is personally liable for the loan.

In this case, if something goes wrong with Plan A, the lender not only has recourse to the pledged collateral, the lender also has recourse to the owner's personal assets (with some limitations).

It is my personal opinion that an individual should never personally guarantee a loan for a church. I say this for a number of reasons. First, unlike the case described above in which the business is owned by an individual who receives the actual profits of that business, the church is not owned by an individual. No individual (legally) receives funds from the church for his or her personal benefit.

Second, the owner of a business has control of that company and therefore is largely responsible for the consequences of decisions that he or she makes concerning that business. In contrast, no one individual has control over the revenues of a church. If top givers from the church relocate or are laid off, the burden of repaying that loan should not fall on one individual personally guaranteeing the loan.

Finally, my caution against personal guaranties from any one or more church members is meant for the health of the church. People guaranteeing church loans that are not church leaders, may believe they now have the right to influence the direction of the church in ways that are not in line with the leaders' vision for the church. Further, these individuals can be locked into the church in ways they do not want to be. If they must relocate to another state for a job, for example, they now are tied financially to a church they no longer attend.

If the person guaranteeing the loan is the pastor and his or her spouse, this latter issue applies as well. That said, there have been cases in which pastors and other key church leaders have stepped forward to personally guarantee a church loan when the bank would otherwise not make the loan. If that is their choice, it can be done. My primary point is that doing so often results in problems after the loan is made, especially if the pastor no longer is a part of that church.

CLOSING THOUGHTS

Understanding the importance of the third C, collateral, is critical when seeking building finance. Excellent character and positive cash flow cannot mitigate a shortfall in collateral value. For a lender, every good loan must have a secondary source of repayment.

The fourth "C"—capital—is important as well. This subject is the focus of our next chapter.

CHAPTER 9

CAPITAL

"The idiomatic expression to have
'skin in the game' means to have incurred monetary
risk by being involved in achieving a goal."
– www.english.stackexchange.com[68]

"I would say raising capital is one of the
weakest things for most entrepreneurs."
– ROBERT KIYOSAKI

Have you ever worked with someone who you thought was not putting in his or her fair share? Most of us can point to others who we believe are not pulling their weight. We may not agree on how "fair share" should be measured, but we can agree that the scales need to be tipped more in our favor.

Lenders feel the same way. Lenders typically contribute the largest portion of financing for a building purchase or construction project and are comfortable with that arrangement, to a point. Lenders believe that a borrower should inject something of significance for the borrower to have a fair share in the overall financing.

---

68 Stack Exchange, online: https://english.stackexchange.com/search?q=skin+in+the+game.

That "something" is called capital, which is our fourth C. Another common term is equity. In the context of building finance, it's the portion of the financing that typically is contributed by individual owners or by the organization itself. Capital may show up in the form of a cash down payment, land that was purchased years before, or any combination of assets not already serving as collateral.

As previously discussed, capital or equity is not the same as cash flow. An organization may have sufficient cash flow and still have insufficient cash equity or capital. One is not a substitute for the other.

Why is capital important? There are two primary reasons: "Skin in the Game" and "The Risks of High Leverage."

"SKIN IN THE GAME"

I previously shared that I worked in a bank's "Workout Loan" department early in my career. The Workout Loan department was the place loans were sent that had problems with repayment, collateral, or some other condition that materially altered the risk profile—and possibly collection—of that loan.

At the time I worked in that department, Dallas, Texas was in the midst of an economic downturn in which real estate values had plummeted. This steep decline in real estate values in 1990 and 1991 caused the Loan-to-Value ratios on collateral real estate to skyrocket above the agreed-upon maximum guidelines. LTV ratios increased well above 100%, meaning the real estate was worth less than the outstanding principal balance on the loan.

A number of these real estate properties were rental properties, primarily apartment buildings and rent houses. Many of our borrowers were the owners of these rental properties.

As in every economic downturn, people lost jobs. When people lost jobs, they couldn't pay their rent to their landlords—our borrowers. When our borrowers didn't receive their rent payments, they couldn't make their loan payments to the bank.

During that time, I saw an interesting phenomenon occur. Those borrowers who had contributed large cash down payments when they purchased their rental property tried very hard to work with the bank. They had used their own cash to purchase the property and they didn't want to lose their investment—which would occur if the bank foreclosed on the property for non-payment.

On the other hand, back in the 1980s, a number of loans had been structured with "zero down payments;" meaning, the bank had provided 100% debt financing on the real estate project. Those borrowers used none of their own cash for the project.

Many of those borrowers who obtained 100% debt financing did something very interesting. They walked into the bank's office, thanked the banker for working with them... and handed over the keys to the apartment building or rent house they had pledged as collateral. Those borrowers told the bankers to take back the property; they'd done all they could and were ready to move on.

The difference? The first set of borrowers fought harder because they had more to lose. The second set of borrowers had no cash of their own in the properties. They had been playing with house money (the bank's) and therefore, could better afford to turn the property back to the bank and walk away.

Banks understand this phenomenon from years of seeing it occur. "Skin in the game" really does make a difference. Individuals and organizations that invest their own funds in a project most often fight harder for the project's success precisely because they *are* invested. They're not just using house money.

THE RISKS OF HIGH LEVERAGE

In my opinion, the second consideration is even more important: the risks associated with "high leverage." Before we discuss "high leverage," however, let's first talk about what "leverage" means.

LEVERAGE

In the context of commercial lending, "leverage" refers to the proportion of debt financing that an organization uses, relative to the amount of equity financing that is contributed.

We already discussed one aspect of leverage in the last chapter: the Loan-to-Value or LTV ratio. As shared, the LTV ratio identifies the percent of debt financing versus equity financing that an organization uses to finance a particular asset. If a church is purchasing an existing building with a 70% LTV, it means the lender will provide 70% of the total purchase price in debt and the church will provide the remaining 30% of the purchase price in equity.

The concept of leverage, however, is not limited to the purchase of a single asset. When commercial bankers evaluate leverage, they also analyze the leverage associated with an organization's entire balance sheet. This leverage often is called "balance sheet leverage."

Commercial bankers most commonly measure balance sheet leverage using an equation called, the "Debt-to-Equity Ratio" or "D/E Ratio" for short. The Debt-to-Equity Ratio is defined below:

$$\text{D/E Ratio} = \frac{\text{Total Liabilities}}{\text{Total Equity}}$$

This ratio is measured at a particular point in time, based on an organization's total liabilities and total equity, as reflected on the balance sheet on that particular date.

So, how and why do bankers use this ratio? Let's look at the example below to answer that question. We'll assume in this example that a church's balance sheet dated as of December 31, 2019 showed the following figures:

- Total Liabilities: $1,200,000
- Total Equity: $ 500,000

What is the existing D/E Ratio as of December 31, 2019? Let's plug the numbers into the equation:

$$\text{D/E Ratio} \ = \ \frac{\text{Total Liabilities}}{\text{Total Equity}} \ = \ \frac{\$1,200,000}{\$500,000} \ = 2.4$$

Bankers would say, "This church has a Debt-to-Equity Ratio of 2.4 to 1" or "Their leverage is 2.4 to 1." These phrases also can be translated as follows: For every $1.00 the church has contributed, its creditors[69] have contributed $2.40. How do we reach that conclusion? Because according to the balance sheet, the church in this example has $1,200,000 in liabilities due to its outside creditors versus $500,000 of its own equity.

Is 2.4 to 1.0 a bad ratio? To answer that question, we would need to know what lenders consider acceptable. In the commercial banking field, lenders consider a D/E Ratio of 3.0 to 1.0 or less to be acceptable. This means that lenders believe a borrower's "fair share" is at least $1.00 for every $3.00 creditors contribute to the total financing. If the ratio climbs higher than 3.0 to 1.0, that contribution ratio no longer seems fair!

Now we're ready to discuss "high" leverage.

HIGH LEVERAGE

In the banking industry, "high leverage" based on an organization's balance sheet typically refers to any D/E Ratio that exceeds 4.0 to 1. This means the organization only contributes $1.00 (or less) for every $4.00 contributed by outside creditors.

I noted above that a D/E Ratio of 3.0 to 1.0 is the maximum level of comfort for commercial lenders. Does this mean an organization can have a D/E Ratio of 3.5 to 1.0 because it's still below the "high-leverage" figure of 4.0 to 1.0 and above? Not so much. Lenders want organizations to have a cushion in the ratio to better shield them from moving into the high-leverage category because of unexpected negative circumstances.

---

69 "Creditors" include lenders, vendors, and all others the organization "owes."

In addition, bankers aren't exactly dancing with delight at a D/E Ratio of 3.0 to 1 either! The 3.0 to 1.0 ratio is the maximum level. A commercial lender's sweet spot typically is a D/E Ratio of 2.50 to 1.0 or below.

RISKS

There are many risks associated with high leverage. The first risk stems from high debt. The higher the debt, the higher the required loan payments. The higher the debt, the less cash is available to fund ministry. Good commercial lenders do not want to overwhelm churches or any other organization with debt because there is a greater risk of non-payment and a greater risk that funds that should be allocated to normal operations instead are allocated to debt. We previously discussed this issue in Chapter 1: "Should You Borrow?"

The second reason may be less obvious but is no less important. The higher the debt, the more vulnerable the church is to downturns in the economy, transitions in their congregation, and other unexpected events that negatively impact giving. Equity financing helps to absorb the negative impact from these occurrences.

On this basis, a church's building loan request may be declined even when the church has sufficient cash flow and has sufficient cash equity for a 75% LTV. Why? Let's look at one final example using the balance sheet figures we showed earlier:

- Total Liabilities: $1,200,000
- Total Equity: $ 500,000
- Existing D/E Ratio: 2.4 to 1.0

In this example, the church has a D/E Ratio of 2.4 to 1.0 as of December 31, 2019. This is an acceptable level. Now let's assume church leaders approach the bank for a $1,000,000 loan to build a family life center in June 2020. Let's also assume they have sufficient cash flow and enough cash for a 75% LTV on the construction. But now, let's calculate what this church's D/E Ratio would be with the new $1,000,000 loan.

$$\text{D/E Ratio} = \frac{\text{Total Liabilities}}{\text{Total Equity}} = \frac{(\$1,200,000 + \$1,000,000)}{\$500,000} =$$

$$\frac{\$2,200,000}{\$500,000} = 4.4$$

In this example, with a new loan for $1,000,000, the church's leverage would increase to 4.4 to 1, which is considered high leverage. As a result, good bankers would decline the $1,000,000 loan request.

Could there be an alternative financing structure rather than a total decline of the loan request? Absolutely, but it might not be to the church's liking! In this scenario, a good banker would advise the church that if they want to build a new family life center at this time, they likely would need to finance the largest portion of the construction costs with even more cash equity. The bank might extend a much smaller loan to help with a portion of the financing (possibly $250,000 or below), but the bulk of the financing would fall on the church.

More likely, however, a really good banker would discuss the merits of that church's waiting to build the center until they had reduced their existing debt. Really good bankers would show church leaders the risks associated with using all their cash balances for a construction project, as well as the risks associated with high leverage and low equity.

The bottom line is that a bank would not decline the $1,000,000 loan to hurt the church. The bank would decline the $1,000,000 loan to not overwhelm the church with too much debt.

ACCUMULATING CAPITAL

What does this discussion mean for you as a church leader? It means that the church can expect to inject some "fair" portion of capital toward the overall financing of its building or building expansion.

First, the church must have sufficient capital to maintain an acceptable Loan-to-Value Ratio (LTV) relative to the appraised value of the collateral. If, for example, the lender required no more than a 75% LTV (75 cents for every $1.00 of total financing need), the church must contribute the remaining 25% in capital or equity. This capital must be available in cash, or in proven collateral value when the loan is closed, not down the road.

Second, if the projected balance sheet leverage is too high, the church would be expected to contribute sufficient capital to bring the D/E Ratio into line. Healthy balance sheet leverage is important not only for a single real estate project, but also for the overall financial health of the church.

CLOSING THOUGHTS

I remember meeting with a pastor who already had spent over $50,000 in architectural fees for a contemplated $11.0 million construction project before I met him. His church wanted to build a new sanctuary and a family life center. Even if the bank were willing to extend a loan with an 80.0% LTV (which is high), this would mean that the church still would need to have 20.0% capital available to make up the difference. What is 20.0% of $11.0 million? The answer is $2,200,000[70] in cash balances, all of which would have to be injected at the start of the project.

This amount of cash was well above the level of cash that the church maintained. We didn't review whether this church's existing cash flow could support the loan payments, nor did we discuss other credit considerations. The capital requirement alone was far greater than this church had available.

Moreover, I assumed a very high LTV in the example above. If lenders were to require the more typical 75% LTV, the up-front cash requirement for an $11 million loan would be even higher: $2,750,000.[71]

I declined this loan request after walking this Godly pastor and his leadership team through the bank's thought process. When I last spoke with them, the church leaders were raising capital funds and evaluating their next steps. They lost $50,000 in architectural fees; however, $50,000 is far less than what could have been lost if they entered into a building project that far exceeded their capacity in terms of capital on hand.

---

70 $11,000,000 x 0.20 (equivalent of 20.0%) = $2,200,000.

71 $11,000,000 x 0.25 (equivalent of 25.0%) = $2,750,000.

Church leaders must think about the amount of capital they need to accumulate before they seek debt financing. It also is critical that church leaders make these calculations before engaging architects and "finalizing" building designs. Finally, it should be remembered that good lenders want churches to have "skin in the game" and don't want them to be overwhelmed with debt. This is not to hurt them, but to help them be financially strong and better able to weather unexpected events.

We're now ready to discuss the fifth and final C: conditions. We've alluded to conditions throughout these chapters. Now we'll do a deeper dive in Chapter 10.

CHAPTER 10

CONDITIONS

"When the seven years of plenty which had been in the land of
Egypt came to an end, and the seven years of famine began to
come, just as Joseph had said, then there was famine in all the
lands; but in all the land of Egypt there was bread."

— GENESIS 41:53–54 NASB

"We can't direct the wind, but we can adjust our sails."

— THOMAS S. MONSON

The fifth C of Credit is conditions. The *Collins English Dictionary*
defines "conditions" simply as "external or existing circumstances."[72] That's an extremely general definition, but it's accurate! Conditions
can be anything and everything that impact us.

Conditions include the state of the economy, industry trends, and
pending legislation relative to a business. As they pertain to churches
in particular, conditions also include the size and make-up of your congregation, succession planning, and denominational characteristics.

---

72 *Collins English Dictionary*, online: https://www.collinsdictionary.com/us/dictionary/english/
conditions.

Conditions even include factors surrounding your building project, such as labor costs, your general contractor, and current interest rate levels.

All of these types of conditions are considered by lenders when evaluating loan requests. These types of factors—often out of the control of church leaders—may affect a church's ability to make loan payments and can impact the value of the real estate. Lenders spend a lot of time seeking to identify risks related to current conditions and evaluating if and how these risks can be mitigated.

Much of this evaluation still comes back to the particular borrower. Individuals can't control the economy, but they can plan. Organizations can't guarantee the future, but they can have systems in place that can help them navigate through unforeseen circumstances. Church leaders also can determine not to live on the financial edge, where they leave no room for a downturn. When obstacles do arise, church leaders still can fulfill the mission of the church with wise planning.

I will use the Biblical account of Nehemiah to frame the discussion regarding conditions. We remember that the book of Nehemiah focuses on the third wave of the Jewish nation who returned to Jerusalem in 445 B.C., following their captivity and exile in Babylon. Nehemiah's task was to rebuild the walls and gates of Jerusalem. That's a real estate construction project!

Nehemiah faced obstacles from without and resistance from within. Nehemiah had *conditions* that impacted his construction project. His conditions were some of the very same conditions church leaders face today.

What types of conditions?

POLITICAL AND ECONOMIC CONDITIONS

I combined these two conditions because, as I believe, many of us would agree, politics and economics are joined at the hip, so to speak. Individuals, businesses, chambers, and churches place and support politicians in office who they believe will advance their economic interests. At the same time, politicians advance philosophies that directly impact the economy.

As the Bible records, after their 70-year exile in Babylon, the southern Kingdom of Judah had no political or economic power. Judah's capital, Jerusalem, was in a severe economic depression. Nehemiah was called to manage a building program during these negative political and economic conditions.

As a result, Nehemiah had to obtain political favor from King Artaxerxes to leave Persia to return to Jerusalem. Nehemiah also needed economic and military resources from the king. All of this was required before Nehemiah could begin his building project. He even obtained what effectively amounted to travel visas from King Artaxerxes for Nehemiah to give to the local governors to be able to cross their borders.

> "And [Nehemiah] said to the king, 'If it pleases the king, and if your servant has found favor in your sight, that you send me to Judah, to the city of my fathers' graves, that I may rebuild it...' And I said to the king, 'If it pleases the king, let letters be given me to the governors of the province Beyond the River, that they may let me pass through until I come to Judah, and a letter to Asaph, the keeper of the king's forest, that he may give me timber to make beams for the gates of the fortress of the temple, and for the wall of the city, and for the house that I shall occupy.' And the king granted me what I asked, for the good hand of my God was upon me." (Nehemiah 2, 7-8 ESV)

Just like Nehemiah and the Jewish nation, all organizations need to be aware of the political and economic conditions that are in place when they're evaluating the purchase or construction of a building. Nehemiah had to manage these conditions on both an international and national level.

We can examine any national and international calamity to recognize the impact of national and international politics and economics on churches—whether it's the negative impact of congregation members losing their jobs or the sharp decline in property values that the church community experiences.

Economic swings also have an impact on interest rates. For example, in December 1980, the Wall Street Journal Prime Rate increased to an all-time high of 21.5% versus the current level of 3.25% that was set in March 2020. For borrowers with floating interest rates, this increase caused loan payments to soar!

Church leaders may never have to operate at an all-time high in interest rates, but it shouldn't be assumed that the economy will continue to operate at the all-time low rates that we've seen over the past decade. Church leaders always should factor in having to navigate negative economic and political conditions, just as Nehemiah did.

Also, allow me to address the common assumption that people return to church in an economic downturn. Pew Research Center found just the opposite. They submitted the following report in the midst of the Great Recession that began in 2008:

> "Contrary to recent media reports suggesting that the country's economic troubles have led to higher levels of church attendance, a Pew Forum analysis of polls by the Pew Research Center for the People & the Press finds that while the Dow Jones Industrial Average has shed over half its value since October 2007, there has been no increase in weekly worship service attendance during the same time period."[73]

Moreover, individuals and organizations are not just impacted by national and international conditions, but also by local economic and political conditions. Looking back to Nehemiah's experience, his building project was held up by two local decision-makers, Sanballat and Tobiah.

> "Then I came to the governors of the province Beyond the River and gave them the king's letters. Now the king had sent with

---

73 Pew Research Center: Religion & Public Life, "Is a Bad Economy Good for Church Attendance?" March 12, 2009, online: https://www.pewforum.org/2009/03/12/is-a-bad-economy-good-for-church-attendance/.

me officers of the army and horsemen. But when Sanballat the Horonite and Tobiah the Ammonite servant heard this, it displeased them greatly that someone had come to seek the welfare of the people of Israel." (Nehemiah 2:9-10 ESV)

Similarly, churches can be impacted by their local municipalities and state governments just as much as, if not more than, decision-making at the national and international levels.

Dr. James Miles, Sr. is a senior strategist on the leadership team of the Multi-Faith Veterans Initiative at DePaul University, and consultant to the Northern Illinois Public Health Consortium. He also conducts participatory research focused on community engagement and Diaspora Citizenship.

I first was introduced to Dr. Miles in 2004 by a friend at her church conference. I never forgot that meeting because of Dr. Miles' insights regarding African-American churches and their impact on economic development in their communities.

I was able to reach Dr. Miles again in 2019 for the purpose of this book to discuss his perspective on what church leaders need to know about building finance. One of Dr. Miles' "checklist items" for church leaders to consider relates to this very area of local political and economic conditions. He posed a question that even as a banker, I never had considered.

Dr. Miles' question was this: "What does your local municipality have planned for the church's neighborhood within the next 10 to 20 years?" What a great question! Dr. Miles' recommendation is that if church leaders don't have that information already in hand, they should obtain a copy of their municipality's plan. He then stated that church leaders should evaluate how aligned their congregation is with that plan! In Dr. Miles' words, church leaders have to "know the pulse of your people."

Dr. Miles also shared that church leaders should ask: "Does your local city embrace churches?" This question is not asking about the City Council's personal spiritual views. This question pertains to their economic and political views. He noted that churches don't pay property taxes into the local government's coffers; therefore, local governments may be reluctant to provide approval for re-zoning requests or required building permits.

I particularly remember that in 2004, Dr. Miles noted that many municipalities do not allow too many churches within a certain proximity of one another, to ensure that for-profit, property-tax-paying businesses will represent the majority interest in their community.

Dr. James Miles' insights are excellent and should be evaluated by church leaders as they pertain to their political and economic conditions.

SOCIAL CONDITIONS

> "Now when Sanballat heard that we were building the wall, he was angry and greatly enraged, and he jeered at the Jews. And he said in the presence of his brothers and of the army of Samaria, 'What are these feeble Jews doing?'" (Nehemiah 4:1-2 ESV)

Nehemiah and the people who were building the walls had to navigate not only political and economic conditions, but also a culture that was overtly anti-Semitic. I discussed mental redlining in Chapter 5 as it pertains to discrimination in the banking industry. Are church leaders aware of other social conditions that pertain to the church industry?

In 2018, *Polling Matters*, a Gallup publication, reported that weekly church attendance had declined from 42% in 2008 to 38% in 2017. According to Gallup, the percentage of attendees from churches, synagogues, and mosques also declined from 49% in the mid-1950s to the mid-30% range in recent years.[74]

Similarly, according to the Pew Research Center, in 2018, 51.0% of Americans born between 1910 and 1945 attended church at least weekly. In comparison, only 27.0% of American millennials born between 1982

---

74 Frank Newport, "Church Leaders and Declining Religious Service Attendance," *Gallup: Polling News,* September 7, 2018, online: https://news.gallup.com/opinion/polling-matters/242015/church-leaders-declining-religious-service-attendance.aspx.

and 2000 reported going to church weekly.[75] Becka Alper of the Pew Research Center wrote:

> "In the United States, religious congregations have been graying for decades, and young adults are now much less religious than their elders. Recent surveys have found that younger adults are far less likely than older generations to identify with a religion, believe in God or engage in a variety of religious practices." For example, the share of U.S. adults under age 40 who identify with a religious group is 17 percentage points lower than the share of older adults who are religiously affiliated.[76]

Further, Joel Mikell, president of RSI Stewardship, a Dallas-based firm that works on church fundraising campaigns, stated that younger worshippers view giving as an option, stating that they, "see the church now as just one place to give" (emphasis added).[77] This trend was in contrast to older churchgoers who may give weekly and with priority to the church.

Mikell wrote that as a result:

> "...many congregations are in no shape to take on big building projects; and, that some congregations even feel pressure to downsize into less-expensive quarters as membership declines."[78]

Jonathan Merritt of *The Atlantic* echoed this same theme:

> "Many of our nation's churches can no longer afford to maintain their structures—6,000 to 10,000 churches die each year in

75 Becka A. Alper, "Millennials Are Less Religious Than Older Americans, But Just As Spiritual," Pew Research Center, November 23, 2015, online: https://www.pewresearch.org/fact-tank/2015/11/23/millennials-are-less-religious-than-older-americans-but-just-as-spiritual/.

76 "The Age Gap in Religion Around the World," Pew Research Center: Religion & Public Life, June 13, 2018, online: https://www.pewforum.org/2018/06/13/the-age-gap-in-religion-around-the-world/.

77 Ben Leubsdorf, "Decline in Church-Building Reflects Changed Tastes and Times," *Wall Street Journal*, December 4, 2014, online: https://www.wsj.com/articles/decline-in-church-building-reflects-changed-tastes-and-times-1417714642.

78 Ibid.

America—and that number will likely grow. Though more than 70 percent of our citizens still claim to be Christian, congregational participation is less central to many Americans' faith than it once was.

Most denominations are declining as a share of the overall population, and donations to congregations have been falling for decades. Meanwhile, religiously unaffiliated Americans, nicknamed the 'nones,' are growing as a share of the U.S. population."[79]

Successful residential developers take social conditions into account when they develop communities—evidenced by the increase in mixed-use developments with an urban flair, rather than single-family houses that millennials are not purchasing. Have church leaders taken these same types of social conditions into account when seeking to build larger edifices or even megachurches?

Further, these poll results were reported in 2018, two years before our current COVID-19 crisis. With the ongoing uncertainty surrounding the transmission of the virus, the timing and willingness to return to church services in physical buildings remain unclear—particularly for older members of our community. These are social conditions that are unprecedented in our lifetime, but which must be addressed by church leaders and congregations worldwide.

SUCCESSION PLANNING

"Now when the wall had been built and I had set up the doors, and the gatekeepers, the singers, and the Levites had been appointed, I gave my brother Hanani and Hananiah the governor of the castle charge over Jerusalem, for he was a more faithful and God-fearing man than many." (Nehemiah 7:1-2 ESV)

---

79 Jonathan Merritt, "America's Epidemic of Empty Churches," *The Atlantic*, November 25, 2018, online: https://www.theatlantic.com/ideas/archive/2018/11/what-should-america-do-its-empty-church-buildings/576592/.

In this passage, Nehemiah recounts his decision to delegate leadership. Another important condition that lenders review is the church's succession plan, or lack thereof, beyond the senior pastor. This plan should include a description of assistant pastors, youth leaders, and elders/board of directors who help lead the organization. If 90% of the decisions go through the lead pastor or even through the lead pastor and his or her spouse, then the church has a dependence problem.

This is particularly the case for non-denominational churches or other churches for which there is no overarching synod or convention that facilitates the transition of leadership if something happens to the pastor.

Why do lenders care about succession planning? Because when they're making a long-term loan, they care if the church can continue operating successfully if the pastor leaves, or quite honestly, if the pastor passes away. If there is an overdependence on the pastor, many lenders will decline the loan request; or at minimum, put provisions in place that help mitigate the perceived risk of overdependence on the pastor without a good succession plan.

What type of provisions? Sample provisions include: Key Person life insurance in the amount of the loan that pays the lender if the pastor passes away, requirements that the pastor must preach a minimum number of Sundays per year, and even an event of default if there is turnover in the pastorate for any reason. Such provision may seem like overreach on the part of the lender, but we know that in many churches, when the pastor is away the congregation will stray!

How can churches prepare for pastoral succession as Nehemiah did? Many times, it's not done because it's a sensitive subject for pastors as they incorrectly infer that the congregation is trying to move him or her out now! This is not the purpose of a good succession plan at all. In fact, I learned in banking that the best succession plans for all types of organizations are those that are put in place long before the leader is expected to leave.

Of course, many mainline denominations traditionally rotate their church leaders by design every three to five years. Whether a rotation is done intentionally or if it occurs by necessity, churches that can show that they not only survive but also thrive after the departure of a pastor, demonstrate that they have strong succession plans in place.

In their book, *Next: Pastoral Succession That Works*, authors William Vanderbloemen and Warren Bird, state the following:

> "Thinking about what's next before they have to—that's what marks the greatest leaders, businesspeople, athletes, and politicians of the world. It's also a common trait of exceptionally wise pastors."[80]

They continue:

> "The Bible also provides many examples of leaders training their successors, including our Lord Himself."[81]

Whether the successor comes from the inner circle, as was the case with Joshua when he succeeded Moses, or from outside the circle, as was the case with the Apostle Paul when Jesus picked him to take Judas Iscariot's place, a well thought-out, well prayed-for succession plan is vital to a lender, and even more vital to a church.

DEMOGRAPHICS OF THE CONGREGATION

Chapter 7 of Nehemiah lists the descendants of those who had been taken into captivity to Babylon by Nebuchadnezzar. Similarly, lenders are interested in the demographics within each congregation, recognizing this information is an important condition. This especially is the case in an era in which older congregants are said to give more to the church than younger congregants, as previously discussed.

---

80 William Vanderbloemen and Warren Bird, *Next: Pastoral Succession That Works* (Grand Rapids, MI, Baker Books, 2014), 19.
81 Ibid., 25.

On the other hand, a church that is concentrated in individuals who are 65 and older with no younger individuals or families shows vulnerability to the long-term viability of the church itself. It does not mean that there is no long-term viability; it just raises a question that must be addressed.

SUSTAINABLE COMPETITIVE ADVANTAGE

In 1985, economist, Michael E. Porter of Harvard Business School first coined a phrase that represents an important condition for churches. In his book, *Competitive Advantage: Creating and Sustaining Superior Performance*, Porter wrote:

> "The fundamental basis of above-average performance in the long run is sustainable competitive advantage."[82]

Porter noted that it's not enough to be able to compete effectively today. Above-average organizations must be able to sustain their advantage over time when others seek to emulate their strategy for success.

One of our mentors, Bishop Kenneth Ulmer, Senior Pastor of Faithful Central Bible Church, put it more succinctly when my husband and I first discussed planting our church with him. Bishop Ulmer asked us this: "Why would anyone drive past 50 churches every Sunday morning to get to yours?" He then said, "If you can't answer that question, you don't need to open another church."

Banks seek to lend to financially successful organizations that operate in industries they understand, that have sustainable competitive advantages. This may not seem to be spiritually correct language when speaking about churches who all desire to love and serve the Lord Jesus Christ, but it's no less important than it is for any for-profit organization.

---

82 Michael E. Porter, *Competitive Advantage: Creating and Sustaining Superior Performance* (New York, NY: The Free Press, 1985), 11.

As Porter states:

> "Being 'all things to all people' is a recipe for strategic mediocrity and below-average performance because it often means a firm has no competitive advantage at all."[83]

In Bishop Ulmer's words:

> "Why would anyone drive past 50 churches every Sunday morning to get to yours?"

CLOSING THOUGHTS

These factors are just some of the conditions that impact churches, that lenders evaluate. Lenders want to know how church leaders addressed conditions that occurred in the past. Lenders also want to know how church leaders address conditions they're facing now, and how they prepare for conditions they may face in the future.

Isn't this the type of leader Nehemiah was? Just a few days after arriving in Jerusalem from Persia, Nehemiah recounts the following:

> "Then I arose in the night, I and a few men with me. And I told no one what my God had put into my heart to do for Jerusalem. There was no animal with me but the one on which I rode. I went out by night by the Valley Gate to the Dragon Spring and to the Dung Gate, and I inspected the walls of Jerusalem that were broken down and its gates that had been destroyed by fire." (Nehemiah 2:12-13 ESV)

Accompanied by just a few trusted leaders, Nehemiah inspected the building project and devised a plan to rebuild. That plan included strategies for addressing the numerous adverse conditions that are

---

83 Ibid., 12.

described throughout the book that bears his name. Nehemiah and his leaders didn't ignore the conditions; they planned for the conditions. And by God's Grace, they succeeded—and in record time!

> "So the wall was finished on the twenty-fifth day of the month Elul, in fifty-two days." (Nehemiah 6:15 ESV)

What obstacles do you as church leaders face and how do you plan to address them? What are the contingency plans? These are questions lenders will be asking, but more importantly, these are questions church leaders should be asking themselves.

This completes our overview of the "Five C's of Credit." The Five C's do not represent the totality of how lenders evaluate building loan requests, but they're a great start. The Five C's also are generic to all commercial loans. In the next chapter, "Unique Guidelines for Churches," we will review lending criteria that are specific to church loan requests.

CHAPTER 11

UNIQUE GUIDELINES FOR CHURCHES

"Boundaries and risk management are very important
parts of living a healthy and positive life."
— BRYANT MCGILL

"Predicting rain doesn't count, building the ark does."
— WARREN BUFFETT

A s shared, the Five C's of Credit are applicable to any commercial loan evaluation across all industries. They're even applicable to loans to individuals. It would be erroneous, however, to believe that only these criteria are sufficient for church financing. Churches have unique characteristics that have caused lenders to develop unique underwriting criteria to address those characteristics.

This chapter provides common underwriting criteria based on my experience, as well as information available on the web. These are not written in stone. Some lenders may use certain benchmarks and not others. Each lender has its own internal Credit Policy and follows, or makes exceptions, to their policy based on their evaluation and perceived risks relative to each credit request.

It also should be noted that as church leaders view the "maximum" and "minimum" guidelines that will be listed in this chapter, the goal is not to reach the high or low points! Just as we don't shoot for a minimum grade of 65 when it's the benchmark for a passing grade, churches shouldn't aim for the minimum or maximum benchmarks that typically are allowed by lenders.

With this in mind, I will highlight key credit criteria used by many lenders.

MINIMUM CHURCH SIZE

Lenders typically require that churches have a minimum number of members. If a church's membership is too small—say, 25 individuals—that congregation's very existence can be significantly impacted by just a few people or families changing membership or moving to another geographical location. The typical minimum church size required by lenders ranges from 100 to 250 "giving units."

A giving unit is equivalent to a household. For example, a husband and wife who jointly contribute to the church would be counted as two individual members, but one giving unit.

MINIMUM AGE OF CHURCH

The U.S. Small Business Administration reports that only about 50% of all newly established businesses survive five years or longer, and only about 33% of newly established businesses survive 10 years or longer.[84] Establishing and sustaining a new business—or church—is hard work!

With this in mind, lenders seek churches that have been in existence for a minimum number of years. For loans up to $2 million in amount, the minimum age required by lenders typically ranges from three to five years. If a loan amount exceeds $2 million, the minimum age required by lenders typically increases to 10 years.

---

84 U.S. Small Business Administration Office of Advocacy, "Frequently Asked Questions About Small Business," August 2018, online: https://cdn.advocacy.sba.gov/wp-content/uploads/2017/08/04125711/Frequently-Asked-Questions-Small-Business-2018.pdf.

As previously discussed, lenders prefer to make loan decisions based on historical information, rather than projections. The longer the financial history, the better banks are able to evaluate a church's historical financial trends.

MINIMUM TENURE OF SENIOR PASTOR

Generally, lenders prefer that a senior pastor has a tenure at his or her current church that ranges from five to 10 years—unless the church is part of a denomination that transitions its pastors every three to five years.

NON-DENOMINATIONAL CHURCHES

There is an interesting phenomenon occurring within American Christianity with regard to formal denominations. On the one hand, according to Gallup, Americans who identify as Christians, other than Catholics or Mormons, increasingly place themselves in a "non-denominational" category, rather than identifying with a specific denomination such as Baptist, Methodist, Lutheran, and Episcopalian.[85]

Per Gallup, others simply refer to themselves as "Christian" without any reference to Protestantism or a specific Protestant denomination. Overall, the number of U. S. adults that identified with a specific Protestant denomination dropped from 50% in 2000 to just 30% in 2016.[86] Non-denominational affiliation is on the rise!

At the same time, many banks are reluctant to lend to non-denominational churches, versus mainline denominational churches. During the Great Recession, the *Wall Street Journal* reported that problems in church real estate loans were concentrated among independent, non-denominational churches. The article cited the lack of a governing body to serve as a backstop to financial hardship, as a key issue.[87]

---

85 Frank Newport, "More U.S. Protestants Have No Specific Denominational Identity," *Gallup*, July 18, 2017, online: https://news.gallup.com/poll/214208/protestants-no-specific-denominational-identity.aspx.
86 Ibid.
87 Banjo, "Churches Find End Is Nigh."

For this reason, it is even more imperative for non-denominational churches to have: A strong internal governing board; clear succession planning; and, a lack of dependence upon what is considered by lenders to be a "personality-driven" congregation. A "personality-driven" congregation is one that is loyal to the pastor, and not necessarily loyal to the church.

MAXIMUM DEBT SERVICE TO ANNUAL UNRESTRICTED TITHES AND OFFERINGS RATIO

This ratio indicates the percentage of debt service (principal and interest payments) that is supported by unrestricted tithes and offerings. A typical range for lenders is 30% to 40% maximum, with 30% being the more conservative figure. Another way of looking at this is that after making required loan payments, the church should have the vast majority of its contributions—60% to 70%—available for ministry operations.

Example:
- Total Debt Service: $144,000 per year in principal and interest[88]
- Annual Tithes and Offerings: $1,200,000
- The Total Debt Service to Annual Tithes and Offerings Ratio: 12%,[89] below the maximum guideline. This is a positive indicator in and of itself.

MAXIMUM DEBT TO ANNUAL UNRESTRICTED TITHES AND OFFERINGS RATIO

This ratio indicates the total debt that is supported by unrestricted tithes and offerings. (Note that this ratio differs from the previous ratio that focused on debt service. This ratio focuses on total debt.) The common benchmark used by lenders for this ratio is that total debt should not exceed 2.5 to 3 times annual unrestricted tithes and offerings.

88 Total debt service of $144,000 per year equates to $12,000 in principal and interest payments per month.
89 $144,000 ÷ $1,200,000 = 0.12 or 12% when expressed as a percentage.

Example:

- Total Debt: $3,500,000
- Annual Tithes and Offerings: $625,000
- The Total Debt to Annual Tithes and Offerings Ratio: 5.6 times,[90] well above the maximum guideline of both 2.5 times and 3.0 times. This is a negative indicator in and of itself.

MAXIMUM DEBT PER GIVING UNIT

This ratio indicates the average donation each giving unit contributes toward the church's debt. A common benchmark for this ratio is a maximum of $2,500.

Example:

- Total Debt: $3,500,000
- Number of Giving Units: 1,100
- Debt Per Giving Unit Ratio: $3,182,[91] above the maximum guideline. This is a negative indicator in and of itself.

MINIMUM CONTRIBUTION PER GIVING UNIT

This ratio indicates the average donation contributed per giving unit. A minimum of $500 per giving unit is a common benchmark.

Example:

- Total Annual Contributions: $2,750,000
- Number of Giving Units: 2,100
- Contribution per Giving Unit Ratio: $1,310,[92] above the minimum guideline. This is a positive indicator in and of itself.

---

90 $3,500,0000 ÷ $625,000 = 5.6. The terminology used by lenders is 5.6x or "5.6 times."
91 $3,500,000 ÷ 1,100 = $3,181.82, rounded to $3,182.
92 $2,750,000 ÷ 2,100 = $1,309.52, rounded to $1,310.

MAXIMUM LOAN-TO-VALUE (LTV) RATIO

I discussed the LTV ratio at length in Chapter 8, sharing that it is the term that lenders use to measure the ratio of the requested loan amount to the total collateral value. The collateral value is determined by the real estate's appraised value. The typical range is 50% to 75% LTV for church loans.

Example:
- Total Requested Debt: $750,000
- Appraised Value of Existing Building: $1,050,000
- LTV: 71%,[93] below the maximum guideline. This is a positive indicator in and of itself.

It is noted, however, that the maximum LTV may be less for new ground-up construction projects. Additionally, if the purchase price for an existing property is less than the appraised value, many lenders base the LTV on the lower purchase price, not on the higher appraised value.

As a case in point, I mentioned that when Christ Community purchased our building in 2005, the appraised value was above the actual purchase price. When we obtained our loan to finance the purchase, the maximum LTV was based on the lower purchase price, not on the higher appraised value.

DIVERSIFICATION OF DONATIONS

Lenders typically require churches to provide a listing of the church's top 10 givers or giving units. The bank typically is not interested in the names of those individuals. What is of interest is the amount each of those members or giving units contributed during the most recent calendar year, and what percentage their donation is of total contributions for that year.

This information is critical because a "concentration" of donations in any one person or giving unit makes the church overly dependent

---

93 $750,000 ÷ $1,050,000 = 0.71 or 71% when expressed as a percentage.

on that donor or donor family. If that donor leaves the church for any reason or is laid off, loan repayment would be negatively impacted. Alternatively, that donor might exert an unusual amount of influence on the church's leaders in ways that may not be in the best interests of the church.

For this reason, lenders prefer that no one individual or giving unit contribute more than 10% of total annual donations. Put another way, lenders want to see diversification of donations.

Example:
- Total Annual Contributions: $875,000
- Total Annual Contributions of the Top Giver: $35,000
- The Ratio of the Top Givers' Contributions to Total Contributions: 4%,[94] below the maximum guideline. This is a positive indicator in and of itself.

MINIMUM LIQUIDITY

A common underwriting criterion for lenders is a minimum "liquidity" requirement; that is, a minimum amount of unrestricted cash that churches have available *after* they make their capital contribution (down payment). The typical requirement is for churches to maintain a minimum of six months of debt service. This requirement often increases to one year of debt service for larger loans or for loans that have a relatively high LTV.

Example:
- Unrestricted Cash Balances after Equity Injection: $75,000
- Monthly Loan Payment of principal and interest: $5,500
- Six Months of Debt Service: $33,000[95]
- 12 Months of Debt Service: $66,000[96]

---

94 $35,000 ÷ $875,000 = 0.04 or 4% when expressed as a percentage.
95 $5,500 x 6 = $33,000.
96 $5,500 x 12 = $66,000.

- Unrestricted Cash exceeds the minimum guidelines of both six months of debt service and one year of debt service. This is a positive indicator in and of itself.

MINIMUM DEBT SERVICE COVERAGE RATIO

The general concept of a Debt Service Coverage Ratio was introduced in Chapter 7: "Cash Flow." In that chapter, we stated that the Debt Service Coverage Ratio shows how well an organization's excess cash flow covers all required loan payments.

The Debt Service Coverage Ratio is an important equation that bankers use to measure this cash flow coverage. The calculation of this ratio is a bit complicated. For that reason, I have included the detailed calculation in Appendix III, and a general example below.

Before I get to the example, however, I want to provide some warnings regarding how some lenders use this ratio in ways that, I believe, harm churches. A minimum Debt Service Coverage Ratio is not unique to churches. Usually that minimum number is 1.20 times debt service; meaning, a borrower's excess cash flow for a certain period must measure 120% of the required principal and interest payments for that same period.

What is unique is that many lenders reduce the minimum coverage ratio for churches. Some lenders reduce the minimum from 1.20 times debt service, to 1.10 times debt service. Other lenders reduce it even further to just 1.0 times debt service. Part of these lenders' rationale for this reduction is that churches are non-profit organizations and therefore, don't need to show an excess balance after expenses and loan payments.

For churches leaders, this reduction initially may sound like a gift from God. It's like telling a student they only need to obtain a 55 to pass the class instead of a 65.

In my opinion, this is flawed thinking that can get churches in trouble—as would teaching a student that 55 is a good grade! Just like for-profit businesses, churches should operate with a cushion or margin each year. This planned cushion absorbs unexpected expenses and events. If such expenses and events never materialize, then that cushion can be moved into savings for future needs.

I am not saying that churches are to operate with a for-profit motive. I am saying that churches should operate with a for-profit strategy that doesn't plan just to break-even every year. It also is noted that the higher the debt service coverage ratio, the more flexibility lenders may give in other areas.

On this basis, I believe that churches should operate with a minimum debt service coverage ranging from 1.15 time to 1.20 times debt service.

Example:

- Annual Debt Service of Principal and Interest: $158,000
- Change in Net Assets ("Profit") before Noncash Expenses and Interest Expense: $354,800
- The Debt Service Coverage Ratio: 2.25[97] This exceeds the minimum guideline and is a positive indicator in and of itself.

OTHER CONSIDERATIONS

Other considerations that lenders typically take into account when under-writing church loan requests include:

- Historical capital campaign performance;
- Stable or growing membership and contributions;
- The size and type of building;
- Church's hierarchical structure and governance (how much control the governing body of a denomination has over property and staff).

CLOSING THOUGHTS

As indicated at the outset, these unique church guidelines are not set in stone and may vary by lender. What has been provided is based upon

---

97 $354,800 ÷ $158,000 = 2.25. By convention, the Debt Service Coverage Ratio is expressed as a decimal, not a percentage. A more detailed discussion of the Debt Service Coverage Ratio and this specific calculation is provided in Appendix III.

my experience over the years in working with both banks and churches. Some lenders may consider some of these benchmarks too conservative, while others may consider them far too loose! These are meant to provide guidelines for church leaders to assess their own credit strength before applying for loans.

In the next and final chapter of Part II, we will discuss the loan evaluation process, focusing on what church leaders can expect once they've submitted a loan package to one or more lenders.

CHAPTER 12

THE LOAN EVALUATION PROCESS

"What happens next is what you always want to know."
— SAMRUDDHI DESIA

"The single biggest problem in communication is
the illusion that it has taken place."
— GEORGE BERNARD SHAW

Thus far in Part II of *Holy Borrowers*, I've discussed how lenders evaluate loan requests. In this last chapter of Part II, I will highlight what church leaders can expect from lenders during their process of evaluating loan requests.

First, it is important to realize that bankers are salespeople. Yes, they also should be trusted advisors, but the skill that is needed to become your trusted advisor is sales.

As is the case in every other industry, there are good salespeople and bad salespeople. There are salespeople who are successful because they truly have the client's and potential client's best interests at heart. Then there are salespeople who are successful because they promise the moon and hope you won't find where they live when the moon isn't delivered!

WHO AND WHERE ARE THE DECISION-MAKERS?

On this basis, when you are speaking with bankers, one of the first things you should find out is what their decision-making process is and who in the organization makes those decisions. Many bankers in the field have little to no credit experience. That means they have little to no ability to understand your financial statements and independently evaluate your loan request!

As a result, these bankers may assure you that the loan request looks reasonable and you move forward with them on that basis—only to discover much later that their credit officer has declined the loan.

A related question that should be asked is this: Where are the credit decisions made? There are several banks that make credit decisions in other states, and at least one that makes them in another country. While this does not mean that correct decisions can't be reached, I strongly recommend that church leaders interact with a bank that has local bankers with local banking authority.

At minimum, if the bank's decision-maker is out of state (or out of country!), then you certainly want to know that your local banker has the juice—the influence—to be able to make a case for your loan request if he or she believes it's a request that should be approved.

Certainly, every loan request will not be approved. I have had loan requests that I strongly supported get denied by my credit officer. But I can assure you, there never was an instance in which I didn't have a voice; and moreover, was not joined by other team members who lent their voices to the discussion. Depending on the loan amount, there were times that I, or my executive management, could override a declined decision, taking responsibility for that approved loan under our own reputation and lending authority.

That said, although many senior bankers have independent lending authority—meaning, they can approve the loan themselves—the preferred protocol is to work with credit officers who have the most expertise for loan decisions. Bankers that are incented financially to make loans may place the bank at risk if their personal motivation outweighs the bank's best interest.

INITIAL REVIEW

Bankers with strong credit backgrounds should be able to evaluate your financial statements and loan request and give you a relatively quick "no" if it's not something the bank can do. In each case, the banker also should be able to provide the reason or reasons the loan can't be done at that time. In many cases, the banker can recommend an alternative structure, including a lower loan amount than originally requested, a different amortization, and/or additional collateral.

In other cases, the loan is not a fit at that time and will not be a fit for some time. An example would be a church that requests a building loan that had just opened its doors a few months before. If there isn't a history of financial giving, this loan is not a fit for banks.

One of the worse things that can happen to a borrower is for a banker to spend a long period of time on a loan request, only to decline the loan based on reasons that were evident at the outset—such as insufficient cash flow or collateral. If your loan request is taking too long without an indication that the banker actually is making progress in the request, then it's a good idea to seek one or more other lenders.

DISCUSSION WITH DECISION-MAKERS

After a banker evaluates the loan request and believes it's a loan that fits the borrower's needs and the bank's credit criteria, the next step typically is to discuss the loan with his or her manager and/or credit officer. At most banks, the credit officer has the authority to approve commercial loans.

Some banks use what's called a "Loan Committee" wherein a number of the bank's executives vote on the loan request. In these cases, the loan request is presented to the Loan Committee and majority rules.

For loan requests exceeding $500,000 to $1,000,000 (depending on the bank), bankers typically create an internal memorandum outlining the nature of the loan request, the parties involved, sufficiency of cash flow to cover expected debt payments, collateral... the Five C's. It need not be a long document, but it should hit the key points that the decision-maker needs to properly evaluate the loan request.

NON-BINDING TERM SHEET INSIDE THE BANK'S CREDIT PROCESS

NON-BINDING TERM SHEET

If the credit officer or other decision-makers believe at that point that the loan request appears reasonable, the next step at many banks is to issue what's called a "non-binding Term Sheet." The key phrase here is non-binding. This means that the banker is communicating what he or she believes the bank *may* approve in terms of loan amount, amortization, pricing, collateral, and other key terms of the loan.

A non-binding Term Sheet is not, however, a loan commitment. This means the lender still can decline the request at any time with no liability. For this reason, most Term Sheets include the following statement or something similar on every page: "For Discussion Purposes Only. This Term Sheet is not Binding."

What's the benefit to church leaders of receiving a non-binding Term Sheet? The benefits are many. First, church leaders can see whether or not the bank is serious about making the requested loan. Second, church leaders receive an early glimpse as to whether or not the bank's contemplated terms and conditions will be acceptable to them.

Moreover, if the church is in discussion with a number of lenders, church leaders can begin to compare and contrast the various terms and conditions between these banks and potentially negotiate a better financing arrangement for the church.

For their part, bankers issue non-binding Term Sheets to see if they are on the same page as a borrower; and if not, figure out where they possibly can make adjustments prior to formal underwriting (discussed below). Good bankers want to be as responsive as possible and Term Sheets allow them to do so.

If the banker has received a full loan package (discussed in Appendix I), a Term Sheet can be produced in a timeframe that ranges from as little as one day to more likely, three to seven business days. Deals that are more complex may take up to two weeks. In no case should a Term Sheet take a month or more, assuming that the bank has received all the requested information from the borrower. If a Term Sheet is taking that long to produce, there is likely something wrong with the banker, the credit process, and/or the information that was submitted by the borrower.

FORMAL UNDERWRITING

By this point, the banker and the credit officer have discussed the loan request, most likely in depth. On this basis, they often have a good idea as to whether or not they can make the loan and if so, under what terms. What, then, is formal underwriting? Formal underwriting allows the credit department to complete more detailed due diligence. Detailed due diligence includes:

- Formal credit checks on key church leaders and on the church itself;
- More detailed financial analysis, including sensitivity analysis that incorporates various cash flow scenarios;
- Identifying any areas they view as key risks to repayment and evaluating how to possibly mitigate those identified risks. For example, if a church is dependent on its senior pastor and there is no succession plan in place, the credit officer might require Key Person life insurance, and sometimes disability insurance.

In most cases, if proper due diligence and evaluation have been completed during the "Term Sheet" phase, the loan request is likely to be approved in underwriting. This is not, however, a guarantee. New information sometimes is uncovered or something may have changed at the church in the interim. In any case, formal underwriting will result either in a bank approval or a bank decline.

In terms of time frame, the underwriting phase can take as little as a few days to two weeks. In most cases, the time frame solely is dependent on what other loan requests the underwriting department is analyzing when your loan request is submitted to them.

FINANCIAL COVENANTS

As part of the loan underwriting, lenders typically establish "financial covenants." Financial covenants are set by the lender and incorporated into the written agreements that a borrower signs.

It is critical that borrowers fully understand every financial covenant before signing their loan documents because lack of adherence to these covenants results in a "technical default." The term "technical default" is used whenever a borrower fails to uphold one or more aspects of the loan requirements other than the regularly scheduled loan payments.

The bank's rationale in establishing these covenants is for the bank to set some measure of financial "boundaries" within which the borrower must operate. Why boundaries? Boundaries are set because the bank should not and cannot operate a borrower's organization. They're not qualified to do so, and it would result in "lender liability" if they tried.

What the bank can do, however, is set boundaries that on the one hand still give the borrower ample room to operate, while on the other, help the borrower maintain its capacity to repay the bank's loan. If an organization no longer complies with these financial covenants, the bank then has the right to meet with the key leaders to find out what's changed or even gone wrong. The bank also has the right to declare a technical default.

What are common financial covenants for churches? They are typically drawn from the very ratios and benchmarks that we discussed in the previous chapter, "Unique Guidelines for Churches," and the Debt-to-Equity Ratio that was discussed in Chapter 9.

For example, a lender's financial covenants might include a minimum Debt Service Coverage Ratio of 1.20 to 1.0,[98] and a requirement that a church maintain minimum cash balances equal to six or 12 months of loan payments.

---

98 See Chapter 11 and Appendix III for further detail.

Another covenant that is typically included for all borrowers (not just churches) is a "No Additional Debt" covenant. This covenant stipulates that the borrower cannot obtain any additional debt above a certain amount (for example, $10,000) without prior written approval from the bank. In some cases, the borrower is not authorized to obtain any additional debt without prior written bank approval.

While this covenant may seem onerous, consider the fact that if the bank underwrites and approves a loan assuming a certain level of debt payments versus existing cash flow, that analysis is moot if the borrower obtains additional debt beyond the debt the bank just funded! This provision is another boundary for the sake of the borrower and the bank.

OTHER COVENANTS

Banks may have other requirements that go beyond financial metrics. As mentioned, a bank may require a lead pastor to preach a minimum number of Sundays in the year. Another may be that it is an event of default if the senior pastor leaves the church. Again, these may seem intrusive, but from the bank's viewpoint, the absence or removal of the senior pastor may cause a decline in members. In turn, a decline in members could lead to a decline in contributions, which leads to a diminished capacity to repay the bank's loan.

Other covenants include the submission of the church's annual membership numbers so the bank can track if the church membership is growing, stable, or in decline. Still another requirement may be an event of default if the church changes denominations.

COMMITMENT LETTER

A Commitment Letter signed by an officer of the bank is the borrower's first written evidence that the bank has approved the loan request under the terms and conditions outlined in the letter. The Commitment Letter looks very similar to the Term Sheet in terms of information regarding the loan amount, pricing, covenants, and so forth; however, there are key differences. These differences include the following:

- The "For Discussion Purposes Only. This Term Sheet is not binding." language has been removed. The Commitment Letter is binding on the bank and therefore is an obligation on which the borrower can rely;
- The Commitment Letter contains covenants that were required as a condition of the loan approval;[99]
- The Commitment Letter usually contains key dates:
  - Date by which the borrower must accept the commitment (typically one to two weeks);
  - Date by which the loan must close (typically within 90 days);
- The Commitment Letter contains language that states the Commitment Letter will be superseded by actual loan documents. These loan documents should not contain information that contradicts the terms and conditions in the Commitment Letter, but contain far more detail or "small print;"
- The Commitment Letter contains a signature block for acceptance by the church, to be executed by authorized signers;
- If the loan is approved in underwriting and a Commitment Letter is issued, it will be approved "subject to" certain conditions or requirements that must be met. If those conditions or requirements are not met, then the bank is not obligated to close the loan. These stipulations are outlined in the Commitment Letter.

As a final note, some lenders don't issue a Commitment Letter, preferring to skip this step and proceed directly to loan documentation. This is not recommended. A Commitment Letter is far easier to read and understand than loan documents. If a bank can't issue a Commitment Letter, there should be reason for concern.

---

99 Some lenders include contemplated covenants in the non-binding Term Sheet as well, but many do not. Some lenders only insert, "To be determined." in the covenant section of the Term Sheet.

ATTORNEY COUNSEL

It is very important for church leaders to obtain good legal counsel prior to signing any Commitment Letter (and any loan documents). The purpose of a good attorney is to ensure that church leaders have a clear understanding of all terms, conditions, and key dates.

The worst thing that can happen between a bank and a borrower is a surprise before closing or complete shock after closing! The banker certainly should review the terms and conditions of the Commitment Letter with you, but independent legal counsel working on your behalf is prudent.

Appendix V is an excellent resource for church leaders in selecting a good attorney to help understand and negotiate real estate loan documents.

APPRAISAL AND ENVIRONMENTAL ASSESSMENT

One of the most important "subject to's" that is included in the Commitment Letter is the receipt of an appraisal and an environmental questionnaire and/or report, if applicable (for example, a Phase I Environmental Assessment). Each of these must be acceptable to the bank in the bank's sole discretion. "Sole discretion" means that even if the borrower believes the reports are satisfactory, it is the bank's opinion that counts! These reports were discussed in Chapter 8: "Collateral."

Most borrowers wait until they have received a formal Commitment Letter from a bank before ordering an appraisal and if needed, a Phase I Report because of the cost involved in each. If time is of the essence, however, some borrowers obtain these items prior to receiving a Commitment Letter. In so doing, these borrowers understand that they are at risk of spending money that may be lost if the loan is not approved.

I also remind church leaders that the appraisal must be ordered directly by the bank if it is to be used by the bank. As discussed, this is a federal requirement for most banks with no exceptions.

The most common practice is to order the appraisal through the bank that is the front-runner for the borrower's business. Banks can use appraisals ordered by other banks, but some banks are reluctant to release appraisals to competitors! Further, sometimes an appraisal that is acceptable to one bank may not be acceptable to another.

TITLE COMPANY, SURVEY, LOAN DOCUMENT REVIEW

The good news is that while the appraisal and Phase I, if needed, are in process, the borrower can move forward with a number of other requirements needed to close the loan.

Most banks close real estate loans through "title companies." Title companies ensure that the legal title to a real estate property is legitimate and issues title insurance for that property. The last thing the church wants to do is to purchase property that doesn't belong to the person offering it for sale! Title insurance protects both the lender (called "mortgagee insurance") and owner (called, "owner's insurance") against lawsuits or claims against the property that result from disputes over the title.

The lender typically selects the title company unless the church already has a relationship with a company. Title insurance rates are regulated by states, so there should be no price differentials. (There certainly can be differences in service!) The rates are based upon the size of the loan and other conditions required by the lender.

The cost for the bank's mortgage insurance is the responsibility of the borrower, not the bank. These are part of "out-of-pocket" closing costs that are above and beyond the cash equity required for the property. These costs are collected at loan closing. Moreover, most title companies also require a current survey certifying the legal boundaries of the real estate property. The cost of the survey also is the responsibility of the borrower unless the borrower can negotiate with the seller to absorb that cost.

The other critical act taking place during this time is that the bank produces draft loan documents for review by the church's leaders and attorney. In most cases, these documents are what are termed, "boilerplate" documents with the idea that they are "stamped out" in a pre-set form. Most banks use nearly identical boilerplate documents for their loans that contain set language and protections for the bank.

Although it is critical for the church's attorney to review the loan documents before closing, there is a limit to how much the banks will negotiate in boilerplate documents. If the borrower's attorney is interested in changing a significant portion of the documents to suit a particular borrower, then attorney-prepared documents will be used instead.

The bank will use its own legal counsel as well—and then charge the borrower accordingly. In contrast, with boilerplate documents, although the borrower still would have to pay for its own attorney, there is no cost for a bank attorney because a bank attorney is not being used.

Boilerplate documents most often are used for loans of $2,000,000 and below. If loan amounts exceed $2,000,000 for many banks and $5,000,000 for nearly all banks, the bank will obtain attorney-prepared documents at the borrower's cost. The rationale for this practice is that the larger loans typically contain more complexity than is captured in boilerplate documents.

LOAN CLOSING!

Once all the bank's closing requirements have been met, draft loan documents have been reviewed and approved, and the title insurance company has issued a clear title commitment, the loan closing can be scheduled! Most loan closings take place at a title company, although some title companies close loans at the borrower's office or the bank as part of their services.

Once all parties sign the loan documents and the seller, if applicable, signs documents on their side, the loan—and the sale—are closed.

As a point of detail, the loan documents must be sent or taken back to the bank and provided to the bank's internal operations department to "book" the loan on the bank's system. This process may take a few hours or may have to be completed the next day if the loan closes late in the afternoon. On this basis, funding is not immediate, but typically takes place within 24 hours at most.[100]

---

100 This discussion assumes the loan is structured to fund when the loan closes. Some loans intentionally incorporate delayed funding arrangements.

DIFFERENT TYPES OF LENDERS

I would note that the timelines and decision-making processes I described in this chapter generally pertain to larger national and regional financial institutions. There are smaller "community banks" in which one or more decision-makers are on the premises. As a result, these banks may be able to provide a loan decision within days.

This is not to say that every church should bank with a community bank. Regional and national banks can be very responsive, particularly when you have an experienced banker driving the process.

IF THE BANK SAYS "NO"

Until this point, everything in this chapter has moved progressively toward the lender's approving and then funding the loan request. That's the happy ending most expect if you have a humble, praying, visionary church and a competent banker and bank.

What happens, however, if the bank says "no"? First, it's important to evaluate if the decline is from one bank while other banks have approved your loan, or if nearly all the banks have declined the request. When multiple lenders decline a loan and one says "yes," that church leaders may assume that the Lord has made a way out of no way and they move forward with that one bank.

In fact, there are times when the one affirming bank is in error. The bankers may have their own agenda, such as booking loans and making money, and are not concerned primarily with the church's best interests.

Therefore, if most or all of the banks say "no," then take the opportunity to recognize that the Lord Himself may be the one saying, "Not now" or even, "Not at all."

In all cases, I would strongly recommend doing two things:

- Gain an in-depth understanding from the bankers that declined the loan regarding their reasons for the decline. It's not enough to have them say, "Cash flow is insufficient." If your church leaders don't understand how they arrived at that conclusion, have the bankers show you the numbers.

- Ask each banker what, if anything, would make your loan one that they could approve. Be careful not to try to lock the banker into an implied commitment; it's meant to be a general conversation. If you can understand what they believe would be needed, you as church leaders will be better equipped to address those issues within your church going forward.

Of course, there is a possibility that if the decline is coming from one bank, that the issue is related to just that one bank. Different lenders have different credit appetites. Some don't even like lending to churches. Therefore, it's never a bad idea to speak with more than one lender to receive multiple viewpoints. It certainly could be the case that the Lord is directing you to a different bank from the one that declined the loan.

The main point is this: Continue to pray with an open mind and don't force the issue. I often think of Jesus' admonition to Saul (Paul):

> "Saul, Saul, why are you persecuting me? It is hard for you to kick against the goads." (Acts 26:14 ESV)

I'm told a "goad" was a strong pole to guide oxen. In short, Jesus used a metaphor to tell Paul it was futile for him to keep trying to work against Jesus and His interests.

When we face roadblocks, we should ask ourselves: Is this a set-back preparing me for a set-up, or is this me trying to bust through a roadblock that the Lord has erected?

CLOSING THOUGHTS

The objective of Part II of *Holy Borrowers* has been to help church leaders better understand how the bank processes, evaluates, closes, and declines commercial building loans; to provide an "inside" look. We're now ready for the next section: "Advanced Lending Topics."

PART III

ADVANCED LENDING TOPICS

"I'm still learning."

– MICHELANGELO

SECTION OVERVIEW

Part III of *Holy Borrowers* is a smorgasbord of topics that have three things in common: they are not naturally intuitive; a lack of understanding can result in significant harm to a church; and, knowledge typically is gained through bad experiences. That's a bad combination!

Chapter 13 of Part III provides church leaders "next steps" after loan documents are signed and the church now has a long-term working relationship with a commercial bank and its bankers.

Chapters 14 and 15 discuss the topics of construction loans and balloon notes, respectively. These subjects were discussed in previous chapters; however, Chapters 14 and 15 provide needed detail that should greatly benefit church leaders.

Chapter 16 provides insight for borrowers who face the unfortunate circumstance of having a loan not perform according to plan. This chapter is for church leaders who face the risk of foreclosure and/or the prospect of having their loan or loans transferred to a bank's "Workout Loan" department.

Finally, as discussed in the *Introduction*, I wrote Chapter 17 after the remainder of *Holy Borrowers* was completed, in light of the current novel coronavirus pandemic. The chapter discusses principles that have been highlighted throughout this book that have been manifested in this crisis.

The overall goal of this section is for church leaders to gain the wisdom needed to effectively lead their congregation through these various contexts now and in the days ahead.

CHAPTER 13

THE LOAN'S FUNDED! NOW WHAT?

"People with good intentions make promises,
but people with good character keep them."

– AUTHOR UNKNOWN

"Bad decisions regarding debt will cripple
a church faster than just about anything."

– J. CLIF CHRISTOPHER[101]

I've attended more loan closings than I can count. It's a wonderful feeling for everyone concerned. The borrower is excited because after so much hard work on all sides, loan documents have been signed by all parties and the loan funds either have been disbursed, or they're ready to be disbursed.

The banker is excited as well! Bringing in new business is not easy, especially in today's highly competitive market. It is no little thing to even secure a meeting with a potential bank client; therefore, bankers spend a

---

101 J. Clif Christopher, *Rich Church, Poor Church: Keys to Effective Financial Ministry* (Nashville, TN: Abingdon Press, 2012), 37.

lot of time developing good referral sources and attempting to meet with organizations' various leaders and employees.

If a meeting is obtained, the banker then has to work with the organization's decision-makers to determine where the bank can add value. As it pertains to lending in particular, the banker must find out if the organization even needs debt financing!

If debt financing is needed, the banker then must work with his or her internal Credit Administration to structure and approve a loan that fits both the organization's needs and the bank's requirements.

If all these steps take place, the banker knows that the potential client still must choose the banker's bank over the many competitors that are in the market. While borrowers work hard to convince banks to approve their loan requests, bankers work hard to convince organizations to bank with them! Commercial bankers' careers and financial compensation are dependent upon their ability to fund loans into the market. On this basis, every loan closing is greatly celebrated within the bank as well.

In sum, loan closing is a happy day all around!

And then tomorrow comes. The individual or individuals who signed the loan documents on behalf of the borrowing entity turn their attention away from the bank and back to their organization. This is natural and expected; however, if those individuals are not careful, they can forget all the promises they made to obtain the loan and solely focus on moving forward with their organization's plans.

Borrowers who have travelled this road before with other banks often make this transition easily. Borrowers that have obtained their first commercial bank loan, however, have a greater likelihood of not incorporating the new loan requirements from the lender into their organization's plans and procedures.

What are the lender's expectations? Simply put, every lender expects the borrower to do what the borrower promised to do in the signed documents. The lender also expects the borrower to look reasonably like the borrower looked when the loan was approved and funded! If there are significant changes in financial performance, staff, or other critical areas, the lender expects the borrower to make them aware of those changes as quickly as possible.

What are some of the typical requirements that lenders expect borrowers to meet after a commercial loan closes?

FINANCIAL REPORTING REQUIREMENTS

When an individual closes a personal home mortgage or a car note, that person rarely hears from the bank unless that bank has sold their loan, or a payment has been missed. This is not the case with building finance. For commercial loans in excess of a certain amount, banks do not satisfy themselves with only sending "payment due" notices and collecting loan payments. Banks monitor the loans in their portfolios above a certain amount to ensure the on-going quality of those loans.

What is that "certain level"? For some banks, that level is $1,000,000 or more in combined outstanding loans. For others, it may be as low as $250,000. Whatever that level is, the requirements will be listed in the loan documents and should be reviewed by the borrower's attorney before the loan closes so that the borrower is aware in advance.

Well-run banks monitor the borrower's on-going financial strength for their own knowledge. Moreover, banks are regulated by federal or state authorities that independently evaluate the loan portfolios of their member banks. Governing authorities want to ensure that deposits entrusted to banks are maintained in financially sound institutions.

On this basis, lenders typically require borrowers to submit financial statements on a periodic basis after the loan closes to ensure that the organization still demonstrates the capacity to repay its loan. For some organizations and loan amounts, financial statements are required annually, within 90 to 120 days of the organization's year end. For others, the financial statements are required quarterly, while other organizations may be required to submit financial statements on a monthly basis.

If the financial statements show evidence of a diminished capacity— for example, if the organization now is losing money—then banks have steps they take. Those steps may include informing the borrower that they have a technical default on their loan.

LOAN COVENANTS

As discussed in Chapter 12: "The Loan Evaluation Process," lenders typically approve loans subject to certain loan covenants. Banks expect the borrower to operate their organization in such a way that they remain in compliance with all loan covenants and do not incur any technical defaults.

The requirement to comply with loan covenants may be one that causes the most problems for borrowers after loan closing. However, if church leaders agreed to comply with the bank's requirement that the church maintain a minimum level of cash equating to six months of loan payments, then it is problematic for church leaders to allow their cash balance to fall below that level for any reason. It's even more problematic for church leaders to argue with the banker after loan closing that they shouldn't have to maintain that level of cash!

KEEP YOUR WORD

At the heart of the matter, banks expect individuals leading their organization to do what they say they were going to do, and not to start doing things they did not disclose before the loan funded. This particularly is an issue if those new actions can become an impairment to repayment of the loan.

CONTINUE TO MEET WITH YOUR BANKER

Thus far, it may appear that a relationship with a bank is like an albatross around your neck! This should be the farthest from the truth. A good banking relationship is one in which your banker wants to meet with you regularly; not to control you, but to better understand what you're trying to do and wherever possible, support that effort.

Good bankers want to be trusted advisors and even needed partners, similar to a board of directors. Good bankers also attempt to be flexible with borrowers as much as they can, while honoring their first responsibility to the bank.

Good bankers also will not want to be your lender alone. Good bankers are interested in providing deposit accounts, cash management, and other services. These types of "non-lending" services can benefit the church because banks most often lower pricing on loans when there is revenue generated from other areas. Good bankers also should be active in the community and be part of an organization that provides financial education, credit awareness, and even classes for youth and children to teach them the principles of money.

If this is not the relationship you have with your bank, then it is up to you to tell them what you're looking for in a partner. If they're not willing to meet what should be reasonable expectations, then it's up to you to take your business to a bank that will.

CLOSING THOUGHTS

The most important consideration raised in this chapter is not to view the closing of your loan as the end of your interaction with your bank. Rather, it should represent the beginning of a new chapter in the life of the church.

Banking ought to be a mutually beneficial relationship full of trust and openness. There is an expectation that you, the borrower, understand your loan documents and after close, adhere to them. There also ought to be an expectation that your bank will continue to work hard for your business, to serve you as a trusted advisor along your journey together.

CHAPTER 14

CONSTRUCTION LOANS

"By wisdom a house is built,
and by understanding it is established..."
— PROVERBS 24:3 ESV

"The loftier the building,
the deeper must the foundation be laid."
— THOMAS À KEMPIS

In 2019, my husband, two adult sons, and I had the wonderful opportunity to vacation together in South Africa. We spent time in the cities of Johannesburg and Cape Town, and in the townships of Soweto and Langa. We toured Nelson and Winnie Mandela's former home in Soweto and visited his prison on Robben Island where he and other men were unjustly held for decades in opposition to apartheid.

One of our hotels was in the heart of Cape Town. Right across from the hotel was the most unusual highway structure. Pictures of this structure are shown on the following page.

Cape Town's unfinished freeway bridge. KYPROS/ALAMY

Another view of the unfinished bridge. ELOYB

As tourists, we found these roads to nowhere to be pretty remarkable! We also noticed, however, that most people around us paid them little mind. Why? Because this highway had remained unfinished for over 40 years!

We went online to get more information and found an article that provided the information we wanted. The article stated that the city of Cape Town began construction of this highway—named the "Foreshore Freeway"—in 1977. Then without explanation, construction suddenly stopped and has not resumed to date.[102]

---

102 Sarah Laskow, "A Highway in Cape Town Has Been Left Half-Finished for 40 Years," *Atlas Obscura*, September 19, 2018, online: https://www.atlasobscura.com/articles/cape-town-unfinished-freeway.

The article stated:

"In the four decades that Cape Town's 'unfinished highway' has stood downtown, locals have imagined all sorts of reasons why the bridges were never finished—hold-out landowners, engineering mishaps. But the official explanation is a simple one: Funding ran out..."[103]

People continue to debate the reasons that Foreshore Freeway became an unintentional talking point rather than a means for vehicles to get from Point A to Point B. Whatever the imagined reasons, I can consolidate them into one overarching fact: Construction projects are complicated!

Which leads me to this question: If mishaps occur when experts in the construction industry are leading the way, what are the implications for church leaders and congregations who don't operate in the construction industry at all?

Construction loans earned their own chapter in *Holy Borrowers* precisely because of their complexities. The goal of this chapter is to increase awareness about some of the complexities associated with construction projects and construction financing. This chapter is relevant to church leaders considering constructing a new building or renovating an existing facility.

TYPES OF BUILDING CONSTRUCTION PROJECTS

GROUND-UP CONSTRUCTION PROJECTS

"Ground-Up" construction projects, as you might guess, describe those in which a building is built from scratch, or from the ground up. There is no existing building before construction starts, and often no infrastructure, such as roads, sewage lines, and utilities.

---

103 Ibid.

RENOVATION CONSTRUCTION PROJECTS

"Renovation" construction projects describe those that involve an existing building that is being improved or modified. The key is that modifications are made to an existing structure. These modifications might involve adding a new wing, upgrading a sanctuary, or reconfiguring office space.

INCREASED COMPLEXITY

Both types of construction projects are more complex than projects involving the purchase of an existing structure. Additional requirements, expertise, and work are needed for construction and renovation projects.

External parties involved in purchasing and financing existing buildings include bankers, real estate agents, attorneys, appraisers, surveyors, environmental officers, and title companies. Construction projects and financing involve all of these parties as well. They also, however, involve these additional parties: architects; general contractors; construction managers; subcontractors (plumbers, electricians, HVAC specialists, foundation companies, etc.); construction inspectors; and, local city government officials who must approve permits, zoning changes, and other requests. Of course, most of these individuals come at a cost.

Additionally, the requirements and structure of construction and renovation financing are more complex. When lenders evaluate construction loans, they are reviewing all of the factors discussed in Part II of *Holy Borrowers*, but also must evaluate numerous other elements specific to construction projects.

Let's touch on some of these requirements associated with both types of construction loans.

FUNDING OF CONSTRUCTION LOANS

FUNDING IN INSTALLMENTS

Loans to purchase existing buildings typically are funded by the lender at or near loan closing in one lump-sum. In contrast, lenders most often fund construction loans over time, in installments.[104] These installments are called "draws."

The lender advances funds in draws as various phases of the building project are completed. Even here, there is a process. The general contractor must submit a "draw request" on a standard industry form detailing the work that has been completed and how that work fits within the previously approved construction contract and budget.

In addition, most lenders hire—typically at the borrower's expense—a construction inspector to visit the construction site and verify the work and costs that the general manager has submitted. Most bankers and church leaders are not construction experts; therefore, it is a good practice to have someone with expertise verify the work. As I love to say: "Trust is not a strategy!"

FUNDING FROM CASH EQUITY

In addition to advancing funds in installments or draws, banks follow another practice for construction loans that catches many church leaders by surprise. That practice is requiring the church to deposit 100% of its cash equity for the construction project in a special reserve account that is owned and controlled by the bank.

That's right. When closing a construction loan, the church will not be able to retain the cash equity in its own bank account and use those funds at its own discretion. Rather, banks want to ensure that those funds will be available for the construction project when they are needed and will not trust a borrower to keep those funds available.

As a result, the church is required to fund the reserve account and the bank, not the church, controls those funds. A banker, not a church leader, also will be the signer on that account.

When are those funds placed into the project? The bank advances those funds into the project first, before advancing any funds from the loan. This practice has the benefit of saving the church interest expense

---

104 Some lenders fund smaller construction loans of $150,000 or less in one lump-sum, but this is not uniform.

on loan funds that are not advanced. It also benefits the bank by keeping their loan funds from being at risk before the borrower has a vested—cash—interest in the project.

REPAYMENT OF CONSTRUCTION LOANS

Because construction loans are not fully funded when the loan closes but rather, are advanced over time via draws, repayment is set up on an "interest-only" amortization schedule during the construction period. Moreover, the interest rate is variable or floating, as discussed in Chapter 4. As a result, the interest rate fluctuates based on a benchmark that the bank chooses, such as the Wall Street Journal Prime Rate.[105]

The construction period is tied to the expected length of time to construct or renovate the building, plus a typical cushion of two to three months. This time cushion allows for unexpected circumstances, such as heavy rains or delays in receiving city approvals. The construction period also incorporates the receipt of a "certificate of occupancy" from the local municipality, certifying that the construction has been completed according to code and that the building is suitable for occupancy. So, by way of example, if the construction period is estimated to be one-year, the loan could be structured as interest-only for 15 months, providing a three-month cushion.

To the positive, this structure results in lower debt payments during the construction period, all else equal. The borrower only pays interest on loan funds that are advanced. The borrower also may pay a lower interest rate than they will have to pay when the loan is fully-funded and loan amortization begins.

What happens after the construction period ends? At that point, the loan should be fully funded, and the loan payments convert to principal and interest payments over the set amortization period. The interest rate

---

105 Today's Wall Street Journal Prime Rate is 3.25%; therefore, if the bank sets the borrower's rate at Wall Street Journal Prime + 2.0%, the borrower's interest rate at that point in time would be 5.25%. If the Wall Street Journal Prime increases from 3.25% to 5.0% over time because of a change in market conditions, the borrower's interest rate will increase to 7.0%.

also may become fixed, which is a positive occurrence in a rising interest rate environment. Most typically, the rate is fixed on the date the payments convert from interest only to principal and interest, based on the level of interest rates at that time.[106]

APPROVAL OF CONSTRUCTION LOANS

I wrote about the funding and repayment of construction loans. It also is important to note that even approval of construction financing takes longer than approval of financing for existing building loans. The approval process is longer for construction financing because both the borrower and the bank require additional information, and the bank must perform additional due diligence.

For the bank to approve and fund a construction loan, the bank needs the following items, in addition to the information required when financing an existing building:

- Architectural plans & specifications ("plans & specs") of the new building(s) or renovations;
- A detailed construction budget submitted by the general contractor;
- The name and contact information of the general contractor;
- An appraisal on an "as-complete" valuation basis. As discussed in Chapter 8, "as-complete" appraisals are needed to estimate what the value of the property will be once the ground-up construction or renovation is completed. This valuation is based heavily on the detailed construction budget that is submitted by the general contractor, but other considerations are incorporated as well.

Let me stop here and make an important note. I stated that these requirements are needed for the bank to approve and fund a construction loan. These are not the same requirements that are needed for a banker to

---

106 In a rising interest rate environment, there may be ways to lock in what the fixed rate will be after the construction period ends, in advance of the payment conversion. This is a discussion that should be held with the bank's interest rate derivatives department if one is available.

simply give his or her *general opinion* as to whether or not a church qualifies for a construction loan, and if so, in what amount.

Why do I say this? Because I have seen pastors and church leaders
spend significant sums of money on architectural plans and specs without knowing if they will qualify for a construction loan from any bank!
In Chapter 9, I shared the story of a church that paid over $50,000 to an
architect for plans and specs for an $11 million project, before knowing if
they qualified for a construction loan. That pastor believed the next best
step would be to obtain detailed plans and specs for his congregation to
see and for the bank to use.

This actually happens quite often, as pastors and church leaders
get far down the road with architects and general contractors who are
happy to take their money. Although a banker will not be able to provide
a formal loan commitment or even a Term Sheet because of insufficient
information, he or she should be able to provide guidance on the *estimated*
loan amount for which a church *might* qualify. Although this guidance
is non-binding, at least it keeps the church from operating with grossly
unrealistic expectations and unnecessary costs.

One other aspect of the approval process is the due diligence the bank
conducts on the general contractor. Many construction projects experience problems because a general contractor led a construction project that
was far larger than any previous construction project he or she had handled;
or, was trying to manage too many construction projects simultaneously.

The questions that banks ask about general contractors are the same
questions that church leaders should ask. These include:

- What is the largest construction project you've ever handled in
  terms of scope and cost?
- What type of financing do you have in place to cover your costs
  between draws?
- What is your experience in building church facilities?
- How many subcontractors do you have available right now for this
  project?

Of course, the background check on the general contractor should not be limited to speaking with the general contractor alone! Banks typically ask general contractors to provide their ten most recent clients and then will ask those clients if their projects came in on time and within budget. I emphasized their ten most recent clients because you don't want the general contractors to cherry-pick their satisfied clients while omitting those clients that were dissatisfied with their work.

The information about the general contractor's financing capability also is important. Draw requests typically are submitted to the bank once a month, and typically no more than twice a month. However, the general contractor's subcontractors typically are paid weekly or upon completion of their work. Further, construction materials must be paid upfront. These "mobilization" expenses should be absorbed by the general contractor and not by the church. Therefore, church leaders must find out if the general contractor has the capability to pay its workers and fund material before receiving funds from the draw request.

If a general contractor cannot fund these interim expenses from the company's own resources, the project will stop. Further, the borrower—the church—ultimately is responsible for paying the subcontractors and every worker on the project, even if the general contractor promised to do so. Those workers have the right to place what's called a "Mechanic's Lien" on the property. A Mechanic's Lien supersedes the bank's lien (which does not make the bank happy either).

Have you ever seen a construction project halted for long periods of time? The source of that stoppage frequently is associated with problems with a general contractor that ran out of money.

CONTINGENCY COSTS

When lenders evaluate construction loans, most banks increase the requested loan amount by 5% to 10% to allow for "contingency costs." Contingency costs are designed to cover cost overruns stemming from required overtime, "change orders" in which the general contractor or the church decides to enhance the original plans and specs, and many other factors.

In my experience, some portion of contingency costs always are needed, and the more expensive the building, the larger the required contingency. Without this contingency, borrowers can run out of funds— much like the Foreshore Freeway in Cape Town.

What is the impact of this requirement on the church's construction budget? The answer is that a contingency amount needs to be added to the church's projected construction costs based on this requirement. For example, if the construction budget is $3,500,000 and the bank requires a 10% contingency amount, the total construction budget will increase to $3,850,000. That's a $350,000 increase![107]

What does this mean for a church? First, the required capital injection will be higher. If the bank requires a maximum LTV of 75%, then the church must inject an additional $87,500 in capital, equal to 25% of $350,000.

Second, the loan amount also will be higher, resulting in higher loan payments and higher required cash flow. Third, the required minimum cash balance will be higher, because it's now based upon six or 12 months of loan payments that have increased.

COMMON PITFALLS OF CONSTRUCTION LOANS

There are numerous pitfalls associated with construction loans. Perhaps the most common relates back to the general contractor and management of construction projects. The likelihood of this problem occurring increases significantly for churches for one reason: the mistake of using individuals from one's own congregation to serve as general contractor or construction manager on the project.

Such individuals may be very well meaning—or they simply may see dollar signs swimming before their eyes. Either way, if they do not have the required experience that a general contractor or construction manager should have, they are not qualified to manage your construction project.

Another common pitfall occurs when churches do not obtain detailed bids from at least three different general contractors, but instead, trust

---

107 10% of $3,500,000 is calculated as $3,500,000 x 0.10 = $350,000. Next, $3,500,000 + $350,000 = $3,850,000.

a lone bid from one general contractor. In these instances, the construction costs can be much higher than they would have been had the church obtained competitive bids.

Similarly, churches experience problems when they obtain bids from three different general contractors and assume that the lowest bid must be the best! If a general contractor's bid is significantly below the projected costs of two other reputable general contractors, it may mean that the general contractor with the lowest costs is "low-balling" the church.

In these cases, the low-bid general contractor may subsequently impose cost overruns on the project because the work can't be done for that lower cost. Alternatively, the general contractor may substitute inferior material, may not be able to complete the work, or a combination thereof.

A third pitfall occurs on the loan side when a church does not prepare adequately for the loan repayment after the interest-only period ends. Remember, I noted that loan payments are lower during the construction period because payments are structured as interest-only. If churches do not incorporate the higher loan payments of interest *and principal* into their budgets in advance, they will not be prepared to make those higher payments when they become due.

These are some of the most common pitfalls involving construction loans, but they by no means are all-inclusive. Potential issues involving mechanics' liens, lien waivers, cost overruns, and change orders, to name a few, highlight the fact that church leaders need trusted advisors with expertise in this field to guide them through this process. Not doing so can result in significant problems down the road, or even in the midst of the construction project.

CLOSING THOUGHTS

Construction loans are far more complex than financing for existing buildings. It is critical that church leaders evaluate the costs of construction prior to spending money with architects and other vendors. It also is critical that church leaders incorporate unexpected events before, during, and after construction, because they so often occur.

With this in mind, we now will address another critical area that when not fully understood, can have significant negative consequences for churches. The next chapter addresses the subject of balloon notes.

CHAPTER 15

BALLOON NOTES

"The 'Rich Church' understands that it needs to manage 'debt principal.' The 'Poor Church' just looks at the 'debt payments.' It is always principal elimination that the church must have a plan for, not only making payments."

— J. CLIF CHRISTOPHER [108]

"The note is a balloon note. It ballooned, and when it ballooned the bank has asked for all their money."

— Senior Pastor [109]

Globophobia, also called balloon phobia, is the fear of balloons. The source of the fear may be the loud SOUND! of the balloon popping. Alternatively, it may be the unexpected timing of the balloon popping that sends a shock through the system. When we were children, my older sister used to love yelling "BOO!" at me from all kinds of hiding places, and watching me then contort in fear. From that standpoint, I might be

---

108 Christopher, *Rich Church, Poor Church: Keys to Effective Financial Ministry*, 38.

109 "Radcliff Pastor Resigns as Gloryland Harvest Faces Foreclosure," WDRB.com, March 25, 2014, online: https://www.wdrb.com/news/radcliff-pastor-resigns-as-gloryland-harvest-faces-foreclosure-still-running/article_76f3a709-9693-5d36-aeee-056320e74e4e.html.

able to relate to individuals who suffer from globophobia. (Thankfully, my sister has outgrown this unkind tendency and has become quite a wonderful woman!)

As discussed in Chapter 4, balloon notes are short-term loans that usually are due and payable within five to ten years, but are amortized over much longer periods—say 20 years.

When a loan has a balloon structure, it can mean that the scheduled payments are structured on an "interest-only" basis for all or a portion of the loan term. More commonly, balloon notes have some level of principal and interest payments scheduled over the entire loan term; however, the payments of principal and interest are lower than the amount needed to pay off the entire loan balance by maturity. As a result, the last "balloon" payment on the loan is the entire principal amount. That is, the entire principal balance is due and payable.

The benefit of balloon notes is that the payments are more affordable for the borrower than payments would be if the principal balance were fully amortized over a much shorter time period. In contrast, fully-amortizing loans are structured so that when the final payment is made, the entire loan has been paid in full.

Here's the thing about balloon notes. At some point, the balance is going to POP! If you as a borrower are prepared for the POP!, it's not an issue. The impact of the matured note will be analogous to the impact of a balloon popping for most of us. We know that popping is part of a balloon's nature so that when it occurs, it's a mild irritation.

If, however, you are not prepared for the POP! of a balloon note, it will cause a significant shock through your organization's system. In the worst case, churches have defaulted on their loans and lost their buildings.

COMPARISON

Let's look at an example of two building loans that have identical principal amounts, interest rates, and maturity dates:

	Church A	Church B
Loan Amount	$1,000,000	$1,000,000
Interest Rate	7.0%	7.0%
Origination Date	October 1, 2019	October 1, 2019
Maturity Date	October 1, 2024	October 1, 2024
Term of Loan	5 Years (60 Months)	5 Years (60 Months)
Amortization Period	5 Years (60 Months)	20 Years (240 Months)

We can see that everything is the same... except for the critical difference that the amortization period for the building loan to Church A is five years, while the amortization period for the building loan to Church B is 20 years.

To put it another way, the building loan to Church A is *fully amortizing* because the amortization period matches the term of the loan—five years. As a result, monthly payments will be calculated to ensure that the loan will be paid in full—that is, fully amortized—by the maturity date.

In contrast, the building loan to Church B is a balloon note. We can tell that it's a balloon note because the amortization period is longer than the term of the loan. The monthly payments will be calculated as though the loan did not have to be repaid for 20 years, even though the balance is due in full in five years. There will be a balloon payment that POPS! and must be paid in five years.

The advantage for Church B? Their monthly loan payments will be much lower than the monthly loan payments for Church A. The disadvantage for Church B? In five years, they will have to apply for a new loan if they don't have the cash available to pay off the balloon note in full!

Individuals in the finance field have enough information from the chart above to calculate both the monthly loan payment and the outstanding balance at the maturity date, when the loan is due in full. The results from placing the information in a financial calculator are as follows:

	Church A	Church B
Monthly Payments*	$19,801	$7,753
Loan Balance at the Maturity Date	$0	$862,566
	(Paid in Full)	(Balloon Payment Due)

* Principal and interest.

Let's take a moment to really consider the ramifications of the balloon note. In this scenario, Church B is approved for a $1.0 million building loan set up with payments they presumably can afford.

But the not-so-small caveat that can be missed is this: The entire balance of Church B's loan is due and payable in five years! If Church B needed and used the $1.0 million building loan to purchase their new sanctuary, it is not likely that Church B will have the cash available to repay the balloon balance in full: $862,566 in five years.

Are there alternatives? Certainly. In our example, when Church B's building loan comes due in five years, if the favorable conditions that were in place when the loan originally was approved in 2019 remain in place in 2024, it is highly likely that the lender will renew their loan; or, that the church can refinance the outstanding balance with a competitor bank.

Did you catch it?

If the favorable conditions that were in place when the loan originally was approved... If those conditions are not favorable for the lender in five years, *the lender is not obligated to renew the balloon loan even if the church has made every loan payment on time, every time.* Unfortunately, this comes as a complete surprise to most borrowers.

We discussed "conditions" in Chapter 10 of *Holy Borrowers*. We also discussed the fact that these conditions can change. What are possible unfavorable changes in conditions?

- A decline in the economy can negatively impact the value of your church building upon which the lender relies to secure the loan, and can negatively impact the church's contributions if members of the congregation are laid off from their jobs;

- A change in lead pastor/other senior leader;
- A church scandal;
- A change in the lender's appetite for lending to churches;
- Negative changes in the church's financial condition for whatever reason.

Now, let's return to our example. Church A has a fully amortizing building loan and in five years, will have no debt. Obviously, Church A would have to have the financial wherewithal to pay the much higher payment of approximately $19,801 per month for five years. If they can, they are debt free if one or more of the conditions above changes.

In contrast, Church B's balloon note structure allowed them to make a much lower loan payment of approximately $7,753 per month—less than half the monthly payment that is paid by Church A. That sounds great going in, but here's the problem: When Church B's building loan comes due in five years, they will have a balloon balance of $862,566. This balance is not much lower, relatively speaking, than the original $1.0 million loan that they used to purchase their sanctuary building.

When the loan comes due, the lender *may* want to renew the loan, *but they do not have to renew the loan, regardless of what a banker or bankers verbally stated at or before loan closing.*[110] Unless it's written in the loan documents, verbal assurances cannot be enforced legally.

Why, then, would Church B proceed forward under this structure? Most often, the reasons involve one or more of the following realities:

1. They've done it before, and it worked out fine;
2. They're simply happy to get the loan and will cross the balloon-bridge when they get to it;

---

110 We also have not discussed the fact that Church B will pay much higher interest expense over the term of its loan than Church A will pay.

3. It's the only structure that will enable the church to be approved for the loan—and the church is desperate to be approved for the loan;
4. The church leaders completely missed the fact that with a balloon note, the lender is not required to renew the loan balance when it matures.

In my experience, most problems involving balloon notes involve a perfect-storm combination of #3 and #4 above. The perfect storm also may involve a banker who is desperate to close the loan for his or her personal production and career goals, and church leaders who are desperate to close the loan to grow or secure the real estate property.

Does this mean that borrowers never should get a balloon note? No it doesn't. The fact is that most real estate loans have some type of balloon structure, particularly loans to churches. Furthermore, in most cases, lenders intend to—and do—renew the outstanding balance of balloon notes when they become due.

Lenders are in the business of making and keeping good loans and good clients and renewing an existing building loan is the lender's goal. In many cases, the borrower also has the option of refinancing the remaining loan balance with another lender.

That said, here's what church leaders always should keep in mind regarding balloon notes: The shorter the loan term, the greater the potential for the church to be exposed to changing conditions that, in turn, may cause the lender not to renew the balloon note at maturity.

More specifically, five years is a short time period for a real estate note. Lenders limit their exposure to that time period to reduce their own risk to changes in conditions. Lenders want the option to *not* renew the loan at maturity. This is in the lender's favor.

What can church leaders do?

- If church leaders are in a position to negotiate, they should require a longer loan term; preferably ten years, but no less than seven. While there always is a risk of conditions changing, the longer

timeframe gives the borrower more time to address those changing conditions before having to reapply for the loan to be renewed.
The longer the loan term, the greater stability the borrower has in
their financing.

- Church leaders always should operate their church under sound
financial principals that adjust to changes in conditions as they
occur, in an on-going effort to stay creditworthy. For example,
if the church's contributions decline because of a change in the
economy or a decline in membership, then it's important to reduce
ministry expenses accordingly. Reducing expenses will help the
church maintain the same level of "profitability" that was in place
when the loan originally was approved.
- Church leaders always must keep in mind that they are working
with borrowed funds that have to be returned!
- Church leaders should understand the terms of their loan, which
require outside legal and financial counsel before closing the loan.
- Church leaders should look for opportunities to reduce principal
ahead of schedule and/or incorporate an operating budget that
allows the church to put aside excess cash to pay down principal
when the balloon note matures. I shared in Chapter 1 that my
church, Christ Community, reduced the principal balance of our
renovation loan by more than 50% in two years—well ahead of the
20-year amortization schedule for that loan. This was done intentionally to reduce our vulnerability to changing conditions.

If church leaders place their church in a position to reduce principal
ahead of schedule or when the note balloons, the church is more likely to
retain an acceptable Loan-to-Value. In turn, this increases the likelihood
of being able to refinance the balance when the loan matures, either under
the current structure or with lower loan payments based on a lower principal balance.

INDICATORS OF A BALLOON NOTE

Here is sample wording from the repayment schedule section of a promissory note:

> "Monthly payments of principal including interest beginning one month from the date of the note, based upon a 120-month amortization schedule. Outstanding principal and accrued, unpaid interest due at maturity."

Remember that balloon notes occur when the amortization schedule is longer than the loan term. In the example above, if the maturity date is ten years from the origination date of the note (equivalent to 120 months), then this is a fully amortizing loan.

Some amortization schedules will underscore this point by saying, "... based upon a 120-month amortization schedule, fully amortizing principal by maturity," and deleting the last sentence, "Outstanding principal and accrued, unpaid interest due at maturity."

If, however, the maturity date in this example only is five years from the origination date, then you know you will have a balloon payment due at maturity. How do you know? Because in this example, the payments have been calculated as though the borrower has 120 months (10 years) to repay the loan, rather than the actual loan term of 60 months (5 years).

WHAT IF THE CHURCH ALREADY HAS A BALLOON NOTE?

It is highly likely that if your church has a building loan, that it is a balloon note. Unlike the manner in which mortgages are structured on a personal residence in which the mortgage loan fully amortizes over 30 years or 15 years, most loans financing commercial real estate in general, and church buildings in particular, are not fully amortizing. A 10-year maturity is quite common; however, five-year maturities occur as frequently.

What should churches do? Two words: Plan Ahead! Church leaders should begin working on their options to refinance their balloon note at least one year prior to the maturity date of the loan. That planning should include these steps:

1. Contact your existing lender.
2. Contact other lenders even if your existing lender has stated they will renew the loan. The competition typically yields the most attractive structure and it provides borrowers a viable back-up plan if the existing lender does not approve the loan.
3. Ask for a one-year extension in your maturity date, before the balloon payment becomes due.
4. Have a banker or other qualified financial advisor review the church's most recent financial statements to evaluate the church's viability for obtaining a renewal. If there are any issues, this gives the church more time to address them.

My other recommendation? Even when the maturity date of your balloon note is 10 years or longer, always keep your loan in mind! You should operate your church as though you have to qualify for a loan each year, even if your loan is not maturing. With this in mind, it will be less of an issue when your balloon note actually matures and the balloon balance comes due.

CLOSING THOUGHTS

Balloon notes can be one of the least understood risks in building finance. To be sure, many notes have a balloon structure and most are repaid or refinanced with little issue. The most prudent borrowers, however, will not allow themselves to be surprised by the POPPING of the balloon; but rather, will prepare themselves for the certainty that the principal balance will need, one day, to be repaid in full.

CHAPTER 16

IF THE LOAN GOES SOUTH

(With Contribution by Sharon K. Simmons)

"I'm sorry to say so but, sadly it's true that
bang-ups and hang-ups can happen to you."
— Dr. SEUSS

"A bend in the road is not the end of the road...
unless you fail to make the turn."
— HELEN KELLER

I mentioned in earlier chapters that I worked from 1990 to 1991 in what was nicknamed, the "Workout Loan" department. Loans were transferred into the bank's Workout Loan department for various reasons.

Some loans no longer were paying according to the original terms of the loan. The borrower might only be able to pay half of the agreed-upon payment amount, or not be able to make any payments at all. Other loans were paying on time, but either had experienced a significant decline in the value of the collateral, or the organization was losing money. As it happens, 1990 was a recession in Dallas, and all of these circumstances were occurring.

Regardless of the reason, a transfer to a Workout Loan department in any bank is an indication that the original repayment plan and/or loan structure no longer is viable. Something has gone wrong with the loan.

If this occurs, what are the best strategies for church leaders to take if the loan "goes south"? This chapter seeks to respond to that question from two perspectives. The first perspective is my own—that of a banker with over 30 years of experience. The second perspective is that of a prominent real estate attorney who has represented both churches and banks in the Dallas/Fort Worth Metroplex. Her recommendations are not to be taken as formal legal counsel; rather, they are provided as general wisdom based on her own vast experience.

A BANKER'S PERSPECTIVE

REMEMBER CHARACTER

One of the things I most remember during that period was how individuals acted when they had problems with their loans and they felt as though their backs were against the wall. I recall working with two main categories of people.

The first category included those individuals that I'd love to do business with anytime, anywhere. Why? These individuals demonstrated character even in the midst of their difficulties. To be sure, they were unhappy and even stressed about their situations, but these individuals tried their best to work with the bank, recognizing that the bank was not at fault either! These individuals had, in my opinion, great character.

The second category included those individuals whose character I considered the polar opposite of those in the first category. The second category of individuals faced similar difficulties and stress, but vehemently blamed the bank and seemed to minimize their own responsibility. Some swore they never understood the loan documents they had signed—even in the many cases in which those documents had been reviewed and negotiated by their attorneys.

To be sure, I realize that in some of those cases, individuals didn't understand what they had signed. Even in these instances, however, the responsibility for this lack of understanding is, at best, shared between the banker who didn't adequately explain the loan documents and the individual or individuals who signed the loan documents. At worst, the borrower is solely responsible.

What the latter category of individuals missed, in many cases, was the opportunity to work with the bank to try to obtain a mutually acceptable solution. Obtaining a mutually acceptable solution is not always possible, but the potential for these solutions increases significantly when borrowers maintain the first of the 5 C's discussed in Part II: character.

Provide Early Warning

Out of all the wishes on a banker's wish list regarding what they'd like all borrowers to do if a loan goes south, I believe the first wish would be this: Please tell your banker as soon as possible!

Too many individuals don't tell their banker that something is wrong because they fear what the bank will do. I'm not going to tell you that there never is cause for fear because banks may exercise options that borrowers don't like.

What I can tell you, however, is that in my experience, banks want to help borrowers find a solution to the problem, for a number of reasons. First, working together to find mutually acceptable solutions helps—you guessed it—get the loan repaid. Additionally, I can tell you that the best bankers sincerely care about the success of their borrowers. Good bankers develop personal relationships with the individuals with whom they do business and are motivated by that organization's success.

When an organization discloses a problem early, it provides the bank many more options. One of my favorite customers used to host quarterly meetings with my credit officer and me and at those meetings, give a power point presentation highlighting their successes, challenges, risks, and, whenever applicable, problems.

For example, on several occasions, this borrower alerted us that they were going to be out of compliance, that is, have a technical default, with their Debt Service Coverage Ratio covenant for the upcoming quarter. The owners provided these alerts months before the financial statements for that quarter were due. They provided these alerts as soon as they became aware that they had a problem. Moreover, they also communicated the source of the problem and what they were doing to address it.

As a result, we developed a great level of trust for this borrower because we knew there would not be any surprises. This borrower worked extremely hard to keep the bank informed. In return, the bank was able to present the borrower with several options when these types of problems arose in their business.

To reiterate: Is early warning a guarantee that banks will not take recourse against their collateral or take other remedies? No, it's not. The bank's main priority when there are problems with loans, is avoiding or minimizing loan losses. Providing an early warning does mean, however, that the borrower and the bank increase the likelihood of being able to find mutually acceptable alternatives.

DON'T PANIC IF THE LOAN IS TRANSFERRED TO A "WORKOUT LOAN" DEPARTMENT

You might ask why loans are transferred to a Workout Loan department. There are several reasons. First, bankers that are responsible for bringing in new business and managing loan portfolios are extremely busy in these tasks—even when loans are performing as agreed. The phrase "bankers' hours" was used to describe short workdays for bankers who rolled into the office at 10:00 a.m., had a business lunch at noon, and was on the golf course by 2:00 p.m.

Bankers' hours must have been before my time because most of my workdays started at 7:00 a.m., went all day, and routinely extended into the evening. Clients, potential clients, managers, staff and co-workers had my cell number, and many used it at all hours. It is a competitive market and good bankers work hard at their craft.

On this basis, bankers don't have the time to work through the complexities of a loan that is not performing under its original terms. Nonperforming and under-performing loans involve much more communication, both externally with the borrower and internally with management and senior credit officers. External communication includes in-person client meetings, telephone calls, and written communication. Internal communication involves the same—plus numerous reports that must be written and provided to executive management.

Second, under-performing loans are transferred to the Workout Loan department because bankers in those departments specialize in keeping the bank from losing money on the loan; and, in working out mutually acceptable solutions with the borrower, if at all possible. Moreover, these officers usually are more objective than the original banker with whom the borrower has developed a personal relationship.

Third, loans are transferred to Workout Loan departments because those bankers specialize in working to restructure loans wherever possible to return them to the original department. As shared, this is not always possible, but it certainly is something banks evaluate. I have seen numerous loans not only return from the Workout Loan department, but even receive additional financing from the bank under mutually acceptable terms.

For all these reasons, having a loan transferred for non-performance or other reasons is not an automatic indication that the relationship with your bank can't be salvaged. There is an opportunity for church leaders to develop a professional working relationship with their new bank officer in the Workout Loan department to potentially work out a viable, mutually satisfactory plan and solution.

RECOGNIZE THE BANK'S PERSPECTIVE

When church leaders experience problems with their loan, stress can rise to indescribable levels. The ministry already carries its own responsibilities and stress points, and now attention must be directed to working with the bank, strategizing with the board, communicating with the congregation, and crying out to the Lord about the problem loan!

It is difficult to recognize another's perspective when facing such challenges, but in any relationship, the best negotiated outcomes arise from seeking to understand the other party's perspectives. Understanding does not necessarily mean agreement. Understanding does mean intentional awareness and perhaps, even empathy for another party.

In that regard, here are several factors for church leaders to keep in mind and even pray about:

- The bankers who made and approved your loan face their own stress. A bank officer's credibility and career can be negatively impacted if it is perceived within the organization that he or she recommended a loan that now is having problems. Moreover, bankers often are penalized financially when loans in their portfolios no longer perform according to the original terms. These penalties can include deductions from their paycheck for incentive compensation they had received when the loan closed, and the cancellation of a planned salary increase. A banker's entire team also can be penalized because the costs associated with managing an under-performing or non-performing loan—including losses—typically are deducted from the entire department's revenues.

- Loans that are not paying as agreed or that have some other structural issue—such as a decline in collateral value—require a significant amount of internal documentation and communication. As shared, bankers are paid to be trusted advisors to clients for their on-going business needs, and they are paid to uncover and close new business. The additional work—whether for the borrower's original banker or from the Workout Loan department—is time-consuming and stressful on their side.

- Lenders do not want to foreclose and own church buildings.

- Lenders do not want to foreclose and own church buildings.

- Lenders do not want to foreclose and own church buildings.

- Lenders... This cannot be underscored enough. Foreclosing is a last resort for the bank as well.

Seek to Address Technical Defaults

As previously discussed, a "technical default" exists when a borrower fails to uphold one or more aspects of the loan requirements other than the regularly scheduled loan payments. An example of a technical default is when a borrower does not reach the minimum required Debt Service Coverage Ratio covenant. This type of default typically results from an unanticipated decline in revenues without a corresponding reduction in expenses; or, an unanticipated increase in expenses that can't be covered by higher revenues.

If the issues that resulted in a technical default are non-recurring and can be remedied, church leaders should tell their banker just that. An example of this type of scenario is damage to the church caused by a tornado or earthquake that has immediate financial consequences—but which will be covered by insurance proceeds in the coming quarter.

If, however, the issue is not temporary—such as a church split or other occurrence resulting in a steep decline in revenues—then other measures need to be taken. How will the church reduce expenses if revenues decline and the church cannot meet its minimum Debt Service Coverage Ratio on an on-going basis? Most options are painful and include reductions in ministry activities and reductions in salary levels or staff count.

Borrowers that make these difficult decisions for the purpose of restoring compliance with their loan covenants, and for the sake of their own organizations, often can avert more drastic steps from being taken by the lender. By so doing, these borrowers also communicate to the bank that they take compliance with their agreed-upon loan covenants seriously.

On the other hand, borrowers that ignore their loan covenants, that constantly complain about their loan covenants, and that don't take any necessary steps to return to compliance with their loan covenants, communicate something quite different to the lender. These were, after all, loan covenants that were set by the bank as a condition of approval, and that were agreed to by the borrower in order to obtain the funding.

OBTAIN GOOD ATTORNEY COUNSEL

This final recommendation is not meant to contradict what I previously wrote regarding maintaining or developing positive working relationships with your bankers. Obtaining an attorney's expertise does not automatically mean you plan to sue the bank, nor does it even mean the borrower has grounds to sue!

Attorney counsel provides expertise in understanding what your loan documents state, what rights the bank has, what rights the church has, and what are the best ways to navigate through unanticipated problems with the financing.

One note: The attorney who is hired should have expertise in working with bank loans. If this is not the case, even the attorney can have unreasonable expectations and can make a potentially salvageable situation unsalvageable. This can particularly be the case if the church's attorney is a member of the congregation with a passion for the church, but with little to no legal training or experience in corporate law or real estate finance.

With that, we now will transition to an attorney's perspective. I asked Sharon K. Simmons to contribute to this chapter (as well as to Appendix V) based on her extensive legal expertise in representing lenders, churches, and developers in all manner of real estate law.

By way of background, Ms. Simmons is a Dallas attorney with over 32-years of experience in real estate and commercial transactions. Ms. Simmons graduated with a Bachelor's degree in Economics from the University of Texas in Austin, and a J. D. Degree from Stanford Law School. She began her legal career in 1986 in the real estate section of the top-tier Dallas law firm, Jenkins & Gilchrist.

In 1993, Ms. Simmons formed her own law firm, Sharon K. Simmons & Associates, PC. Since that time, Ms. Simmons has represented commercial institutional lenders in connection with all types of loans. She has documented and negotiated term loans; revolving loans; and, construction and permanent loans secured by real estate, equipment, accounts receivable, and other types of collateral. Moreover, in over 15 years of representing one of the largest banks in the country, Ms. Simmons and her firm have handled over 525 commercial loan transactions with loan amounts ranging from $100,000 to $27 million.

At the core of Ms. Simmons' practice is the review, drafting, and negotiation of complex contractual agreements, including complicated financial covenants; restrictive use covenants and reciprocal agreements; office and retail leases; tri-party agreements; all manner of loan documents; and, partnership and corporate documents.

Ms. Simmons has represented numerous borrowers, including churches and prominent real estate developers. I first met Ms. Simmons through a mutual real estate client in the 1990s. I'm happy to report that Ms. Simmons also is the attorney I lauded in Chapter 1 who has represented Christ Community for the past 15 years.

One final note: I did not provide Ms. Simmons' extensive background, nor did she contribute to *Holy Borrowers*, for her to gain new clients! The sole motivation for Ms. Simmons' contribution to *Holy Borrowers* is to equip church leaders—the very purpose of this book. Ms. Simmons is a strong Christian who loves God's church and desires for church leaders to gain from her experience.

On this basis, the next portion of this chapter will come from Ms. Simmons, with my gratitude for her time, thoughts, and insights.

AN ATTORNEY'S PERSPECTIVE—
CONTRIBUTED BY SHARON K. SIMMONS

Perhaps, not surprisingly, the decisions made at the beginning of the loan process and the actions taken during the loan term directly impact what happens, should problems with church loans arise. One of those decisions is hiring the right lawyer to represent the church at the beginning of the loan process and having that lawyer—or another "right" lawyer—help church leaders should problems arise. Therefore, my first recommended strategy when dealing with an under-performing or non-performing loan is to ensure that you, as a church leader, have competent and experienced legal representation.[111]

111 See Appendix V for "Guidelines in Selecting an Attorney."

Having said that, be wary of attorneys who see litigation as the solution to a loan the church no longer can pay. Suing your lender is rarely a good option. Moreover, should your lawyer immediately suggest something like that, you might want to get a second opinion. At the end of the day, your church accepted money from a bank and agreed, in writing, to pay it back. If those two things have occurred, "equity"[112]—that is, what is considered fair and just—demands a certain deference to the lender.

This does not mean that the church may not have rights to exercise against the lender in the event of actual wrongdoing by the lender. But these rights will rarely, if ever, allow a church to avoid paying the debt because, again, equity generally demands that the lender be repaid.

In addition, loan documents are designed to protect the lender because they have, after all, taken on significant risk in loaning funds, and loan documents are constantly being revised to provide even more protection to the lender. Even with a good lawyer representing the church and negotiating the documents on the church's behalf, that is not going to change—and church leaders should not expect anything different.

On a related note, I've seen many borrowers try to "game the system" when a loan goes south. Over all my years in the legal field, I can't think of one situation where this has worked. First, there really aren't any new tricks to pursue that someone hasn't already tried; and, the loan documents, bank policies and practices, and even government regulations have been adapted to address these attempted "tricks."

Second, as stated above, equity always will step in to protect a bank even if that bank has made a technical error of some kind. A technical error might include not providing timely notification that a balloon note is about to mature and will not be renewed by the bank. Finally, the most important reason to avoid "gaming the system" is because it is inconsistent with good character. And as stated throughout this book, character matters.

---

112 In this context, "equity" is a legal term with no relation to its usage in the 5 C's of Credit or financial statements.

As a case in point, I had one non-church client who, against my advice, went to court to argue that a commercial loan was somehow invalidated because the bank had sold the loan multiple times and my borrower client had never been properly informed. This client lost this case in court... spectacularly. Their business situation was far worse after this failed litigation. It should be noted, this client was represented in court by a "brilliant" and very successful litigator. Again, be wary of attorneys who see litigation as the solution to a situation involving a non-performing loan.

Given that I seem to be discouraging aggressive legal action should the loan go south, you might wonder what I, as a lawyer, would recommend. Frankly, my experience as an attorney who has represented banks and borrowers is consistent with the banker's perspective mentioned above: Identify and disclose the problem early to your banker *and* to your lawyer. Whatever assistance I can give my clients as a lawyer requires that I be engaged very early on to help them navigate the situation.

If borrowers are calling me because they already have received a certified letter from their lender, the most I can do for them at that point is tell them how long they have before the lender takes the next and subsequent steps. Yes, I can call the lender on their behalf, but if the lender is sending certified letters, the borrower probably doesn't have many options available to them at that point. In that case, all I can do is "beg" for more time. For the record, begging by the lawyer at this juncture is not likely to work.

On the other hand, here are some possible options that borrowers may have if the loan goes south and there is early notification to the bank and to the attorney.

First, if it is a temporary situation, a bank will consider restructuring the loan. This is typically done through a loan "modification agreement" entered into with the borrower. A modification agreement does exactly what the title states: It modifies some aspect of the terms of the loan.

The modification agreement could modify the interest rate, it could require a principal pay down to bring the loan into balance, or it could modify a covenant such that the covenant can now be satisfied, and the technical default is addressed. Sometimes these modifications are temporary, and sometimes the modification will remain in place for the remaining term of the loan.

Another type of document that comes into play less frequently with non-performing or under-performing loans is called a forbearance agreement. A forbearance agreement typically states that the lender will refrain—or forbear—from taking certain actions, such as foreclosure, as long as the borrower is following certain agreed-upon actions.

If a borrower enters into a modification or forbearance agreement early enough, the borrower sometimes can avert a more dire situation from happening. And, just as a lawyer can assist with the original loan documents, a lawyer can assist church leaders in understanding and negotiating a modification or forbearance agreement. By the way, these types of agreements are rarely "standard" or boilerplate; therefore, they are more subject to negotiation between the bank and the borrower.

To reiterate, early identification and disclosure of a temporary situation can often avert a more dire situation. I would argue, however, that the main reason for early identification of a problem is that it best positions you, as a church leader, to address a situation if the loan is not performing or under-performing *due to a systemic or a permanent* reason.

Avoiding or ignoring the problem will not make it go away. Typically, it will only get worse. But through early identification of a loan going south, church leaders, with the assistance of the church's lawyer, can gain a number of benefits. Let me say at the outset, however, that *these listed benefits do not assume that in a worst-case scenario, that the church will be able to retain its real estate property.* This is a reality that has been discussed elsewhere in this book and is one that church leaders certainly have to face if a loan cannot be paid according to the stated terms.

With that said, here are potential benefits that I've identified from early notification:

EARLY RECOGNITION OF THE PROBLEM ALLOWS CHURCH
LEADERS TO POSSIBLY SELL THE REAL ESTATE PROPERTY TO
REPAY THE LOAN.

If the reason the loan is under-performing or non-performing is because
the church no longer can afford the mortgage, the most obvious solution I
see is to sell the property and pay off the mortgage. But selling real estate—
particularly special purpose real estate—can take several months, if not a
couple of years. So again, facing the problem early is required to pursue
this option.

By way of example, one of my church clients experienced a church
split. Over the course of two years, the church saw half of its membership
depart, and giving declined directly as a result of this split. Because of the
church leader's history of monitoring their finances carefully, the leaders
could see that their situation was not sustainable.

Because of their prudent business practices and a significant amount
of cash reserves on hand, these church leaders projected that they would
at least be able to pay their mortgage for the next few years. They identified where they could cut expenses, and they did. They determined the
church could undertake stewardship campaigns to increase giving, and
they did. Ultimately, however, they also knew their ability to do ministry
was severely hampered by trying to keep the building, and that at some
point, they would not be able to pay their mortgage.

By the way, their lender appeared very reluctant to work with the
church. The implicit message was that the bank didn't see the situation
as sustainable either. Based on all these considerations, these church
leaders made the hard decision that the building would need to be sold.
Truthfully, from the moment the church split occurred, leadership
was aware of the possibility that they might not be able to maintain
the building.

These church leaders had the emotional and spiritual maturity to
recognize that the building was merely a tool to help them do ministry.
The building, itself, was not their ministry. So, they were able to properly see what was coming and take the necessary steps. In this case, that

necessary step was to sell the building and continue their ministry in a building they could afford.

It should be noted that when church leadership made this decision, they had never missed a loan payment and did not anticipate missing a loan payment any time soon. But they knew it would take time to prepare the congregation for the loss of the current facility and a move to a new location. They also knew it would take time—possibly as much as a year—to actually sell the facility. Even as they pursued this option, however, they stayed open to the possibility that God might somehow enable them to keep the building.

EARLY RECOGNITION OF THE PROBLEM GIVES CHURCH LEADERS TIME TO MAKE ARRANGEMENTS FOR A FUTURE LOCATION.

If church leaders have to sell their facility to avoid foreclosure, or if the bank obtains the facility through foreclosure, church leaders will need another location to continue the ministry. Unless God has led the church to believe that they should no longer continue the ministry, the loss of the facility should not be the end of the ministry.

Early recognition of the problem allows church leaders time both to vacate the facility and to identify alternative locations to continue their ministry. It also gives church leaders time to make whatever financial adjustments may be needed to make an alternative location feasible.

There is another related advantage to early recognition. If church leaders are facing a foreclosure situation, typically the church will be expected to vacate the premises after the foreclosure. If the church hasn't vacated the premises, the lender will pursue eviction.

This could, however, be subject to negotiation. If the church has acted in good faith, demonstrated good character, and has been working with their lender throughout this time, the lender may give the church additional time to vacate the premises. The lender may even lease the premises to the church for a period of transition after the foreclosure. Perhaps not. The point is, early disclosure and good character creates the opportunity and the desire for someone, even your lender, to extend the church grace.

EARLY RECOGNITION OF THE PROBLEM ALLOWS CHURCH LEADERS TO PREPARE THEIR CONGREGATION THROUGH EFFECTIVE MESSAGING.

The loss of the building does not, and should not, automatically mean the end of the church's ministry. But it can be traumatizing and will likely negatively affect the congregation. With enough time, careful planning, and thoughtful leadership, church leaders can prepare the congregation through messaging designed to focus the congregation on the future of the ministry, and to mitigate some of the negative emotions and trauma that might result due to the loss of the building.

EARLY RECOGNITION OF THE PROBLEM ALLOWS CHURCH LEADERS TO APPROACH THE LENDER WITH THE OPTION OF A DEED IN LIEU OF FORECLOSURE.

With a Deed in Lieu of Foreclosure, the borrower voluntarily transfers the property to the lender pursuant to an agreement between the borrower and the lender. A voluntary transfer can avoid the embarrassment of the more public foreclosure process. Lenders typically do not consider this because a foreclosure is a "cleaner" approach to taking title. But Deeds in Lieu of Foreclosure do occur and if a borrower has given the lender enough time to consider and process this, and if the borrower has acted with good character, their lender may be open to a Deed in Lieu. It is certainly an option that can be put forward, assuming church leaders have been proactive and provided early notice of the problem.

CLOSING THOUGHTS

I (Lisa) understand this chapter is a difficult one for any church leader to read. Sharon Simmons and I covered a range of scenarios that all fall under the umbrella of a loan "going south." It is recognized that this chapter did not provide a happy, fix-all remedy for many church leaders who face this reality.

In some cases, borrowers may have a temporary glitch, either with a technical default or a short-term inability to pay the loan in a timely manner. This scenario is not to be minimized, but with timely and transparent communication to the lender and the church's attorney, there often is a satisfactory outcome for both the borrower and the bank. The church gets back on track, and the loan returns to a satisfactory status within the bank. Even if the loan is transferred temporarily to a bank's Workout Loan department, there can be a good resolution and the problem loan can be placed in the church's rear-view mirror.

In other cases, the problem is far more serious. A matured balloon note that will not be renewed and cannot be repaid, a split congregation that results in a sharp decline in revenues, or a significant economic downturn that negatively impacts debt service capacity and real estate values, all can have a long-term impact on the church loan. In these scenarios, churches and lenders may face the unwanted prospect of foreclosure to repay the loan, having to sell the property, or other hard measures. This is reality.

I close with two thoughts. First, for those who do not have a problem loan, my prayer is that you, as church leaders, truly understand what can happen if a loan goes south. The purpose of *Holy Borrowers* is to help church leaders greatly reduce, if not eliminate, the likelihood of this occurring.

Second, for those who are facing the potential loss of their building, my prayer is that as Ms. Simmons shared, steps will be taken that will allow the ministry to continue, even if ownership of the building does not—as painful as that will be. Please know that I fully understand the deep sentiment that is tied to a church building. I have that same sentiment for ours.

It is *The Place* where the Lord meets with us and where we meet with one another. It is *The Place* where ministry takes place and lives are transformed. It is our history. It is our sanctuary. But at the end of the day, if it is not our future, it can be deeply grieved and then released... as are so many other things in this life. We can walk in the knowledge that despite a tragedy on Friday, resurrection power can show up early Sunday morning.

This chapter originally closed out Part III of *Holy Borrowers*; however, COVID-19 emerged before this book went to print. Given the significant parallels between the principles already outlined in this book and financial lessons that emerged during the current pandemic, I prayerfully added a chapter to this section entitled, "In the Midst of COVID-19."

Part IV of *Holy Borrowers* will immediately follow Chapter 17. Part IV focuses on key lessons shared by two highly-successful churches. These are lessons that also highlight many of the principles discussed throughout this book and are lessons from which we all can learn.

IN THE MIDST OF COVID-19

"Yea, though I walk through the valley of the shadow
of death, I will fear no evil: for Thou art with me;
Thy rod and Thy staff they comfort me."

— PSALM 23:4 KJV

"But I know, somehow, that only when it is
dark enough can you see the stars."

— REV. DR. MARTIN LUTHER KING, JR.

On a beautiful Sunday afternoon on January 26, 2020, I was sitting in my niece's apartment in Washington, D.C. and heard the word, "coronavirus" for the first time. I would be flying back to my home in Dallas in just a few days and Brianna admonished me to take precautions as I traveled. I had no idea what she was talking about and didn't give it much thought at that time—particularly after we learned that Kobe Bryant's helicopter had crashed that same morning.

A few days later when I traveled through Reagan National Airport to DFW International Airport, I noticed three or four individuals in each of the airports wearing masks to cover their noses and mouths. It was quite a bizarre sight. My niece had shared that the "coronavirus" was rocking

China, but I thought it was awfully strange that individuals in the United States apparently were guarding themselves against a contagion that seemed so far away.

It only was after I returned home that I learned that a man from the state of Washington who had traveled to Wuhan, China, had been diagnosed with novel coronavirus on January 22nd.[113] Then on January 30th, the World Health Organization declared the novel coronavirus a "public health emergency of international concern,"[114] and our world changed.

It's now May 18, 2020 and I'm writing these words from my shelter-in-place office. Johns Hopkins University currently is reporting 1,487,447 confirmed cases of COVID-19 in the United States and 4,744,216 cases worldwide. Moreover, they currently report that 89,567 individuals in the United States and 315,822 worldwide have passed away from the virus.[115] These numbers continue to increase throughout the day, every day. So many people lost.

Glaring structural imbalances also are center stage yet again in the United States, as a grossly disproportionate percentage of cases and deaths among African-Americans and Latinos have been attributed to COVID-19. AmfAR, the Foundation for AIDS Research, has reported that Black people make up a disproportionate share of the population in 22% of U.S. counties, and that those counties account for more than 50% of coronavirus cases and nearly 60% of COVID-19 deaths.[116] The virus also

---

113 "Maps & Trends: New Cases of COVID-19 in World Countries," Johns Hopkins University & Medicine Coronavirus Resource Center, May 8, 2020, online: https://coronavirus.jhu.edu/data/new-cases.

114 "Rolling Updates on Coronavirus Disease (COVID-19)," World Health Organization, May 7, 2020, online: https://www.who.int/emergencies/diseases/novel-coronavirus-2019/events-as-they-happen.

115 "COVID-19 Dashboard by the Center for Systems Science and Engineering at Johns Hopkins University," Johns Hopkins University & Medicine Coronavirus Resource Center, May 18, 2020, online: https://coronavirus.jhu.edu/map.html, accessed May 18, 2020 at 9:00 a.m. CST.

116 Vanessa Williams, "Disproportionately Black Counties Account for Over Half of Coronavirus Cases in the U.S. and Nearly 60% of Deaths, Study Finds," *Washington Post*, May 6, 2020, online: https://www.washingtonpost.com/nation/2020/05/06/study-finds-that-disproportionately-black-counties-account-more-than-half-covid-19-cases-us-nearly-60-percent-deaths/.

has spurred even further divisions in this country surrounding shelter-ing-in-place, wearing masks, and perceived personal freedoms.

Then there is the economic front. The unemployment rate in the United States rose to a record 14.7% in April and payrolls plummeted by an unprecedented 20.5 million individuals.[117] At this time, nearly 36.5 million people have filed for unemployment insurance since the start of coronavirus shutdowns[118] and businesses are fighting to survive.

As the economy slid off a cliff, Congress passed its $2.2 trillion "Coronavirus Aid, Relief and Economic Security Act" ("CARES" Act) on March 27, 2020. That initial relief package included $350 billion under the U.S. Small Business Administration's "Paycheck Protection Program" ("PPP") for loan amounts up to $10 million.[119] The CARES Act provided unprecedented benefits to businesses, including: an annual interest rate of 1.0%, no required collateral, no required personal guaranties, a six-month moratorium on loan payments, and of course, potential forgive-ness of all principal and accrued interest if PPP funds are used appropri-ately for payroll and other eligible expenses.

When I learned with the rest of the country that for the first time, the U.S. Small Business Administration ("SBA") would allow churches, non-profits, and other 501(c)(3) organizations access to government-guaranteed loan funds, I turned my attention to helping those organi-zations and small businesses become educated about PPP financing. I helped many determine if the PPP and other measures were appropriate for their organizations and employees, and helped several organizations obtain approval and needed funding.

---

117 Sarah Chaney and Eric Morath, "April Unemployment Rate Rose to a Record 14.7%," *Wall Street Journal*, May 8, 2020, online: https://www.wsj.com/articles/april-jobs-report-coronavirus-2020-11588888089?mod=hp_lead_pos1&mod=article_inline&mod=hp_lead_pos1.

118 Sarah Chaney and Gwynn Guilford, "Nearly Three Million Sought Jobless Benefits Last Week," *Wall Street Journal*, May 14, 2020, online: https://www.wsj.com/articles/unemployment-benefits-weekly-jobless-claims-coronavirus-05-14-2020-11589410374.

119 "Business Loan Program Temporary Changes; Paycheck Protection Program," *Federal Register: The Daily Journal of the United States Government*, April 15, 2020, online: https://www.federalregister.gov/documents/2020/04/15/2020-07672/business-loan-program-temporary-changes-paycheck-protection-program.

Lenders first began accepting PPP loan applications on April 3rd. As is well known by now, $349 billion of the original $350 billion allocation was depleted by April 16th, just 13 days later. An additional $310 billion was made available by the SBA on April 27th; however, as of 5:00 p.m. on May 10th, only $120 billion of those funds remained and many lenders have stopped accepting PPP applications.[120] Like musical chairs on steroids, many organizations, including churches, will be left without a seat.

As I became involved in the PPP process, I was able to assess some "takeaways" that I believe are applicable to church leaders from a finance standpoint. I recognize that the primary purpose of PPP financing was not buildings, as is the focus of this book. I prayerfully added this chapter, however, because several principles that arose during the PPP process underscore principles that we have highlighted throughout *Holy Borrowers*.

I've identified four such principles below.

KNOW YOUR BANKER

The PPP Loan rollout unveiled the vast gulf between the "have's" and the "have-not's"—in this case, those church and business leaders who have personal relationships with commercial bankers and those who do not. Much attention has been given to the fact that larger organizations received the personal attention of individual bankers, while smaller organizations were relegated to navigating their way through bank websites.

Here's the issue: This is not new. Banks are structured such that even in normal economic environments, smaller business loan requests—say under $100,000—typically are processed through some kind of portal with minimal human touch. Most of these loan decisions are based on the credit score of the individual business owner or owners.

Why is this the case? Efficiency! It is far more efficient and cost effective to "credit score" a large volume of loan applications under a certain size than it is to hire bankers to manually review each

---

120 Mat Sorensen, "PPP Loan Developments: Only $120 Billion Left, Favorable Forgiveness Guidance from SBA and IRS Tax Pitfall," *Entrepreneur*, May 10, 2020, online: https://www.entrepreneur.com/article/350444.

application submitted. This process also benefits the borrower that is able to receive a response far more quickly than would be the case if their organization had to wait for a banker to finish a manual review of every loan application. Greater speed is a benefit to organizations waiting on funding. Lower cost is a benefit to banks when processing smaller loan requests.

On the other hand, larger loan requests—particularly those exceeding $500,000 and $1,000,000—warrant the individual attention of commercial bankers for businesses, and "private bankers" for wealthy individuals. There are several reasons.

First, larger loans involve more complexity in underwriting, hopefully, as demonstrated in this book! Larger loans also have a more significant impact on the lender's financial performance if the loan goes south. Second, relationships with larger organizations hardly ever are limited to loan requests. Deposit accounts, treasury management services, international banking services, investment services, and retirement services typically are needed by larger organizations. These additional services also require more personalized attention.

Finally, let's state the obvious: larger clients typically generate higher revenues. That's not news either. By way of illustration, let's look at the difference between a fast food restaurant that operates on high volume and low pricing, and a higher end restaurant that operates on lower volume and medium-to-high pricing. We all would expect a higher degree of attention if we were paying $100 or more per person for our meal, than we would expect if we were ordering a sandwich or salad in the drive-through lane!

In sum, the practice of processing smaller loan requests through online portals and larger loans through personal bankers was not introduced during the PPP process. The PPP just shined a spotlight on what has long been the case.

On a related note, I've also heard criticism that banks chose to serve their own customers first for PPP loan requests, before serving those who were not their customers. There are some who believe "first-come, first-served" should have been applied by lenders, meaning: If an organization that was not yet a bank customer submitted its PPP application before an existing bank customer submitted its PPP application, then the "non-customer's" PPP application should be processed first.

Let me ask this of church leaders: In the case of sickness, would you go to the bedside of your long-term member first or to the bedside of someone in the community whom you have not yet met? If there are expressed financial needs, would you as church leaders serve the individuals in your own congregation first or individuals in someone else's congregation? Would your answer change if the member of your congregation made his or her request after the non-member made his or her request? I could be wrong, but I believe the answer in all cases is, "Of course not."

In the same way, I do not believe it was a sin for bankers to give priority to their existing clients during the emergency PPP loan process, especially given their limited time and resources. It actually was sound business and an attempt to provide excellent customer service.

What does all this mean for church leaders? As I stated in Chapter 3, "Getting Ready Before You're Ready," this means it is critical for church leaders to establish a personal relationship with a commercial banker now. This way, you too can pick up a telephone or send an e-mail or text and be known by the banker on the receiving end!

If a bank is not willing to give you that kind of attention and service, then it is time to find another bank! Many regional banks and community banks thrive on giving personal attention to their commercial clients. Further, if you are a smaller church with less than 100 members, it is even more critical that you establish a banking relationship with a smaller bank where you are not just a customer number to them.

With that said, please let me digress a moment to give a shout out to the good bankers. From the first day that PPP was launched, bankers I know literally worked around the clock to prepare to accept PPP applications and to process those applications once they were authorized to do so. When I write, "literally" I mean just that. Receiving an e-mail from a banker that was sent at 2:00 a.m. in the morning was not unusual during this time. These individuals were committed to processing as many PPP loan requests as possible. In many banks it was all hands-on-deck. Anyone who could read an application was expected to do *something*.

Further, remember all of those online portals that collapsed under the weight of the number of PPP applications being received by banks and by the SBA? Someone inside a bank with technical skills that I don't possess had to design those systems on the fly, and then fix those systems when they collapsed.

Many bankers shared how stressed they were during this time. I know that many people can echo that feeling in the midst of COVID-19. What has been missed, however, is that bankers also have been essential personnel during this crisis. Regrettably, most have not been recognized as such. These bankers have the same levels of stress as individuals that others face—children at home instead of school, distancing from elderly parents and grandparents, fear for their jobs, and fear of getting COVID-19 themselves. Of course, bankers have become ill too.

Are there some bankers who, with their clients, gamed the system? There always are. My personal belief, however, is that the vast majority of bankers worked hard in the midst of their own personal challenges to get up to speed on the PPP and to serve as many clients and prospective clients as possible, often without complaint. In my opinion, these bankers should be applauded for doing so.

Overall, as church leaders develop personal relationships with commercial bankers going forward, it is important to recognize the role bankers can play and have played in supporting our churches and business community overall. More specifically, it is essential that church leaders recognize the role they can play in supporting your church.

SOUND PAYROLL SYSTEMS

In Chapter 3, I also discussed the importance of sound payroll systems and recommended that churches consider contracting with reputable payroll processing companies to process their payroll and payroll taxes. Good payroll systems always are a necessity for one major reason: You don't want to play with Uncle Sam and tax dollars because he always wins that fight! Payroll taxes should and must be paid on time.

During PPP, however, the need for sound payroll systems emerged for other reasons. A prerequisite for obtaining a PPP loan was proof of 12 months of payroll for each employee, as well as proof that payroll taxes were paid in a satisfactory manner. If an organization could not readily produce that information, it could not obtain a PPP loan.

In contrast, not only did payroll processing companies provide this information for their clients at the touch of a computer key stroke, many of them even produced the specific reports that were needed for the PPP application! The ability to access this information in a timely, accurate manner saved time, and time was a critical commodity for organizations racing to submit their applications.

Further, these same types of reports will be required by banks and the SBA when organizations submit documentation requesting to have their PPP loans forgiven. A lack of accurate payroll reporting will make it challenging, if not impossible, for these organizations to have their loans forgiven. This will leave them with PPP loans that must be repaid.

1099 CONTRACTORS V. EMPLOYEES

I also mentioned in Chapter 3 that I'm not an accountant. That fact has not changed 14 chapters later! On that basis, I will not presume to advise church leaders as to whether pastors and other key staff members should be classified by the church as W-2 employees or as 1099 independent contractors. Many employers consider it more advantageous to hire staff as 1099 independent contractors rather than W-2 employees. This is because an employer does not have to withhold a contractor's income taxes or payroll taxes, nor pay the employer side of payroll taxes. On the flip side, there are various debates regarding which classification is more advantageous for the individual worker in terms of taxes they must pay as a 1099 contractor versus a W-2 employee.

Let me say two things. First, the decision that is made in classifying an individual as a W-2 employee or a 1099 independent contractor is not supposed to be based upon which classification is more advantageous for either the employer or individual worker! Rather, it's supposed to be based upon guidelines established by the Internal Revenue Service ("IRS"). Discerning these classifications for each staff member is a conversation that should be held with the church's accountant, consistent with IRS guidelines that are listed on their website. (See footnote below.[121])

Second, I spoke with a number of pastors during the race for PPP dollars who regretted the fact they were classified by their respective churches as 1099 contractors, rather than W-2 employees. Why? Because the PPP regulations did not include 1099 compensation within "eligible payroll expenses" in an organization's PPP loan application, nor in eligible payroll for loan forgiveness. Rather, 1099 contractors were required to apply for PPP loans on an individual basis.

Moreover, while lenders began accepting PPP loan applications from churches and other organizations on April 3rd, those who were classified as 1099 independent contractors had to wait one full week before they were allowed to apply. This requirement proved to be extremely disadvantageous to these individuals, given that the first round of PPP funds was exhausted in less than two weeks.

With this in mind, the PPP process may serve as a call to some to make sure their staff members are properly classified—first, because it's the right thing to do and second, because it may come back to haunt the church if you don't. I stressed, "may" because as stated, this is a decision that church leaders should make in conjunction with their accountant and IRS guidelines.

THE IMPORTANCE OF A CUSHION

In Chapter 9 of *Holy Borrowers*, I wrote this statement:

> "The higher the debt, the more vulnerable the church is to downturns in the economy, transitions in their congregation, and other

---

121 "Understanding Employee vs. Contractor Designation," Internal Revenue Service, July 20, 2017, online: https://www.irs.gov/newsroom/understanding-employee-vs-contractor-designation.

unexpected events that negatively impact giving. Equity financing helps to absorb the negative impact from these occurrences."

At the time I wrote this statement, I obviously had no idea that "other unexpected events" would include the events surrounding COVID-19! At the same time, the principle is true at all times: Churches and other organizations always should maintain a cushion because "the unexpected" always occurs!

A few weeks ago, I received a letter that underscores this point. The letter was written by Christian philanthropists, John and Ellen McStay, and directed to members of the "Faith-Based Forum." The Faith-Based Forum was formed by John and Ellen in 2007 to facilitate collaboration among faith-based entities in Dallas that are "dedicated to providing basic human needs to disenfranchised individuals and communities." Wil McCall, CEO & President of Dallas Leadership Foundation, was one of the members who received this letter, and he e-mailed a copy to me.

The letter contains great wisdom for the Forum members from start to finish, but one section in particular jumped out in the context of this discussion. I share this portion with John and Ellen's permission:

> "...we suspect that even the best managed entities among you will find solace in a renewed commitment to focusing on your balance sheet. Ask yourself if you have had the proper respect for fiscal responsibility? Did you establish 'Rainy Day Funds' in past years? How about the proper creation of reserves for the inevitable problems (catastrophes) that will continue to confront you? You should assume your next three years will be very different from your last three-year plan. This will also be the case with your two-year and one-year plans. COVID-19 can be the impetus you need to strategize and plan for the future."

Let the Church say, "Amen." Let the Church say, "Amen" again! The principle is clear: Rainy Day Funds and reserves—that is, cushion—should be an integral part of every organization's on-going financial strategy.

That's not all. I shared in Chapter 11 that lenders typically require churches to maintain minimum cash balances equating to six to 12 months of debt service on their loans. That criterion can seem so onerous to church leaders in prosperous times, but in the current economic environment, it should be recognized that this type of liquidity cushion is extremely valuable for paying current expenses and providing greater peace of mind.

Finally, let me reemphasize the importance of maintaining a cushion when preparing budgets and projections. I wrote the following in Chapter 7:

> "I am not a fan of including capital campaign contributions in cash flow to evaluate debt service coverage. Rather, I believe the best practice is for church leaders to rely on historical cash flow from tithes and offerings when establishing your loan amount, and even there, to use about 75% to 80% of tithes and offerings to leave the church a cushion."

As I have shared then, projected revenue does not cover present-day expenses. Of course, even a 2020 budget that was based conservatively on 75% to 80% of 2019 tithes and offerings still would not have compensated for the sharp decline in actual giving that many churches have experienced during this COVID-19 pandemic. It would, however, have placed these churches in far better positions than budgets that provided no cushion whatsoever; or even worse, budgets that relied on an increase in projected tithes, offerings, and capital campaign donations.

DÉJÀ VU: IF YOUR LOAN GOES SOUTH

If these previous sections feel like I'm pouring salt on the wounds of churches that did not have any cushion, that is not my intent. If your church had a building loan before COVID-19 and now has insufficient cash flow to cover loan payments, this is the epitome of your loan "going south." In this case, the information provided in Chapter 16 may not have been relevant to your church before COVID-19, but it's certainly relevant now.

The most important message of that chapter is to contact your banker as soon as possible if you have not done so already—along with an attorney with expertise in commercial real estate loans. (As a reminder, Appendix V provides guidelines for selecting a qualified attorney.) In so doing, remember that this is not a time to approach the bank as an adversary. Rather, this is the time to collaborate with your banker to prayerfully work out a solution that is mutually satisfactory to both the church and the bank.

CLOSING THOUGHTS

I wrestled mightily with adding this chapter. I recognize that the impact of COVID-19 on human life never can be reduced to takeaways and principles, and I feared implying this was the case. As important as these principles are, they pale in comparison to the lives lost and the on-going emotional and economic toll that still is unfolding. At the same time, my continued desire is for you, as church leaders, to understand and implement financial principles that will help you successfully lead your churches financially now, and in the years ahead.

I close both this chapter and Part III of *Holy Borrowers* with this important truth: Through it all, we serve a God who has revealed Himself in Jesus Christ, our Resurrected Savior, who calls us to trust in Him at all times. COVID-19 pales in comparison to Him! I grieve with each of you for every life lost. I also give the Lord thanks for every person healed and for every person who has not needed that type of healing.

Our entire world has been shaken to its foundations in so many ways. In this shaking, however, we can see afresh that Jesus alone is our rock, and that everything else is sinking sand. As He said:

> "Everyone then who hears these words of mine and does them
> will be like a wise man who built his house on the rock. And the
> rain fell, and the floods came, and the winds blew and beat on

that house, but it did not fall, because it had been founded on the rock." Matthew 7:24-25 ESV

We also can cherish the encouraging words of the prophet, Jeremiah:

"'For I know the plans that I have for you,' declares the LORD, 'plans for welfare and not for evil, to give you a future and a hope. Then you will call upon Me and come and pray to Me, and I will hear you. You will seek Me and find Me, when you seek Me with all your heart.'" (Jeremiah 29:11-13 ESV)

Let the Church say, "Amen."

PART IV

LESSONS FROM
SUCCESSFUL CHURCHES

"Leadership and learning are
indispensable to each other."
— JOHN F. KENNEDY

SECTION OVERVIEW

My church in general, and my husband, Terrence, in particular, have been blessed to be mentored by other pastors who are leading highly-successful ministries, as measured by any number of standards. Two of these pastors and ministries are located in the Dallas/Fort Worth Metroplex, affording me the opportunity to speak with them and their leaders about their own experiences with building finance.

Both ministries are led by dynamic pastors and leadership teams. Both have sizeable congregations numbering in the thousands that continue to grow. And, both have financed sizeable building projects, obtaining construction financing in the multi-million-dollar range. There is much we can learn from them.

With great appreciation and respect, I close *Holy Borrowers* with lessons from these two church ministries: Mt. Hebron Missionary Baptist Church in Garland, Texas, led by Pastor Leonard O. Leach; and, Friendship-West Baptist Church in Dallas, Texas, led by Dr. Frederick Douglass Haynes, III.

CHAPTER 18

LESSONS FROM MT. HEBRON MISSIONARY BAPTIST CHURCH

"There were probably three or four years before
taking on new debt, to prepare, to build up our cash
reserves and cushion, and to make the down payment.
We started our capital stewardship campaign."
— Member of Mt. Hebron's Finance Committee Board

"Just because they say they can do it for those prices,
doesn't necessarily mean the 'better bid' is actually the
better bid. They said, 'We can do it for this money.
We can save the church some money.'
That definitely wasn't the case."
— Former Chairman of Mt. Hebron's Finance Committee Board

BACKGROUND

Founded in 1958, Mt. Hebron Missionary Baptist Church ("Mt. Hebron")
is the largest predominantly African-American church in Garland, Texas,
a suburb located about 20 miles east of downtown Dallas. Affectionately
known as "The Mount," Mt. Hebron's current membership exceeds 3,500
individuals, with 250 new members, on average, joining each year.

Mt. Hebron's primary worship and ministry center consists of a two-story, 77,102 square foot facility located on 14 acres of land on Highway 66 in Garland. Ground-up construction of this facility began in January 2003 and was completed in December 2004. This facility is the base for most of Mt. Hebron's numerous ministries.

Mt. Hebron also owns a 16,582 square foot multi-purpose facility on Dairy Road in Garland. This property previously served as Mt. Hebron's main sanctuary prior to the construction of its current worship facility. The Dairy Road property includes an educational and classroom wing, a multi-purpose hall, and a full-service kitchen. This property houses Mt. Hebron Christian Academy which serves children attending kindergarten through the third grade.

Seven senior pastors have led Mt. Hebron over its 62-year existence. Its seventh and current pastor, Pastor Leonard O. Leach, is the most tenured of them all, having served as Mt. Hebron's shepherd for over 24 years.

My husband and I first met Pastor Leach 30 years ago in 1990 when he served as the Assistant Pastor of the historic Concord Baptist Church in Dallas. We immediately admired both him and his wife, and our admiration for them both only has grown stronger over the years. We know his entire family very well and count them among our many blessings.

With this information as the backdrop, I am going to highlight four lessons regarding church finance that I believe we can learn from Mt. Hebron.

LESSON #1: QUALITY OF FINANCIAL REPORTING

I've written at length about the importance to banks of having "high quality" financial reporting. It is clear that high quality financial reporting is a priority for Mt. Hebron as well. How do I know? I accessed the church's website and almost immediately noticed the following logo: [122]

---

122 Mount Hebron Missionary Baptist Church, online: www.onthemount.org.

What is ECFA? The letters represent the acronym for "Evangelical Council for Financial Accountability." The following description is found on ECFA's website:

"Founded in 1979, ECFA provides accreditation to leading Christian nonprofit organizations that faithfully demonstrate compliance with established standards for financial accountability, fundraising and board governance."[123]

ECFA ascribes to "Seven Standards of Responsible Stewardship™" drawn from Scripture. Two of these standards directly relate to the organization's financial accountability: Standard 3—Financial Oversight and Standard 5—Transparency.[124]

Mt. Hebron was accredited by the ECFA in 2017. Since that time, Mt. Hebron's leadership has submitted its financial reports not only to their external CPA, but also to the accreditation standards of this external organization. Mt. Hebron's commitment to its financial transparency is so strong that anyone can find the church's key financial metrics for 2016, 2017, and 2018 on EFCA's website, with 2019's information to be uploaded at the time these words were written.

What were Mt. Hebron's total revenues for the year ending December 31, 2018? Nearly $2.9 million. What was Mt. Hebron's total change in net assets ("profit") for that same year? Almost $206,000. Mt. Hebron's total assets as of December 31, 2018? Approximately $7.7 million, with total liabilities of $3.6 million. For those of you with a calculator, these figures translate to an excellent Debt-to-Equity Ratio of 2.14 to 1.0 as of that date.

That's not all. If you look across the top of Mt. Hebron's Home Page,[125] you'll see a page title I've not seen on any other church website I've ever

123 ECFA, online: https://www.ecfa.org/Content/GeneralBackground.
124 ECFA, online: https://www.ecfa.org/Standards.aspx.
125 Mount Hebron, online: https://www.onthemount.org/.

visited. The name of the page is: "State of the Church." When I accessed that page, I found links to three documents:

- The Agenda for Mt. Hebron's next churchwide meeting on January 22, 2020;
- Detailed minutes from Mt. Hebron's previous churchwide meeting on October 23, 2019;
- A detailed, 16-page copy of Mt. Hebron's 2020 expense budget.

The third item intrigued me the most. These detailed budgeted expenses for 2020 included, among others, the amount of support each missionary and mission receives from Mt. Hebron; the budgeted amount for the church's Christian Education curriculum; total salaries for full-time and part-time staff; and, projected principal and interest payments for 2020.

Further, Mt. Hebron's 2020 budget was completed and available on its website within a few weeks of December 31, 2019. I found it even more noteworthy that Mt. Hebron's church leaders made this detailed budget available not just to their own congregation, but to any person, anywhere, who accessed their website. That's financial transparency!

I'm not stating that every church needs to place their financial details on the worldwide web. What I am saying is that from a banker's perspective, Mt. Hebron's financial transparency is a dream come true, and certainly, is a key credit strength. Mt. Hebron provides an excellent example of maintaining a level of financial reporting that is clear, transparent, and readily available.

LESSON #2: PASTORAL SUCCESSION

In Chapter 11: "Conditions," I wrote that an important condition that banks evaluate is the succession plan for the senior pastor and other key leaders.

As shared, lenders like seeing churches change pastors. Why? Because a church's surviving—and thriving—after a change in its senior pastor demonstrates that the congregation is not dependent on one leader.

Such is the history of Mt. Hebron Missionary Baptist Church. While the current pastor, Rev. Leonard O. Leach, has had a significant impact on the church over his 24-years of leadership—and maintains that same impact today—he has not been Mt. Hebron's only pastor. As previously mentioned, over Mt. Hebron's 62-year history, seven pastors have made their mark on this church.

In fact, one might say that just as King David laid the foundation for his son, Solomon, to build the temple in the next generation,[126] Mt. Hebron's former pastors successfully laid a foundation on which each successive pastor could stand.

I created the chart below based on the historical narrative that Mt. Hebron provided on its website:[127]

Senior Pastor	Real Estate Purchase	Debt Repayment
W. J. Davis	September 1983: Tract of land on Dairy Road	
Carey Casey		1984—Dairy Rd. land paid off in full
James B. Rodgers	March 1987: Completed Phase I of four-phase building program on Dairy Road	
James B. Rodgers	1988: Purchased 28 acres of land at Highway 66 and Country Club Road	20 acres owned free and clear
James B. Rodgers	March 1991: Completed Phase II of building program on Dairy Road (Educational and Classroom wing with multi-purpose hall and kitchen)	
Leonard O. Leach	1997: Mt. Hebron Christian Academy in the Education wing on Dairy Road	
Leonard O. Leach		1999—All debts on Dairy Rd. buildings paid off in full.
Leonard O. Leach	January 2003—December 2004: First two buildings of a new worship and ministry center were constructed and completed	

---

126 1 Chronicles, Chapter 28.
127 Mount Hebron, online: https://www.onthemount.org/new-here/history/.

In the previous chart, we can see that four different pastors oversaw Mt. Hebron's significant real estate projects. The land on Dairy Road originally was purchased in 1983 under the leadership of Pastor W. J. Davis—and the debt on that land was paid off under the leadership of Pastor Carey Casey in 1984. Then, Pastor James B. Rodgers was the senior pastor when the Dairy Road facility was constructed on that debt-free land in 1987.

Pastor Rodgers also was the leader when Mt. Hebron purchased 28 acres of land on Highway 66, a portion of which serves today as the site of Mt. Hebron's Worship and Ministry Center. In 1999, just three years after Pastor Leach became Mt. Hebron's Senior Pastor, the church paid off all debt on the Dairy Road building.

I'm not writing this section to recommend that all senior pastors immediately transition their leadership! Rather, I'm highlighting Mt. Hebron's demonstrated succession planning. There is a lesson to be learned in how to move a church from glory-to-glory, from one leader to the next.

LESSON #3: MT. HEBRON'S CHURCH FINANCING

Lesson #3 highlights the manner in which Mt. Hebron's church leaders have managed the financing of their buildings. For this purpose, I was blessed to meet with two of Mt. Hebron's leaders who at that time, were the primary liaisons between the church and the banking community.

The first, whom I'll call, "David," was at that time, the Chairman of Mt. Hebron's Trustees, as well as the Chairman of Mt. Hebron's Finance Committee Board. The second, whom I'll call "Mark," served as a Trustee and as a member of the Finance Committee Board. He also held the office of Treasurer.[128]

The two men had been chosen to evaluate financing options for the church, and then offer recommendations to Pastor Leach and the Joint Board

---

128 At their request, I have used fictitious names for both leaders to avoid indirectly linking their respective full-time employers to this interview, because both are officers at their respective companies.

of Trustees and Deacons. At that time, if a banker were interested in winning Mt. Hebron's business, he or she needed to start with these two men.

Mt. Hebron's history highlights a church culture that prioritizes paying off debt prior to taking on additional financing. This theme continued to be underscored in my conversation with David and Mark. They discussed, in particular, the intentionality of Mt. Hebron's leaders in paying off the debt on the Dairy Road facility before beginning construction on the new 77,102 square foot facility. This priority was followed even though it meant delaying construction of the new building.

When the debt on the Dairy Road property was paid off in 1999, Mt. Hebron held a note burning ceremony during its Sunday morning service. Mark shared that this event was particularly memorable for him because the note burning ceremony was held on his first Sunday visiting the church.

Mt. Hebron's leadership then took it one step further. Although the Dairy Road debt had been paid in full, and although Mt. Hebron had no debt on the land on Highway 66 where their new facility would be located, they did not immediately apply for a new construction loan to build their new facility. They were not declined by a bank. The leadership reached this decision on their own accord. Why?

Mark provided the explanation:

> "There were probably three or four years before taking on new debt, to prepare, to build up our cash reserves and cushion, and to make the down payment. We started our capital stewardship campaign."

Part of that capital stewardship campaign included a feature that David introduced to Mt. Hebron's leadership team. David serves as Senior Managing Partner of a private equity firm and brought his significant financial expertise to the church.

Specifically, David introduced the strategy of establishing a "Gifting Account" for the church with a well-known financial firm. This Gifting

Account enabled Mt. Hebron's members to give non-cash assets to the church's Capital Stewardship Campaign—including stocks, bonds, and even cars.

David recalled that in some cases, Mt. Hebron retained a donated car for ministry purposes, while in other cases, the church sold the donated cars for cash. In both scenarios, the donor received a tax write-off for the charitable donation to the church. David taught Mt. Hebron's membership about this donation strategy by first speaking briefly about the concept on Sunday mornings and then holding more in-depth follow-up classes once a month.

Mt. Hebron's leadership team also exercised discipline in its planned construction loan in other ways. First, David stated the team was very conservative in performing their own calculations as to the amount of debt the church could afford. David stated:

> "We always relied on historical numbers with a cushion, rather than hoping they will come."

Additionally, Mark shared how the church leaders decided to scale back the design of their new facility on Highway 66. He said:

> "They built in parts. They originally planned to do a sanctuary, fellowship hall, and other items—but they dropped the fellowship hall when we didn't have the funding."

Let me reemphasize the last portion of that statement: Mt. Hebron dropped the fellowship hall when they didn't have the funding. This is an example of the type of financial discipline that allows church leaders to simply acknowledge: "We can't afford this."

Ultimately, Mt. Hebron saved enough cash to make a significant equity injection toward their construction financing in 2003. David shared that a number of banks bid on their financing. What stood out to these lenders? Mt. Hebron's cash reserves, unencumbered real estate property, a demonstrated history of repaying building debt ahead of schedule, strong financial reporting, proven succession planning across seven different senior pastors, and an active leadership team beyond the senior pastor.

These events occurred between 1999 and 2003. Mt. Hebron continues to exercise this same type of conservatism toward debt today. David shared, for example, that Mt. Hebron started planning for further expansion to support its continued growth and ministry nine years ago. These plans included obtaining architectural renderings for a new facility. Mt. Hebron has not yet moved forward beyond these preliminaries, however.

One need only look to Mt. Hebron's website to learn why the expansion plans have not yet been implemented. In the minutes from Mt. Hebron's State of the Church Meeting on October 23, 2019, the following excerpt was provided by members of the Financial Committee Board, pertaining to the debt on the Highway 66 facility:

> "Structured, 7-year balloon note which means the whole balance come due. We are due to refinance the church in 2023 and we are paying $12,000 to $14,000 dollars a month in interest alone... our goal is to burn the note for the church."

In other words, Mt. Hebron is actively managing its balloon note more than three years before its maturity date.

In sum, Mt. Hebron's financial discipline has served this church extremely well over many decades and in the most recent years. Their conservative practice has enabled them to weather downturns and have a financial cushion.

LESSON #4: WHAT MT. HEBRON WOULD HAVE DONE DIFFERENTLY

While there are many lessons to be learned from Mt. Hebron from practices they have followed that led to their success, David and Mark also shared decisions the church made that they would not make today. These decisions involve the construction of their current, 77,102 square foot Worship and Ministry Center on Highway 66.

THE PARKING LOT

As shared, the construction of Mt. Hebron's current Worship and Ministry Center, was started in January 2003 and was completed on schedule in December 2004. Initially, the project appeared to be entirely satisfactory and the congregation transitioned its worship and ministry activities to the new facility with great joy.

David stated that about three years after the construction was completed, however, problems emerged with the parking lot that was built in conjunction with their new facility. The parking lot surrounding the facility began to crumble and decay in multiple places and continued to deteriorate with each passing month. Ultimately, it was found that the parking lot had been poorly constructed. The parking lot wasn't level and the drainage system that had been put in place was defective.

The problems with the parking lot became even more apparent in inclement weather. David recalled, "Not only did we have water standing in the parking lot when it rained, we had water flowing back into the building, going under doors! It was a mess."

Eventually, Mt. Hebron was forced to obtain a few hundred thousand dollars in additional bank financing to repair their parking lot's faulty drainage system. Mt. Hebron took the construction firm to court for damages, but only was awarded a few hundred thousand dollars from the suit—largely offset by their legal fees. No other recourse was available to the church because eventually, the construction company went out of business.

David recounted his feelings about that experience:

> "It was very frustrating. We felt very taken advantage of. We felt duped by this construction company when we were trying to do the right thing... All together, these were multiple millions of dollars' worth of mistakes in terms of repairs, problems, litigation, and legal battles."

I asked David and Mark what lessons they had learned from this experience. David spoke first and shared the following wisdom:

"Just because they say they can do it for those prices, doesn't necessarily mean the 'better bid' is actually the better bid. They said, 'We can do it for this money. We can save the church some money.' That definitely wasn't the case."

Mark followed with this insight:

"We also learned we needed a Construction Manager to oversee all of the contractors to make sure they were doing what they were supposed to be doing,"

to which David added:

"We had a retired church member who said he was an expert, who was going by on assigned days and sitting out there—but he wasn't an expert. We won't do that again."

The two lessons shared here are invaluable. Both are common mistakes made by many churches. First, the lowest bidder is not always the best provider. Many times, we really do get what we pay for. Second, no matter how many individuals in your congregation assure you that they can manage the construction project, obtaining a trustworthy expert should be an absolute requirement for every project.

CLOSING THOUGHTS: THE PASTOR'S ROLE

At the end of our conversation, I asked David and Mark what level of involvement Pastor Leach has in the church finance process. Here's what David said:

"We talk to him regularly about what we're doing; about what we think makes sense. He's involved in the discussions with the leaders. It's really helpful because it's never about carrying out the orders of the pastor. Then we bring those things to the Trustee Board and then the Joint Board for discussion.

He's not directly hands-on like some pastors are, but he's not far away. His mentality is, 'You guys have the expertise. I've got some good brothers who love the Lord and are trying to do the right thing. You guys lead on this and keep me updated.'"

Mt. Hebron provides an excellent model of, on the one hand, a senior pastor who allows those around him with financial expertise to "run point" on making recommendations concerning significant financing decisions; and on the other hand, a financial team who is worthy of the trust their pastor has placed in them! Mt. Hebron's financial team has the best interests of Mt. Hebron at heart.

Here's my question as we close this chapter: What happens when a senior pastor extends the same level of trust in individuals that Pastor Leach extends, but those individuals are *not* found to be trustworthy? What happens when those advising the senior pastor about church financing decisions do not even have the best interest of the church at heart? Moreover, what happens when *the lender* does not have the best interest of the church at heart either?

This is exactly what occurred with Friendship-West's Baptist Church's construction financing. We will learn from their experience in the next chapter.

CHAPTER 19

LESSONS FROM FRIENDSHIP-WEST BAPTIST CHURCH

"These people know what makes you tick. What they will do is they will quote Scriptures and before you know it, you're doing church at the table instead of business at the table."

– VETA HOLT, Chief Operating Officer,
Friendship-West Baptist Church

"Do not ignore the language of business. I did and we had to pay for it in ways I have repented for and God has forgiven me—but we paid the price."

– DR. FREDERICK D. HAYNES, III, Senior Pastor,
Friendship-West Baptist Church

BACKGROUND

Friendship-West Baptist Church ("Friendship-West") was founded in 1976 by Pastor Robert L. Castle, III. Six years later, Pastor Castle passed away unexpectedly, and Friendship-West was left without a pastor. At that time, the church had approximately 80 members.

The congregation invited Frederick Douglass Haynes, III, then a young minister at Bishop College, to serve as its Interim Pastor. Dr.

Haynes served in that role until his graduation in August 1982. After the church was led for a short period under a different interim pastor, Dr. Haynes returned to take the mantle full-time. He was officially installed as Friendship-West's senior pastor in April 1983.

Since that time, under Dr. Haynes' servant leadership, Friendship-West's membership has grown to over 13,500 individuals, with an average of 800 to 1,000 people completing the New Members Curriculum each year. Friendship-West actively engages in ministries that, "exalt the Savior, evangelize sinners, emancipate those who suffer, and equip the saints for service." The church's vision statement is to be, "a game-changing Christian movement connecting people to Jesus Christ and fighting for justice while creating the beloved community."[129]

Friendship-West is one of the largest employers in South Dallas, with a full-time pastoral and support staff that exceeds 45. The church's 45+ ministries include a credit union, a state-of-the-art printing company, and the Frederick Douglass Human Services and Justice Center that provides a food pantry, skills training, and a myriad of other needed services for the community.

Friendship-West's national and international impact also is significant. The church long-ago adopted Emmanuel Baptist Church in Harare, Zimbabwe, helping to fund the construction of a worship auditorium, day care center and school; and, launched Emanuel Care—a hunger-relief program designed to help provide food to at least 150 families in Harare, Zimbabwe. Friendship-West has donated over $1 million to Historically Black Colleges and Universities and over $2 million in scholarships to students both in the church and the greater Dallas community.

Friendship-West also has planted a number of churches domestically. I can personally attest to this because my church, Christ Community, was Friendship-West's first church plant. Dr. Haynes has been a mentor to my husband and me; and he, his wife, and their daughter are lifelong friends.

---

129 Friendship-West Baptist Church, online: https://www.friendshipwest.org/about-us.html#/.

BUILDING PROJECTS AND DEVELOPMENT

Friendship-West has undergone two significant building projects and real estate developments over Dr. Haynes' 37-year tenure, to accommodate the church's significant growth. In June 1991, Friendship-West purchased a 39,680 square foot existing facility on Kiest Boulevard in the Oak Cliff section of Southern Dallas, about 10 minutes south of downtown Dallas. The Kiest property was significantly larger than their 3,100 square foot church building where they had worshipped, and which they had outgrown.

Friendship-West's membership accelerated even more in their new facility. The church moved from three worship services to four, but eventually, the Kiest facility couldn't accommodate their continued growth.

Therefore, in 2005, Friendship-West purchased 60 acres of land along Interstate 20 and Wheatland Road, approximately five minutes from its Kiest facility. The church used a portion of this land to construct its current worship and conference center: a beautiful 174,000 square foot, two-story facility that is alternatively called, "the Taj Mahal in Oak Cliff" and "the Palace in Southern Dallas."[130]

Notably, Friendship-West's new construction and overall presence in the new location on Wheatland Road and Interstate 20 also spurred significant commercial development in the surrounding area. Before the church broke ground, there was not a single national or even regional business in the area. After Friendship-West completed the construction of its new facility, national and regional businesses followed, including Target, banking institutions, warehouses, and trucking firms.

THE DEBT FINANCING

Friendship-West Baptist Church obtained a total of $30 million in bond financing in 2005. As discussed in Chapter 5, Friendship-West had been approved by a bank for a $19 million construction loan. It was no small amount, but it was $11 million less than the bond financing that was arranged for them by a church broker.

---

130 Ibid.

The bond company's financing included $25 million for ground-up construction of the new 174,000 square foot facility and $5 million for the facility's new audio-visual system. If this sounds like wonderful news, you'd be in full agreement with what the leaders of Friendship-West originally thought. In the end, however, this financing arrangement could have destroyed the church financially, and did severely damage the ministry for many years.

Dr. Haynes and Friendship-West's Chief Operating Officer, Veta Holt, have been extremely transparent regarding the challenges Friendship-West faced through this financing. Dr. Haynes explained their transparency and outright enthusiasm for contributing to *Holy Borrowers* with these words:

"I want God's church to be protected."

With these words as a backdrop, here are lessons all church leaders can learn from the financing associated with Friendship-West's current facility, and the wisdom these church leaders have gained.

LESSON #1: RECOGNIZE THE SIGNS OF PREDATORY LENDING

In the "Introduction" to *Holy Borrowers*, I listed three elements, any one of which is an indication of predatory lending. Two of those three elements are evident in the $30 million in bond financing that Friendship-West obtained. I'll reiterate those two elements here:

- Making unaffordable loans based on the assets of the borrower rather than on the borrower's ability to repay an obligation;
- Engaging in fraud or deception to conceal the true nature of the loan obligation, or ancillary products, from an unsuspecting or unsophisticated borrower.

Further detail will be provided in the pages to follow, but I will highlight key features of Friendship-West's $30 million financing structure here. In this final chapter of *Holy Borrowers*, see if any of these stand out!

CAPITAL REQUIREMENT AND RESULTING LOAN-TO-VALUE

As shared, Friendship-West received $30 million in bond financing. This financing was secured by their new land and soon-to-be constructed new facility. Do you know what the appraised value was for that property when their financing was approved? $30 million.

Do you remember what we said about acceptable LTV ratios for church buildings? Correct: 50% to 75% as a normal range, with some banks increasing that maximum to 80% or even 85%. Friendship-West received 100% debt financing on their property.

At the time, not being required to inject any cash equity for the construction project sounded like a great blessing to the church—as did receiving $11 million more than the $19 million construction loan Bank of America had offered them. But, as we discussed in previous chapters, overloading a church with debt is never a blessing for numerous reasons: money diverted from ministry functions and increased vulnerability to economic downturns.

Did you notice what year Friendship-West obtained their financing? The church closed on their loans in 2005—three years before the beginning of the Great Recession. The church was walking into a brick wall saddled with 100% debt financing.

By the way, the $19 million offered by Bank of America would have equated to a conservative 63% LTV on their collateral real estate, based on the $30 million "as-complete" appraisal valuation. This may be considered too conservative for some, but it certainly would have better positioned the church for the recession that was soon coming.

Bad Structure and False Verbal Assurances Surrounding a Balloon Note

Friendship-West received a separate note for $5 million to finance the new audio-visual equipment in the new facility. That's a lot of AV equipment, but 174,000 square feet is a big facility! Because AV equipment has a shorter "useful life" than does a real estate asset, the $5 million note was structured as a balloon note with a short five-year maturity.

Further, the church broker structured the balloon note with interest-only payments for the entire five-year term. Think about the ramifications of this structure. The church was not required to make any principal payments whatsoever on this note, with 100% principal due and payable in five years. Why would the lender structure the note in this way? This was done to make the payments *affordable*.

Did anyone at the church question what would happen at the end of the five years when the note matured? They did, and by all accounts, church leaders were assured, verbally, that the loan balance would be renewed at maturity. They also were provided a document to this effect with one important facet: There were conditions for renewal that were listed in that document that were not fully explained.

Here's what Ms. Holt stated:

> "...they worked out a deal for a $5 million, five-year balloon. He told us, 'It's going to mature in five years but when it does, we're going to roll it into the main bond mortgage.' The first mortgage was set for 25 years; $25 million for 25 years. So, then we had to get another $5 million for AV. So, they gave us a document saying that when it matures in five years, you don't have to worry about a thing. We're just going to roll it into the big mortgage."

Rising Interest Rates on the Bonds

Friendship-West had one more problem at the outset, the ramifications of which were not immediately felt. The interest rate on the bonds not only were much higher than interest rates on conventional (non-bond) financing, the interest rate on their church bond financing also increased every six months! Ms. Holt stated that at the highest level, their interest rate on the church bonds was 8.5% per year, versus rates on conventional loans of 4.0% to 4.5% per year at that time.

Ms. Holt was not on staff when Friendship-West obtained its church bond financing, but she became heavily involved in managing the financing once she was hired. She shared this:

> "So, what they did with Friendship-West, [the loan payments] started out at $160,000 per month, and then every six months after a certain date it went up. It continued to go up every six months. When I came into the picture and read the letter and realized what was going to happen, I was worried that even if they rolled it in, we couldn't afford the new payment because the agreed-upon interest rate would have been 9.0%."

Friendship-West's bond financing is a present-day example of predatory lending and is one from which all church leaders can learn. As we continue, the remainder of this chapter includes lessons that Friendship-West learned from mistakes they made that contributed to their financing problems. Dr. Haynes and Ms. Holt were equally transparent about these.

LESSON #2: READ AND UNDERSTAND THE LOAN DOCUMENTS FOR YOURSELF

Both Dr. Haynes and Ms. Holt discussed the need for pastors and church leaders to understand church financing for themselves. She cautioned against relying on external advisors who are motivated by self-interest, rather than the best interest of the church. The individuals Ms. Holt referenced are loan brokers, general contractors, architects, and yes, lenders.

Ms. Holt shared the following:

> "One of the myths is that if you're not an accountant or a mathematician, you can't understand the numbers. Yes, you can. It just

may take a little bit of time and you need to have them go over it. Because if you're paying these people, their major concern is getting paid. YOUR major concern is your church growth and your church's sustainability.

Be aware of letting them use words you don't understand and leaving out people who really need to be in the room. Take notes. Even though you are a senior pastor or executive pastor or other leader, it is a MUST that you understand your mortgage."

Dr. Haynes echoed Ms. Holt's statements. He said:

"When I look back on these 37 years of ministry, one of the things I've learned, and I try to share with younger pastors coming up, is to make sure you have some business sense; not only spiritual sense. Make sure you have some business sense and make sure you pay attention to the business of ministry.

I trusted people and they had their own motives. I only looked at the line that said, 'sign here' because I trusted the person who was putting the documents in front of me. I didn't read anything; I trusted them. This is one of the biggest regrets of my pastoral ministry.

I was so busy doing the spiritual work and the community work, that I left the business of the ministry to other people. I thought they would recognize that this is God's work and 'Who would dare do God wrong?' I was wrong. I had spiritual blindness in the Name of Jesus.

This caused me to overlook a lot of stuff, even when the Holy Spirit was giving me warning signs to say this was something you need to read. But I ignored the Holy Spirit and trusted other people. And those people had their own agenda. That's why Dr. H. Beecher Hicks, Jr. got an M.B.A. toward the end of his ministry.

I tell them, 'Do not ignore the language of business.' I did and we had to pay for it in ways I have repented for and God has forgiven me—but we paid the price."

The reflections that both Dr. Haynes and Ms. Holt shared do not negate the need for qualified attorneys to review the loan documents and even commitment letters before signing. Rather, they are calling for church leaders not to blindly trust others—even attorneys—without gaining a first-hand understanding of the information for themselves.

I'll add this sage advice that I received from a senior credit officer at the beginning of my banking career: He told me:

> "If it's too complicated for you to understand it, then it's too complicated for us to do it."

I've never forgotten that counsel. That same advice applies to church leaders.

LESSON #3: DON'T SUBSTITUTE SPIRITUAL VERBIAGE FOR BUSINESS DISCUSSIONS

In Chapter 2 of *Holy Borrowers*, I discussed the role of faith when making business decisions. Ms. Holt spoke about similar concepts when we met. She said,

> "These people know what makes you tick. What they will do is they will quote Scriptures and before you know it, you're doing church at the table instead of business at the table. That is a ploy of the devil to throw you off from what they're trying to hide. For these discussions, this is a business conference table. We don't leave faith out, but we need to talk business! It's not time for a sermon.
>
> So, preachers, listen to your business managers, not the people who make you feel good, because they know how to make you feel good. They know what makes you tick. They know how to use the words that preachers love."

Ms. Holt also noted that in her experience, outside advisors attempt to speak to the senior pastor or executive pastor alone, without the presence of a business manager or financial advisor. She strongly advises church leaders to include these advisors in all meetings with banks, architects, and general contractors. She shared:

> "There has to be someone else in the pews, there has to be someone else you can bring in, regardless of the size of the church, to give you some balance. But if you only have a cheerleader, you're going to have problems. Somebody needs to tell you where the red flags are. If you can figure out how to bridge the gaps, fine. But you may find there are some gaps you can't bridge."

LESSON #4: STAND BY YOUR VISION

In my experience, the best bankers are those who have the interest of the client or potential client firmly at heart when providing advice and recommendations. The best bankers do not first look out for their own personal interest. This is a matter of personal integrity, but it also is the best way to build a career in which the banker earns the reputation of trusted advisor.

If a smaller loan is better for the organization than a larger loan, the banker should recommend the smaller loan, even if he or she receives less compensation and recognition for it. If the client has too much excess cash in an interest-free checking account, bankers should call and let them know about interest-earning accounts or investment accounts—even though the bank and banker will earn less money on that account once those funds are transferred.

Regrettably, this "client-first" counsel too often is not what borrowers receive. Many individuals are self-motivated, and it's important that church leaders recognize this fact when receiving counsel from them.

Dr. Frederick Haynes recounted his experience with the architect who designed Friendship-West's current facility.

> "When we gave the architect what we wanted the building to look like, it looked nothing like what I originally envisioned. I wanted a facility that would seat 3,000 people and would be multi-use.

They came back with this design that was for 7,500 seats and the price tag was more than double."

Dr. Haynes recalled the architect's response when he told the architect that he had not asked for him to design a 7,500-seat facility. As mentioned, Dr. Haynes was preaching four services in the Kiest facility at that time. He said the architect told him:

"Pastor, the people on your staff don't want you preaching all those services. They want you down to one service."

Dr. Haynes said that he continued to push back against the new goal of having one service, even telling the architect that church members and guests don't want to be limited to one service time. In response, the architect revised the plan and returned with plans and specs... for a 5,000-seat sanctuary! Dr. Haynes said that this process continued and that with each iteration, Friendship-West was required to pay the architect for the revisions.

Dr. Haynes then made this telling statement:

"And there were people around me who bought into this and were supporting the architect's vision."

In sum, the vision that Dr. Haynes had was for a worship facility and conference center that would seat 3,000 people and would be multi-use. The architect heard this and still more than doubled the size. The architect, as well as the general contractor, were motivated by greed. A larger facility meant more money for them.

In addition, there were others who were advising Dr. Haynes who were motivated by their care for him, who wanted him to preach less often. This, however, was not what he had envisioned either!

Ultimately, Friendship-West's 174,000 square foot facility, while magnificent in scope, did not fit the original vision that Dr. Haynes believes the Lord had shown him. He recalled counsel from Dr. Zan Holmes, Pastor Emeritus of St. Luke United Methodist Church, that he regrettably did not follow. Dr. Haynes said:

> "I went to see Zan Holmes before we built, when I was praying and envisioning what the new facility would be like. Zan told me, 'Do not allow the vision God has given you to be kidnapped by all the "experts" who will get involved. That includes the architect, the contractor, the bankers, and others. They want to build their reputation on your project.'"

Dr. Haynes then said:

> "This proved to be completely true."

LESSON #5: THE DOWNSIDE OF CHURCH BOND FINANCING

Church bonds are defined as certificates of indebtedness that are issued by the church as the borrower and sold by a church broker or church "broker dealer" who acts as the lender. These types of bonds are purchased by church members and other investors at a public sale.[131]

While a conventional bank loan typically involves a single lender—or at most, two to three lenders for larger church loans—a bond program involves many lenders. Based on Friendship-West's experience with bond financing, Ms. Holt now has an extremely low view of this type of debt instrument for churches. She stated the following very emphatically:

> "A bond loan should be your absolute last resort and you need to thoroughly understand what you're getting into. And when I say that, I mean, the pastor needs to thoroughly understand it, and

---

131 Peachstate Financial Services, "Church Bonds," online: https://www.peachstatefinancial.com/church-bonds/.

the people who are not getting paid by the bondholders need to thoroughly understand it.

Bonds are a last resort; bonds are expensive—especially because of the upfront costs because they make sure they get all of their money up front. In case something falls apart, they have their money.

People also don't understand that bonds are sold to 1,000, 2,000, 5,000 people. And you desire one day, 'Oh, I want to add this building.' Well, you can't because you have to get the approval of those 1,000, 2,000, 5,000 people! And they don't know who you are. They're just interested in you for their money because your interest rate is higher than what they earn at a bank."

When reflecting on Friendship-West's decision to use bond financing rather than conventional bank financing, Ms. Holt shared this:

"The mortgage the bank offered did not fit the coveted design and build, so we went with the bond company. What really should have been done was the scope of the design should have been decreased."

LESSON #6: THE DOWNSIDE OF BALLOON NOTES

Holy Borrowers opened with true stories of churches that had experienced bank foreclosures when their balloon notes matured during the Great Recession and they could not renew their loans. I provided a more in-depth discussion regarding the risks associated with balloon notes in Chapter 15.

I submit that the challenges that Friendship-West underwent with their balloon note structure should sensitize church leaders to the potential pitfalls of balloon notes once and for all!

Friendship-West entered into a balloon note structure because of the required financing on the audio-visual equipment for its new facility and extremely poor counsel from the church's advisors at that time. And, as is the case with so many other churches during economic recessions, the bond company refused to renew Friendship-West's $5 million, 5-year balloon note when it matured.

Ms. Holt recalled:

> "Well, the economy fell apart in that fifth year and they wouldn't honor the document they gave because there were different criteria we had to meet that wasn't discussed when the loan was made. We found out only two months before it was to mature and roll into the large mortgage, that they weren't going to do it at all. It was too late to scramble to get something else. Because the mortgage was so big, we didn't have the amount of money in savings that the bank required."

The collateral value of Friendship-West's real estate property had plummeted during that time period and they did not have cash to reduce principal to achieve an acceptable LTV. As mentioned earlier, the original "as-complete" appraised value of their new property on Wheatland was $30 million.

Five years later, when the bottom had fallen out of the economy, Ms. Holt stated that the appraised value plummeted to $20 million. The church's outstanding principal balance on the bonds now exceeded the value of the real estate pledged as collateral. Of course, this issue was exacerbated by the fact that the bond company had provided 100% financing at the outset!

Ms. Holt also provided this additional insight: She stated that the appraiser that valued their property during the recession was not someone that specialized in appraising churches. She shared that because of that lesson, she now knows to insist that any firm appraising their real estate must have significant experience in appraising churches.

LESSON #7: DEMONSTRATE CHARACTER AND PERSEVERE!

The final lesson is a great testimony. It is the testimony of how Friendship-West Baptist Church persevered, did not lose its church building, and ultimately refinanced their debt with a conventional lender. Ms. Holt testified to God's grace and wise counsel, saying:

> "Only by the grace of God, we didn't lose a thing. Thank God we had good attorneys. We had good people around. You know, a lot of churches can't even find attorneys. I would do my research and then call and rely on different people who helped."

Although Friendship-West's bond trustee and bondholders would not renew the $5 million balloon note when it matured, the church persevered in trying to work out a mutually acceptable solution. Friendship-West could not pay off the balloon note nor make full loan payments at the higher interest rate, but the leaders determined the amount they could pay and paid that amount consistently. The church also continued to work through their attorneys to keep negotiations open with the bondholders and trustee.

Sharon Simmons and I mentioned in Chapter 16: "If the Loan Goes South," that a borrower that demonstrates good character and that seeks to work with the lender, has better outcomes than borrowers that won't work with their lenders when loan problems occur. Friendship-West serves as an example of these recommended practices.

The church continued its payment plan and dialogue with the bond trustee until two breakthroughs occurred. First, the bondholders and the trustee finally agreed to have discussions regarding restructuring the bond debt. Ms. Holt stated:

> "God so blessed us. Thank God, the bondholders were active in their churches. They had philosophies totally different from ours. But they loved the Lord, they liked Pastor Haynes, and they wanted to see us succeed. The trustee did too."

As a result, in 2010, Dr. Haynes, Ms. Holt, and other church leaders met with the bond trustee and three representative bondholders. Ms. Holt recalled that Friendship-West's presentation included information that Friendship-West's attorneys and financial counselors had provided, as well as communication from staff members. Ms. Holt shared that they talked about the vision of the church and why they needed to have a bond modification.

At the end of the presentation, Ms. Holt said the following occurred:

> "So, we left them alone for about an hour and the three men from the bondholders and the trustee came back with a counterproposal to our requested modification, and it still was a win for us."

Ms. Holt recounted that after the agreed-upon bond modification, the bond trustee combined the $5 million balance of the AV note with the balance of the original $25 million note. This modification eliminated the balloon feature and consolidated both sets of payments into one note. Friendship-West's new combined loan payment measured $240,000 principal and interest. Ms. Holt stated that in contrast, the combined payments under the original amortization schedule would have totaled $290,000 per month at the current interest rate. Ms. Holt said:

> "We weren't pulling in that kind of money at that time because of the recession. We would have had to let people off payroll to manage that. What we did do was reduce staff through natural attrition."

And the church broker that arranged Friendship-West's original bond financing? Ms. Holt stated that firm went out of business during the Great Recession because so many churches with whom the company had done business shut down.

The second breakthrough occurred eight years later in August 2018. After years of trying without success to refinance their bond debt with conventional bank financing, Friendship-West finally was able to do so with a national bank in Dallas. Ms. Holt found the bank through a loan broker that the church had hired.

The church's loan payments were further reduced from $240,000 per month to $148,000 per month principal including interest, based on a 20-year fully-amortizing note. No balloon! Their interest rate is locked in for seven years and will reset every seven years until maturity.

One of the largest obstacles that Friendship-West had faced in attempting to refinance their loan was the fact that they didn't have the minimum level of cash that banks typically require—in this case, 10 months. Friendship-West was able to negotiate a structure with this bank in which they committed to paying an extra $25,000 per month into their savings account to build up the minimum required cash balance over time. Ms. Holt estimates that it will take the church approximately three years to do so.

How was Friendship-West able to negotiate this unusual loan covenant? First, they had the decision-makers at the table—a Commercial Market President and a Senior Vice President, who were able to structure the provision on the spot. I have experienced the benefit of calling on clients with my Credit Approval Officer. It makes a huge difference on all sides!

Second, the appraised value of Friendship-West's facility improved with the economy and with the commercial development that Friendship-West had originally stimulated. The seed they had sewn in their community bore fruit for them!

The appraiser valued their facility and land at *$35 million*, compared with $30 million when the loan was approved and $20 million at the low point of the Great Recession.

It also helped that Ms. Holt had learned from the experience with the previous appraiser who had no prior experience appraising church properties. She insisted on obtaining an appraiser with church experience and the church leaders prayed for both the right appraiser and the right appraised value!

The principal balance that Friendship-West refinanced in August 2018 was $21 million. The resulting LTV based on the new $35 million appraised value was 60%—well within the acceptable range for lenders.

Dr. Haynes is pleased with his current banking relationship but has not forgotten the lessons he learned. He shared this:

> "We definitely have the type of banking relationship now that we always should have had. They are people of faith and they are deeply involved in their own churches and ministries. But here's what's really sad. I made the mistake of thinking the people around me were competent, and they were people I had confidence in. Just as you can get burned by one love relationship, move into a new relationship, and the new relationship suffers the impact, the same hold true in business. Now I'm reading, I'm asking, and I'm being as conversant as I can. Even if I don't understand it, I'm going to ask questions about it."

CLOSING THOUGHTS

In this last chapter of *Holy Borrowers*, so much of the information that was discussed throughout the book is demonstrated in the actual financing experience of Friendship-West Baptist Church. I'm going to close this chapter with some final excerpts from my conversations with Ms. Holt Holt and Dr. Haynes.

First, Ms. Holt provided these two insights:

> "If we would have understood the original loan document, we wouldn't have been in this situation. We wouldn't have a building this size, but we wouldn't have been in this situation. Your banker is not your enemy, and don't let anybody convince you of that. Because if the banker says, 'You can only afford this,' and they're doing an analysis of your current circumstances, as well as your future circumstances and situations, believe them. They're using analytics to give you their best answer."

I asked Ms. Holt if she had anything else she wanted to share. She noted that the larger churches, such as Friendship-West Baptist Church, are available to help smaller churches that are interested in building projects and financing. She said:

> "The larger churches don't mind helping, and we won't charge you anything. But don't get mad at us if we tell you, 'Now is not the time.' Because believe me, we know this from experience."

Dr. Frederick Douglass Haynes, III will have the last word. He stated:

> "I am so transparent with this next generation of churches and pastors. I wish someone had stopped me. I don't know if it's possible to be an ego-less pastor or an ego-less visionary. So we all need someone who doesn't mind, in love, telling you: 'I know you have an ego, but you might want to see what God is saying here.' I still believe God spoke and He has graciously brought us through. But pastors must leave our egos at the door."

He then made this statement that effectively summarizes this entire book:

> "God is preparing the church for whatever comes in the future, and this is part of it."

CONCLUSION

"For we are His workmanship, created in Christ Jesus
for good works, which God prepared beforehand,
that we should walk in them."
— EPHESIANS 2:10 ESV

In December of 2019, I was blessed to do something that had been on my bucket list for a very long time. That bucket-list item was co-leading a team of women from my church (Team USA!) on a short-term mission trip to Ghana, West Africa. And so, 19 women from Christ Community joined me in co-hosting a women's empowerment conference, *Designed for Noble Activity*, in Koforidua, Ghana, with our wonderful mission partners, Full Gospel Church International (Team Ghana!) and WorldVenture.

Now, a second burning item has been completed: this book. *Holy Borrowers* has been on my heart for years, and I believe, on the Lord's heart before the foundation of the world! With my prior full-time employment in banking and on-going work in church ministry, I was not able to complete it. In April 2019, however, the Lord led me to retire early from banking and here I am, checking off bucket list items and serving the Lord full-time in a new way.

I pray that *Holy Borrowers* is helpful to church leaders. I pray that it is just one more tool that can be used for the upbuilding of your ministry.

May the Lord richly bless you and empower you to know His will for your ministry, to victoriously navigate you through previously uncharted waters; and, move forward in the direction He desires you and your congregation to take.

I'd like to close with this encouraging reminder. The Bible speaks about a number of buildings that God's people erected to house His Great Presence. Solomon built the first temple and Ezra led the rebuilding of a temple following the Jewish nation's exile in Babylon. The second temple was not as physically glorious as the first, but it was no less a testament to the greatness and grandeur of Almighty God.

The prophet Ezekiel then saw a vision of a temple that God will build one day in the land of Israel, recorded in Ezekiel chapters 40 through 42. In Chapter 43, Ezekiel wrote:

> "As the glory of the LORD entered the temple by the gate facing east, the Spirit lifted me up and brought me into the inner court; and behold, the glory of the LORD filled the temple." (Ezekiel 43:4–5 ESV)

And so, the Bible reminds us of temples great and small, filled with the glory of the Lord. But then comes Paul who tells us about other temples, other buildings, which far exceed them all. Paul writes:

> "For we know that if the tent that is our earthly home is destroyed, we have a building from God, a house not made with hands, eternal in the heavens." (2 Corinthians 5:1 ESV)

What building? Jesus tells us!

> "'In My Father's house are many rooms. If it were not so, would I have told you that I go to prepare a place for you? And if I go and prepare a place for you, I will come again and will take you to

Myself, that where I am you may be also. And you know the way to where I am going.'

Thomas said to Him, 'Lord, we do not know where you are going. How can we know the way?' Jesus said to him, 'I am the way, and the truth, and the life. No one comes to the Father except through Me.'" (John 14:2–6 ESV)

In our quests for buildings and building loans, I pray we never forget—or are distracted from—the preeminent reason we are here. We are here to point our congregations and the world to the King, the Savior, the Deliverer, Jesus the Messiah; to stand in Him as instruments of evangelism, justice, and empowerment. When we are connected in relationship to Him, His Glory will fill our temples and we will be with Him forever in buildings not made with hands. May God bless you and keep you.

APPENDICES

SAMPLE CHURCH LOAN APPLICATION CHECKLIST

M any lenders have an application that can be completed online; others will provide a paper application for the borrower to complete. Whatever the format, church loan applications typically will request the information that is listed below.

LOAN INFORMATION

- Requested Loan Amount
- Purpose of Loan (Choose one or more of the following):
    – New Construction
    – Purchase of Existing Building
    – Purchase of Land
    – Renovations
    – Refinance of Existing Loan
    – Other (for example, a "bridge" loan)

CHURCH INFORMATION[132]

- Legal name of church
- Taxpayer identification number (for example, 75-2764385)

---

132 If any of this information is available on the church's website, the banker typically will access the information from that source.

- Inception date of church
- Organizational documents
- Denomination, if any
- Physical address including the name of the county
- Church telephone number
- Key Contact (name, title, mobile number, e-mail address)
- Organizational Structure and Governance
- Number of full-time employees; number of part-time employees
- Number of church services; dates and time
- Membership Information
  - Number of Giving Units as of the three most recent calendar year-ends
  - Number of Members as of the three most recent calendar year-ends
  - Date the membership list was last purged/updated
  - Demographics of Members (gender, age)
  - Weekly Worship Attendees
- Church history
- Website address/ Church app

SENIOR PASTOR

- Length of time with the church
- Length of time as a senior pastor overall
- Pastor's background/resume
- Bi-vocational (Yes/No)
- Age
- Pastor's prior experience with a building program

OVERALL LEADERSHIP STRUCTURE

- Background information on other key leaders
- Succession plan
- Identity of those person(s), board and/or committee(s) who make the financing decisions

EXISTING CHURCH BUILDING WHERE CHURCH CURRENTLY HOLDS SERVICES [133]

- Physical Address including the name of the county, if different from church's physical address
- Square footage of building(s)
- Square footage of land
- Age of building
- Seating capacity of current facility
- Length of time at current location
- If church *owns* the property:
  - Date facility was acquired and the purchase price
  - If the purchase was financed with debt, details about that loan (see "Debt Schedule" below)
  - Description, year completed, and cost of any past building improvements
- If church *leases* the property: a copy of the existing lease agreement

FOR FINANCING PURCHASE OF AN EXISTING BUILDING

- Physical Address including the name of the county, if different from the church's physical address
- Proximity (miles and/or minutes) to current facility
- Square footage of building(s)
- Square footage of land
- Age of building
- Seating capacity of new facility
- Purchase price of land and building
- Required closing date
- Copy of signed Purchase-Sale Agreement[134]
- Existing bank-ordered appraisal report, if available

---

133 This list assumes a single-property worship location. If church is a multi-site organization, the same information will be required for each property.

134 Lenders can work with unsigned Purchase-Sale Agreements if the buyer and seller still are in negotiations.

- Existing environmental risk assessments or reports, if available
- Copy of most recent survey, if available

FOR FINANCING PURCHASE OF LAND AND GROUND-UP CONSTRUCTION OF A NEW BUILDING

The applicable requirements listed above for purchase of an existing building, *plus* the following:

- Projected Cost of Construction
- Name and contact information of architect
- Name and contact information of general contractor
- Name and contact information of construction manager (if applicable)
- Cost Estimates (a detailed construction contract will be required for approval)
- Preliminary architectural plans and specifications
- Project expenses incurred to date (for example, architectural fees)
- Estimated length of construction
- Required audio-visual equipment
- Required furniture and office equipment

Note: As a reminder, these items are required for loan *approval*. They are not all required if church leaders are seeking a *general estimate* regarding a loan amount for which they *might* qualify.

FINANCIAL INFORMATION

HISTORICAL FINANCIAL STATEMENTS

- Annual Statement of Activities (Income Statement) and Statement of Financial Position (Balance Sheet) for the three most recent calendar years.
- Interim year-to-date Statement of Activities (Income Statement) and Statement of Financial Position (Balance Sheet) dated within

the last 90 to 120 days of the loan application. Many lenders also require the comparable interim financial statements for the corresponding prior year period.[135]

BUDGET
- Existing budget for the current calendar year
- Budget for the upcoming calendar year if loan request is submitted in the latter part of the year

DEBT SCHEDULE
Detailed listing of all outstanding debts (including accounts payable to vendors) in a format similar to the chart below:

SCHEDULE OF LIABILITIES
Date of Schedule: _____ (*Loans, Leases, and Accounts Payable*)

Name of Creditor	Original Amount	Original Date	Present Balance	Current or Delinquent?	Maturity Date	Monthly Payment	How Secured

BANK AND INVESTMENT STATEMENTS
- Bank statements for the three most recent months for each depository account owned by the church.
- If applicable, brokerage or investment statements for the three most recent months.
- If a church accepts contributions or payments via credit cards, many banks will request the three most recent merchant card statements to reflect that activity. As a note, this request is not

---

135 For example, a lender may require interim financial statements as of September 30, 2020 and also require the corresponding prior year interim financial statements as of September 30, 2019.

always tied to the credit decision, but to the bank's interest in bidding on that business as well.[136]

- Evidence of required cash equity and any minimum required cash balance in one or more accounts

TOP DONORS

- Individual amounts given by top 10 donors (names need not be provided)

CAPITAL CAMPAIGN (IF APPLICABLE)

- Start date of campaign
- Length of campaign
- Amount pledged to date
- Amount collected to date
- Any pledges listed over $25,000 and/or measuring more than 10% of total pledges
- If the campaign is led by a professional fundraiser, that person's or firm's information.
- History of past campaigns and success rate (actual amount collected, amount pledged, amount requested)

COLLATERAL

- Listing of collateral church expects to pledge to lender for the loan

---

136 The church is not required to award its merchant services business to a bank as a requirement of the loan. As mentioned in Chapter 13, however, awarding this business may result in better pricing on the loan and/or other services.

APPENDIX II

SAMPLE
FINANCIAL STATEMENTS

SAMPLE STATEMENT OF FINANCIAL POSITION
(BALANCE SHEET) AS OF DECEMBER 31, 2019

	12/31/19
ASSETS	
Checking & Money Market	$ 250,000
Certificates of Deposit	$ 350,000
Total Cash & Equivalents	**$ 600,000**
Total Current Assets	**$ 600,000**
Property & Equipment	
Building & Improvements	$ 2,500,000
Vehicles	$ 150,000
Furniture & Fixtures	$ 175,000
Audio/Visual Equipment	$ 300,000
Computer Equipment	$ 75,000
Gross Fixed Assets	**$ 3,200,000**
Accumulated Depreciation	$ (945,000)
Net Fixed Assets	**$ 2,255,000**
Intangible Assets (Net)	$ 25,000
Total Non Current Assets	**$ 2,280,000**
TOTAL ASSETS	**$ 2,880,000**
LIABILITIES & EQUITY	
Revolving Line of Credit	$ -
CP Long-Term Debt - 1	$ 64,000
Total Current Portion LTD	**$ 64,000**
Accrued Expenses	$ 25,000
Total Current Liabilities	**$ 89,000**
Total Long-Term Debt	$ 1,632,795
Less: CP LTD	$ (64,000)
Total Long-Term Debt	**$ 1,568,795**
TOTAL LIABILITIES	**$ 1,657,795**
Net Assets - Unrestricted	$ 1,147,205
Net Assets - Restricted	$ 75,000
TOTAL NET ASSETS	**$ 1,222,205**
TOTAL LIAB. + EQUITY	**$ 2,880,000**

Noteworthy Items

- "Current Assets" include cash, deposits, and investments, as well as assets that are expected to convert to cash within the next 12 months through normal operations.

- "Non-Current Assets" include those that are not expected to convert to cash within the next 12 months. Property & Equipment and Intangible Assets are types of Non-Current Assets. (It is recognized that Property & Equipment can be sold for cash; this, however, is not the primary operation of a church. Therefore, these assets are considered non-current.)

- CP Long-Term Debt shows this church must pay $64,000 in principal within the next 12 months. These principal payments are in addition to interest expense on the debt.

- Accrued expenses include such items as semi-monthly payroll that has been earned, but not yet paid.

- Nearly all of this church's Net Assets (Equity) are Unrestricted.

SAMPLE STATEMENT OF ACTIVITIES AND CHANGES IN NET ASSETS (INCOME STATEMENT) FOR THE YEAR ENDING DECEMBER 31, 2019

		1 Yr. To 12/31/19
Revenues		
Tithes & Offerings	$	1,175,000
Capital Campaign Funds	$	102,000
Interest Income	$	750
Other Donations	$	30,000
Total Revenues	**$**	**1,307,750**
Operating Expenses		
General & Admin. Expenses	$	80,000
Bank Fees	$	14,000
Missions	$	130,775
Ministry Expenses	$	107,696
Church Salaries	$	380,000
Benevolence	$	10,146
Landscaping	$	5,139
Insurance	$	40,000
Utilities	$	34,204
Professional Fees	$	70,000
Repairs/Maintenance/Cleaning	$	30,990
Supplies	$	50,000
TOTAL OPERATING EXPENSES	**$**	**952,950**
% of Total Revenues		72.9%
OPERATING PROFIT	**$**	**354,800**
OPER. PROFIT MARGIN		**27.1%**
Other Income	$	-
Interest Expense	**$**	**98,000**
Other Expense	$	-
CASH EXCESS/ (DEFICIT)	**$**	**256,800**
CASH EXCESS/ (DEFICIT) %		**19.6%**
Amortization (non-cash)	$	3,571
Depreciation (non-cash)	$	160,000
CHANGE IN NET ASSETS	**$**	**93,229**

Noteworthy Items

- Revenues are grouped together in the top section and are detailed by category. It is helpful to be able to separate Unrestricted Tithes & Offerings from other sources of revenue.

- Operating expenses are listed next. Banks request that churches provide detailed expenses, as shown here.

- Interest expense on loans typically is listed after the operating expenses.

- In this statement, (non-cash) depreciation and amortization expenses are listed toward the bottom. In many presentations, these expenses are included with other operating expenses.

- This statement reflects that this church generated $93,229 in "profit" in 2019.

SAMPLE STATEMENT OF CASH FLOWS
FOR THE YEAR ENDING DECEMBER 31, 2019

	1 Yr. To 12/31/19
Net Revenues	$ 1,307,750
CASH FROM REVENUES	**$ 1,307,750**
SG & A Expense	$ (952,950)
Change in Accruals	$ 25,000
Miscellaneous Transactions	$ -
Cash Operating Expenses	$ (927,950)
CASH AFTER OPERATIONS	**$ 379,800**
Income Taxes Paid	$ -
NET CASH AFTER OPERATIONS	**$ 379,800**
Interest Expense	$ (98,000)
NET CASH INCOME	**$ 281,800**
Current Portion Long-Term Debt	$ (60,000)
CASH AFTER DEBT AMORTIZATION	**$ 221,800**
Capital Expenditures - Tangible	$ (35,000)
Capital Expenditures - Intangible	$ -
CASH AFTER CAPITAL EXPENDITURES	**$ 186,800**
FINANCING SURPLUS/(REQUIRED)	
Extraordinary Income/Expense	$ -
Change in Long-Term Debt	$ 30,000
Change in Short-Term Debt	$ -
Change in Equity (Accounting Adjustments)	$ -
TOTAL EXTERNAL FINANCING	**$ 30,000**
Cash After Financing	**$ 216,800**
Actual Change in Cash	**$ 216,800**

Noteworthy Items

- As discussed in Chapter 3, the Cash Flow Statement is a true indicator of cash generated or spent over a period of time.

- In 2019, this church generated $379,800 in cash flow from its normal operations. They spent it on $158,000 in interest and principal payments ($98,000 + $60,000), and on capital expenditures or "CAPEX" of $35,000 (such as equipment, furniture).

- The church obtained $30,000 in additional debt in 2019—likely to finance the $35,000 asset that was purchased.

- Total Cash Flow for 2019 was $216,800 even after debt payments. This cash flowed into their accounts ("Actual Change in Cash").

CALCULATION OF DEBT SERVICE COVERAGE RATIO

The Debt Service Coverage Ratio ("DSC Ratio") was introduced in Chapter 11. In that chapter, the following example was provided:

EXAMPLE:
- Annual Debt Service of Principal and Interest: $176,000
- Change in Net Assets ("Profit") Before Noncash Expenses and Interest Expense: $264,000
- The Debt Service Coverage Ratio is 2.25. This exceeds the minimum guideline and is a positive indicator in and of itself.

The calculation that was provided was not detailed in full because I did not, at that time, provide the formula for calculating the Debt Service Coverage Ratio. I will provide that information here.

First, let's assume the following for the organization that was highlighted above, for the year ending December 31, 2019:

Sample Statement of Activities and Change in Net Assets

	1 Year ending 31-Dec-19
Total Revenues	$ 1,307,750
Total Expenses	
Operating Expenses	$ 952,950
Depreciation Expense	$ 160,000
Amortization Expense	$ 3,571
Interest Expense	$ 98,000
Total Expenses	$ 1,214,521
Change in Net Assets (Profit)	$ 93,229
Annual Loan Payments	$ 158,000

DEBT SERVICE COVERAGE RATIO FORMULA

Now let's look at the actual formula for calculating the DSC Ratio:

$$\text{DSC Ratio} = \frac{\textit{Change in Net Assets} + \textit{Depreciation} + \textit{Amortization} + \textit{Interest Expense}}{\textit{Debt Service}}$$

The DSC Ratio is calculated by totaling the church's Net Change in Assets (or "Profit"), Depreciation Expense, Amortization Expense, and Interest Expense, and then dividing that total figure by the church's debt service for that same period.

Using the information in the chart above, we can plug in the figures as follows:

$$\text{DSC Ratio} = \frac{(\$93{,}229 + \$160{,}000 + \$3{,}571 + \$98{,}000)}{\$158{,}000} = \frac{\$354{,}000}{\$158{,}000} = 2.25$$

The DSC Ratio is 2.25, or put in the language used by bankers, the Debt Service Coverage Ratio is written as "2.25x" and verbalized as "2.25 times."

WHAT DOES THIS MEAN?

In general terms, the Debt Service Coverage Ratio is a quick and conventional tool that bankers use to evaluate an organization's ability to cover its loan payments from its profits over a specific time period. Remember Chapter 7 regarding cash flow? The Debt Service Coverage Ratio is a short-cut used to evaluate an organization's cash flow coverage.

In the example above, the DSC Ratio of 2.25x tells us that this church covered its loan payments in 2019 by 225% or 2.25 times. Put another way, for every $1.00 of loan payments over this period, this church had $2.25 to cover those payments.

Is that good? Absolutely! If the church really needs only $1.00 to cover $1.00 of payments, this calculation shows that this church has a cushion of $1.25. This type of cushion is important because it means that the church can have an unexpected decline in revenues or an unexpected increase in expenses and still have a cushion to make loan payments.

A DEEPER DIVE

For those who want to dive even deeper (bless you!), let's now look at the formula itself. The numerator or top of the fraction adds back three expenses to the church's Net Change in Assets; that is, how much the church clears after expenses. Those three expenses are: depreciation expense, amortization expense, and interest expense. Why are these three expenses added back?

First, depreciation expense is added back because it is not a cash expense. Rather, depreciation is an accounting convention in which an organization "writes off" a portion of its real estate and equipment assets over time. Without getting bogged down in the accounting, let's focus on two words: *writes off*. Depreciation expense is an accounting entry. It is not an expense in which an organization is necessarily spending cash on that asset in that particular period. For that reason, the organization gets the benefit of having this non-cash expense added back to the formula.

Amortization expense is added back for the same reason: It is not a cash expense either. Similar to depreciation expense, amortization is an accounting convention used to write off intangible assets, such as goodwill and loan fees.

What about interest expense? Interest expense is added back in the numerator because it's going to be captured in the denominator; that is, the bottom half of the fraction. Loan payments or debt service include principal *and interest*. Therefore, it's added back on top so that the ratio does not "double-ding" the organization for its interest.

Overall, the Debt Service Coverage Ratio is calculated without penalizing the organization for non-cash expenses and without double-dinging the organization for interest expense.

SUMMARY

As discussed in Chapter 13, the DSC Ratio also is a ratio that likely will be included as a loan covenant; therefore, it is one that church leaders—and their accountants—should understand.

SAMPLE TREND ANALYSIS

I first shared in Chapter 3 that bankers use an organization's historical financial statements to evaluate loan requests. To reiterate, bankers prefer at least the three most recent annual statements and if needed, interim year-to-date financial statements.

Part II of *Holy Borrowers* provided an overview of the bank's credit process and various analytical ratios that bankers use when evaluating loan requests. This Appendix provides a more in-depth view of an important tool that bankers use: Trend Analysis.

Trend analysis involves evaluating an organization's financial performance by looking at patterns in their various financial statements over time. More specifically, bankers analyze financial trends that an organization shows over the most recent periods; typically, the most recent three years.

The premise is that if historical trends can be understood, then future performance—and the ability to repay the loan—can be better evaluated as well. Of course, trend analysis is not a guarantee of future performance, as previously discussed. It does, however, provide a reasonable basis for evaluating the likelihood of loan repayment.

Bankers receive extensive training in trend analysis. This Appendix is not a substitute for that training. Rather, it is meant to provide church leaders introductory insights into trend analysis.

PRELIMINARY STEPS IN TREND ANALYSIS

The first step that bankers take when receiving financial statements is to "spread them;" that is, lay the financial statements out side by side to better see the changes in the same account categories over times. Most banks have specialized financial software that bankers use to input the financial data, but programs such as Excel can be just as useful. (I created the charts below in Excel.)

The second step that bankers take is utilizing a skill that pastors use extensively when studying a Biblical text. That skill is observation: What do you *see*? While bankers are trained to look in key areas, a person without financial training still can observe trends when the financial statements are laid out properly. Financial statements tell a story if you look in the right places and ask the right questions.

Bankers perform trend analysis on all categories of financial statements and on benchmarks, such as the Debt Service Coverage Ratio. For purposes of this Appendix, however, we will just highlight preliminary trend analysis using an Income Statement.

SAMPLE SPREAD OF THE REVENUE SECTION OF INCOME STATEMENTS

	1 Yr. To 12/31/16	1 Yr. To 12/31/17	1 Yr. To 12/31/18	1 Yr. To 12/31/19
Revenues				
Tithes & Offerings	$ 1,160,000	$ 1,025,000	$ 1,130,000	$ 1,175,000
Capital Campaign Funds	$ -	$ 50,000	$ 80,000	$ 102,000
Interest Income	$ 450	$ 325	$ 600	$ 750
Other Donations	$ 24,000	$ 33,000	$ 50,000	$ 30,000
Total Revenues	**$ 1,184,450**	**$ 1,108,325**	**$ 1,260,600**	**$ 1,307,750**

The table above provides an example of a financial "spread" using just the revenue section of a church's income statement. Note how the financial information does not include just one year, but multiple years spread side by side. This format better facilitates analysis of financial trends, rather than trying to analyze a single year or period.

The next step is to observe. What do you see? Look at the top line of tithes and offerings. What stands out? Did you notice that tithes and offerings increased in each of the last two years, from $1,025,000 in 2017 to $1,130,000 in 2018, and $1,175,000 in 2019? That would be viewed as a positive trend—especially if the increase is supported by an increase in membership.

Every banker worth his or her salt, however, also would focus on the $150,000 decline in tithes and offerings from 2016 to 2017. The banker would ask the church leaders to explain what happened that year. Was the $1,160,000 in 2016 an anomaly? Was there a special, non-recurring contribution that year? Or, did a problem occur in 2017? Was there a church split? Did something else occur?

The banker would not be able to answer these questions by observing the numbers alone, but the numbers would spark a conversation. I would hope to hear a good report from the church leader as to why contributions increased. I also would hope that whatever caused revenues to decline in 2017 is not something that is likely to occur again in 2020. Most of all, I would hope that church leaders would give me an accurate account about what has transpired, whether positive or negative.

It also is noted that the church started a Capital Campaign in 2017. Is this campaign successful? It would not be possible to answer that question without knowing what the campaign goal is! Was the $50,000 that was given in 2017 above tithes and offerings or does the $50,000 represent tithes and offerings that were reallocated to the capital campaign?

Finally, I also would want to know what "Other Donations" are. They appear to be consistent and certainly are increasing, but the detail would be important.

Next, we will review a spread of the historical Income Statements in their entirety. These not only include the revenue section, but also include expenses and net assets (profit).

SAMPLE SPREAD OF HISTORICAL INCOME STATEMENTS

		1 Yr. To 12/31/16		1 Yr. To 12/31/17		1 Yr. To 12/31/18		1 Yr. To 12/31/19
Revenues								
Tithes & Offerings	$	1,160,000	$	1,025,000	$	1,130,000	$	1,175,000
Capital Campaign Funds	$	-	$	50,000	$	80,000	$	102,000
Interest Income	$	450	$	325	$	600	$	750
Other Donations	$	24,000	$	33,000	$	50,000	$	30,000
Total Revenues	$	**1,184,450**	$	**1,108,325**	$	**1,260,600**	$	**1,307,750**
Operating Expenses								
General & Admin. Expenses	$	45,000	$	64,000	$	70,000	$	80,000
Bank Fees	$	10,000	$	11,000	$	13,000	$	14,000
Missions	$	118,445	$	110,833	$	126,060	$	130,775
Ministry Expenses	$	113,118	$	129,187	$	129,098	$	107,696
Church Salaries	$	325,000	$	350,000	$	375,000	$	380,000
Benevolence	$	23,459	$	24,746	$	17,595	$	10,146
Landscaping	$	10,310	$	8,519	$	7,691	$	5,139
Insurance	$	35,000	$	37,000	$	37,000	$	40,000
Utilities	$	33,064	$	33,709	$	34,456	$	34,204
Professional Fees	$	25,000	$	27,000	$	30,000	$	70,000
Repairs/Maintenance/Cleaning	$	11,588	$	33,314	$	40,130	$	30,990
Supplies	$	57,000	$	59,000	$	60,000	$	50,000
TOTAL OPERATING EXPENSES	$	**806,984**	$	**888,308**	$	**940,030**	$	**952,950**
% of Total Revenues		68.1%		80.1%		74.6%		72.9%
OPERATING PROFIT	$	**377,466**	$	**220,018**	$	**320,570**	$	**354,800**
OPER. PROFIT MARGIN		**31.9%**		**19.9%**		**25.4%**		**27.1%**
Other Income	$	-	$	-	$	-	$	-
Interest Expense	$	108,000	$	105,000	$	101,000	$	98,000
Other Expense	$	-	$	-	$	-	$	-
CASH EXCESS/ (DEFICIT)	$	**269,466**	$	**115,018**	$	**219,570**	$	**256,800**
CASH EXCESS/ (DEFICIT) %		**22.8%**		**10.4%**		**17.4%**		**19.6%**
Amortization (non-cash)	$	19,744	$	19,755	$	3,228	$	3,571
Depreciation (non-cash)	$	195,000	$	190,000	$	185,000	$	160,000
CHANGE IN NET ASSETS	$	**54,722**	$	**(94,738)**	$	**31,342**	$	**93,229**

As before, the question is: What do you see? It's important not to have your eyes overwhelmed by a sheet full of numbers. Again, there is a story here. A good practice is to let your eyes move horizontally across the years for each expense category. If anything jumps out, write it down.

Three things jump out to me. First, the church in this example "tithes" its revenues in missions; meaning, the mission contributions each year equals 10% of total giving for that respective year. For example, total revenues in 2019 measured $1,307,750. The mission expense in 2019 was exactly 10% of that revenue figure: $130,775.[137] This factor would be incorporated into my analysis.

Second, I notice that benevolence expense has declined since 2017. I would ask the church leaders if there was a specific reason for this decline. Was this intentional on the part of the church leadership or are fewer individuals asking for benevolence?

Finally, did you notice that professional fees more than doubled from 2018 to 2019? Professional fees include fees paid to accountants, attorneys, architects, consultants, campaign managers, etc. This would be an area that the banker would explore with the church leader. Importantly, if this category includes a fee that is non-recurring, that would be important to note for cash flow analysis.

You also may have noticed some percentages in the Income Statement above. An "Operating Profit" represents the profit an organization makes from its normal operations, before interest expense and before any unusual income or expense items. Bankers evaluate profit as a percentage of revenues. Do you notice that operating profit as a percent of revenues has increased since 2017? That is a positive indicator of good expense management.

On the other hand, I also noted that the operating profit margin declined from 2016 to 2017. Although the decline occurred several years ago, a good banker still would ask why. The more recent positive trend would be more important, but a complete analysis still would obtain insight on the decline that one year.

"COMMON-SIZED" INCOME STATEMENT

Bankers use another tool in trend analysis called a "Common-Sized" Statement. This statement shows every category on the Income Statement as a percent of total revenues. This presentation allows the bankers to quickly understand two things over the analyzed periods: The major

---

137 $1,307,750 x 0.10 (the equivalent of 10%) equals $130,775.

components of total revenues and which expenses make up a larger or smaller percentage of revenues. An example of a Common-Sized Statement is shown below.

	1 Yr. To 12/31/16	1 Yr. To 12/31/17	1 Yr. To 12/31/18	1 Yr. To 12/31/19
Revenues				
Tithes & Offerings	97.9%	92.5%	89.6%	89.8%
Restoration Giving	0.0%	4.5%	6.3%	7.8%
Interest Income	0.0%	0.0%	0.0%	0.1%
Other Giving	2.0%	3.0%	4.0%	2.3%
NET REVENUES	100.0%	100.0%	100.0%	100.0%
Operating Expenses				
General & Admin. Expenses	3.8%	5.8%	5.6%	6.1%
Bank Fees	0.8%	1.0%	1.0%	1.1%
Missions	10.0%	10.0%	10.0%	10.0%
Ministry Expenses	9.6%	11.7%	10.2%	8.2%
Church Salaries	27.4%	31.6%	29.7%	29.1%
Storehouse Ministry (Benevolence)	2.0%	2.2%	1.4%	0.8%
Landscaping	0.9%	0.8%	0.6%	0.4%
Insurance	3.0%	3.3%	2.9%	3.1%
Utilities	2.8%	3.0%	2.7%	2.6%
Professional Fees	2.1%	2.4%	2.4%	5.4%
Repairs/Maintenance/Cleaning	1.0%	3.0%	3.2%	2.4%
Supplies	4.8%	5.3%	4.8%	3.8%
TOTAL OPERATING EXPENSES	68.1%	80.1%	74.6%	72.9%
OPERATING PROFIT	31.9%	19.9%	25.4%	27.1%
Other Income	0.0%	0.0%	0.0%	0.0%
Interest Expense	9.1%	9.5%	8.0%	7.5%
Other Expense	0.0%	0.0%	0.0%	0.0%
CASH EXCESS/ (DEFICIT)	31.9%	19.9%	25.4%	27.1%
Amortization (non-cash)	1.7%	1.8%	0.3%	0.3%
Depreciation (non-cash)	16.5%	17.1%	14.7%	12.2%
CHANGE IN NET ASSETS	4.6%	-8.5%	2.5%	7.1%

This statement is one of the most useful to bankers who analyze trends. This statement highlights the changes in expenses as a percent of revenues for each expense category, and over a number of periods. For example, if we had viewed this statement first, we could have immediately noticed that mission expense equals 10% of total revenues.

If we look at church salaries, we notice that although church salaries have increased over the last two years, from $350,000 in 2017 to $375,000 in 2018, and $380,000 in 2019, church salaries actually declined as a percent of revenues over that same period. Church salaries decreased from 31.6% of revenues in 2017 to 29.7% of revenues in 2018 and 29.1% in 2019.

What does this mean? Overall, it means that although church salaries have increased, revenues are increasing faster, which would appear to be a positive trend. Put another way, this trend may indicate strong management as the investment that the church makes in its staff may be a key reason that revenues—and the number of members—are increasing.

These are just a few examples of the types of trend analyses that lenders perform. Lenders review trends in balance sheets, cash flow statements, and key ratios as well. One of the major takeaways is that financial statements tell a story when the person reviewing them knows where to look!

GUIDELINES FOR SELECTING AN ATTORNEY

(Contributed by Sharon K. Simmons)

I t has been stated throughout *Holy Borrowers* that churches should hire an attorney to provide counsel when obtaining bank loans, and that the attorney should have expertise in working with bank loans. I think it important to expound upon that because, believe it or not, lawyers often don't know what they can or cannot do.

So, you may ask a lawyer in your congregation if they could help you by reviewing your loan documents. They will say, "yes" because they are eager to help and because they have reviewed legal documents during the course of their career. Therefore, they think this qualifies them to review a loan agreement or a promissory note.

Unfortunately, this does not qualify that person to assist you with your loan. I offer the following information so that church leaders can be wise and discerning in your hiring decision in case the lawyers you contact are not.

SPECIALIZATION

The first thing church leaders should know is that lawyers are almost as specialized as doctors. Just as you wouldn't hire a cardiologist because you are having problems with your eyes, you shouldn't hire an employment lawyer to read and advise you regarding your real estate loan documents. Some commercial real estate lawyers spend their days reading and drafting retail leases; that gives them limited experience reviewing loan documents. And, a lawyer who specializes in corporate transactions will likely have a familiarity with loan documents, but they will be less familiar with the nuances found in *real estate* loan documents.

The ideal lawyer for church real estate loans is an attorney who specializes in commercial real estate transactions *and who represents lenders or borrowers in real estate transactions on a weekly, if not daily, basis.* Further, the ideal attorney should have significant experience reviewing *real estate* loan documents in particular, not just loan documents. It also is noted that a lawyer who specializes in commercial transactions generally does not do litigation at all, but rather, spends most of his or her time, every day, involved in real estate transactions.

When in doubt, church leaders should ask the prospective attorney to describe in detail his or her experience reviewing and drafting real estate loan documents. The "right" attorney will give you an answer that is reassuring and screams, "experience" with real estate loans.

WHAT CHURCH LEADERS SHOULD EXPECT FROM THEIR ATTORNEY

The average person and the average church do not regularly use lawyers. Therefore, even if church leaders hire the "right" lawyer, they may not fully understand what their attorney can and should do for the church. That being the case, I offer the following guidance as to what church leaders should expect from their lawyer.

TRUSTED ADVISOR

First, just as a good banker wants to be, and should be a trusted advisor, your attorney should be as well. Your attorney should be someone you trust and someone who can be, and act like, part of your team. I am a commercial real estate attorney, but because I am a trusted advisor (to my church and non-church clients alike), my clients usually come to me with legal matters that are not in my area of specialty.

In these situations, they desire two things from me: first, my *general* counsel about the situation; second, where appropriate, assistance in finding the "right" lawyer to help in any situation that does not fall within my area of expertise. On this basis, a church may have a trusted *employment* attorney; use them to identify the "right" attorney to help with the church's real estate loan.

EXPLAIN THE LOAN DOCUMENTS

Second, the church's attorney should help church leaders understand the real estate loan documents. This does not mean that church leaders don't need to understand the loan documents! It means that church leaders have someone with experience who can help make sense of the documents.

Do not rely on your banker to explain the documents to you! A good banker will want you to understand the documents and they will certainly provide assistance with explanations. But a banker's primary obligation is to serve the interests of his or her bank. Your attorney's primary job is to serve *your* interests. And please do not rely on your mortgage broker or the title company to explain the documents or some aspect of the transaction to you! That is not their job and they are not equipped to perform this function.

NEGOTIATE LOAN DOCUMENTS

Third, your attorney should help church leaders understand which provisions of the loan documents could possibly be negotiated. An experienced lawyer that is, the "right" lawyer who has done many, many real estate loan transactions, will know what provisions require negotiation and they will have a sense of what negotiations will actually be fruitful.

In this regard, covenants and reporting requirements often require some negotiation or "tweaking" because these are the provisions that will determine whether the church is in technical default of your loan or not.

An experienced lawyer will have some sense of which of these covenants can be negotiated and how far you can push. Further, they will have solutions and compromises that the bank is likely to accept, if the solutions and compromises are reasonable.

CONSIDER WORST-CASE SCENARIOS

The "right" attorney should help church leaders contemplate and prepare for possible worse case scenarios. My job is to help clients understand the implications of the terms and provisions they are agreeing to when they sign the loan documents. Sometimes that means refining a financial covenant that was too loosely drafted or that does not take into account the way your church operates. Sometimes that means making sure church leaders understand what can happen if they don't fulfill various requirements.

It takes a level of experience to contemplate possible worse case scenarios, so this again underscores the importance of having a lawyer who has several years of experience, and many transactions, under his or her belt. While it is not necessary to have a church-goer or even a Christian as your lawyer, a lawyer who *is* a church-goer and an active member of a church—within your denomination in particular—will be helpful because he or she will be able to help you anticipate terms and provisions that are inconsistent with church practice and peculiarities.

COUNSEL IF THE LOAN GOES SOUTH

As discussed in Chapter 16, "If the Loan Goes South," the church's lawyer should help church leaders understand the process. Understanding what comes next and when can be invaluable.

Sometimes, clients are uncomfortable asking questions, asking for concessions, or bringing up uncomfortable subjects. A lawyer is an advocate and as an advocate, I am often asked to bring up and discuss topics and subjects that my client either is not equipped to bring up or is reluctant to bring up. When necessary, I even play the "bad cop" to my client's "good cop."

Now, the drawback to this is that the bank will want your lawyer to speak to their lawyer, and banks typically expect the borrower to pay their attorney's fees. So, some discretion is required when using an attorney in this manner to not unnecessarily run up legal fees. But the "right" attorney will help you navigate this situation.

Further, an experienced lawyer can add a certain degree of credibility to your church and your church's operation. I have often seen bankers take a slightly different tone once they realize that the "novice" in the transaction has competent and knowledgeable legal representation.

OTHER BENEFITS
As a final note, a lawyer with the experience to help church leaders with real estate loans also will likely have the experience to help the church acquire or sell real estate, as well as help church leaders with construction contracts and other related documents.

CLOSING THOUGHTS
If you, as a church leader, do not feel you are getting any—or all—of these areas of expertise from your lawyer, I would suggest that you may not have the "right" lawyer for your church!

ACKNOWLEDGMENTS

H oly Borrowers: Equipping Church Leaders for Building Finance, has been a step of faith and a labor of love.

I am indebted to many who over the years continued to ask me, "Where is your book?" or "How is the book coming?" Some of you said there was a book "in me" early on; others consistently checked in on the progress (or lack thereof!) of this current work. It mattered. My heartfelt gratitude to Rev. Dr. Cassandra Jones, Rev. Cokiesha Bailey Robinson, Rev. Crashana Suddeth, Pastor Godwin Dela and Lady Cynthia Fiagome, Doris Howard, Evadna Nesbit, Jackie Reed, Jeanette Patterson, Juermelda Swift, Kathy Byrd, Rev. Lloyd and Jan Chinn, Shella Gillus, and Rev. Viveca Potter.

Thank you also to that "certain woman" who walked up to me after I preached at a conference in Arkansas to tell me that I'm supposed to be writing. You told me my books will go where I cannot go and will remain long after I'm gone. Years have passed, but I never forgot your loving reprimand.

Thank you to Pastor Gladys Henderson Williams and to Adina Cucicov for sharing your great expertise for the benefit of Holy Borrowers.

To my creative genius friend and Director of Operations for Christ Community, Rev. Tonya Neal, thank you for allowing the Lord's amazing artistry to flow through your mind, heart, eyes, and hands. The cover of Holy Borrowers was in place long before the book was completed, and it inspired me to keep writing! Thank you for everything you've contributed to bring this work to fruition.

To Dr. James Miles who imparted such wisdom 16 years ago that I had to track you down to provide needed input for this book! Thank you for sharing your strategic insights with us all.

To Sharon Simmons, thank you for your years of service to Christ Community and the Kingdom of God overall. Thank you for keeping our church safe! Thank you for your tremendous written contribution to *Holy Borrowers*.

To Dallas Diggs, thank you for excellence in leadership and for being a resource to me and so many. Thank you for your support of *Holy Borrowers*.

To Pete Carey, thank you for providing such a tremendous learning platform in the area of Credit. Thank you for never saving, "no" to a loan without first explaining in detail why—and without first looking for possible alternatives to get to a "yes." Thank you for your support of *Holy Borrowers*.

To all those who taught, challenged, and inspired me during my banking career, thank you. To all those who do banking the right way as trusted advisors, thank you.

To Pastor Brenda Brooks Alexander, co-founder of Eirene Christian Fellowship, now known as Christ Community: You were such an instrumental partner in our launch and early years! Here again, you are an instrumental partner in the launch of *Holy Borrowers*. I salute you as a tremendous woman of God and leader in our community. Thank you!

To Pastor Leonard O. Leach, my deepest appreciation to you for allowing us all to learn from you and from Mt. Hebron Missionary Baptist Church. I praise God for the example you set for us. Special thanks to "David" and "Mark," two wonderful brothers in Christ, for allowing me to interview you. Your time and insights made such a difference.

To my long-term sister, Veta Holt, thank you for meeting with me and sharing your wisdom. From the days at 616 W. Kiest Boulevard until now, you have been a blessing. May you continue to lead at Friendship-West with grace and skill.

To Dr. Frederick Douglass Haynes, III—forever, "Pastor Haynes" to me: I cannot possibly thank you enough for serving as God's launching pad for so much of our ministry and life. You and my sister, Debra, were the first individuals we met when Terrence and I moved to Dallas in 1990, and over these past 30 years, the Lord amazingly demonstrates what a Divinely-strategic, "it came to pass" meeting that was. You have opened doors at great personal cost through which so many of us have followed. I am honored to call you my life-long pastor, brother, mentor, and friend. To Debra Peek-Haynes, thank you for your enduring and inspiring friendship. I would not be here without you. Thank you, Friendship-West Baptist Church, for your years of encouragement and support.

To my church family, Christ Community: No words are enough. I love you with all my heart and thank God that I have the honor of serving Him and this world with you. You are an *amazing* church family who makes my heart glad every day. God bless each and every one of you.

To Dad and Mom, Rev. Clabon and Frankie Autry, thank you for the privilege of being your daughter-in-love; no, your daughter period. You helped lead me to Christ so long ago and your unswerving faith and fortitude are a model for us all.

To my best friend, Rev. Jada Elizabeth Jackson, I pray that when you see *Holy Borrowers,* you also see the fruit of your incomparable friendship, counsel, prayers, and encouragement. It spurred me on when I wanted to stop. Thank you for keeping me on task in completing this book. You are the Lord's great gift to my life and to all who know and love you.

To my sisters, Leslye Miller Fraser and Lori Miller White, I pray this makes you proud. You are the other part of me; I cannot see myself without seeing you both. I am grateful that the "beauty of character" our mother charged us with emulating shines so deeply through you. To my brothers-in-law, Darryl Fraser and Grady White; nieces and nephews, Brittney Fraser, Michael Fraser, Pooja Fraser, Brianna Crayton, Nigel Crayton, and Angela White; and to my entire family: I'm so grateful the Lord blessed me with each of you!

To my beloved sons, Terrence Autry, II and Daniel Autry, I'm so privileged to be your mother. I could not be more proud of you. Thank you for being such dynamic young men. You daily inspire your father and me. I thank God every day for you.

To my amazing husband, soul mate, life partner, and pacesetter, Dr. Terrence Autry—I love you more than you'll ever know. Thank you for asking me to join you on this wonderful journey that is our life together. I wouldn't be where I am without you and would never want to be. I just love being your wife.

A special thanks to Brenda, Dallas, Jada, Pastor Haynes, Pete, Sharon, and Terrence for previewing the manuscript and confirming its impact. Extra gold stars to Jada for re-reading the manuscript so many times!

Above and beyond, the Lord Jesus can never be on a list. He is my totality, my all-in-all. He is the reason for my being, the source of all I do, and the only one I love with all of my heart, with all of my soul, with all of my mind, and with all of my strength. *Holy Borrowers* has been a labor of love. I pray Your will is done through this book and through my life, for Your Great Glory. Amen.

BIBLIOGRAPHY

(n.d.). Retrieved from Friendship-West Baptist Church: https://www.friend-shipwest.org

(n.d.). Retrieved from Collins English Dictionary: https://www.collinsdictio-nary.com/us/dictionary/english/conditions

(2020, January 21). Retrieved from Mt. Hebron Missionary Baptist Church: https://www.onthemount.org/

(2020, January 19). Retrieved from Evangelical Council for Financial Accountability: www.ecfa.org

Alper, B. A. (2015, November 23). *Millennials Are Less Religious Than Older Americans, But Just As Spiritual.* Retrieved December 19, 2019, from Pew Research Center: https://www.pewresearch.org/fact-tank/2015/11/23/millennials-are-less-religious-than-older-americans-but-just-as-spiritual/

Baker, S. (2014, May 20). Arlington's High Point Church Faces Foreclosure on 107-Acre Property. *Fort Worth Star-Telegram.* Arlington, TX. Retrieved June 1, 2019, from https://www.wfaa.com/article/news/local/tarrant-county/arlingtons-high-point-church-faces-foreclosure-on-property/254909446

Banjo, S. (2011, January 25). Churches Find End Is Nigh. *Wall Street Journal.* Roseville, CA. Retrieved June 3, 2019, from https://www.wsj.com/articles/SB10001424052748704115404576096151214141820

Banks, B. (2010, December 27). Foreclosure Threatens Survival of Longtime Lithonia Church. *Atlanta Journal-Constituion.* Retrieved February 27, 2020, from https://www.ajc.com/news/local/foreclosure-threatens-survival-longtime-lithonia-church/mrL8SRHGOG8moCr7MqdAdO/

Burkett, L. (1985). *Using Your Money Wisely: Biblical Principles Under Scrutiny.* Chicago, IL: Moody Publishers.

Business Loan Program Temporary Changes; Paycheck Protection Program. (2020, April 15). Retrieved May 18, 2020, from Federal Register: The Daily Journal of the United States Government: https://www.federalregister.gov/documents/2020/04/15/2020-07672/business-loan-program-temporary-changes-paycheck-protection-program

Cambridge Dictionary. (n.d.). Retrieved March 1, 2020, from https://dictionary.cambridge.org/us/dictionary/english/collateral

Chaney, S., & Guilford, G. (2020, May 14). Nearly Three Million Sought Jobless Benefits Last Week. *Wall Street Journal.* Retrieved May 18, 2020, from https://www.wsj.com/articles/unemployment-benefits-weekly-jobless-claims-coronavirus-05-07-2020-11588813872?mod=article_inline

Chaney, S., & Morath, E. (2020, May 8). April Unemployment Rate Rose to a Record 14.7%. *Wall Street Journal.* Retrieved May 8, 2020, from https://www.wsj.com/articles/april-jobs-report-coronavirus-2020-11588888089?mod=hp_lead_pos1&mod=article_inline&mod=hp_lead_pos1

Christian Standard Bible. (2017). Nashville: Holman Bible Publishers.

Christopher, J. C. (2012). *Rich Church, Poor Church: Keys to Effective Financial Ministry.* Nashville, TN: Abingdon Press.

Church Bonds. (n.d.). Retrieved from Peachstate Financial Services: https://www.peachstatefinancial.com/church-bonds/

Churches in Financial Distress. (2009, June 19). Retrieved from Religion & Ethics Newsweekly: https://www.pbs.org/wnet/religionandethics/2009/06/19/june-19-2009-churches-in-financial-distress/3281/

Clark, J. (1938). Conference Reports of The Church of Jesus Christ of Latter-day Saints. 108th Annual Conference April 1938. Salt Lake City: The Church of Jesus Christ of Latter-day Saints. Retrieved November 7, 2019, from https://archive.org/details/conferencereport1938a/page/n103/mode/2up

Conway, D. (1999). Clergy as Reluctant Stewards of Congregational Resources. In M. Chaves, & S. L. Miller (Eds.), *Financing American Religion* (pp. 100-101). Lanham, MD: AltaMira Press.

COVID-19 Dashboard by the Center for Systems Science and Engineering at Johns Hopkins University. (2020, May 18). Retrieved May 18, 2020, from Johns

Hopkins University & Medicine Coronavirus Resource Center: https://coronavirus.jhu.edu/map.html

Due. (2017, October 24). Retrieved March 1, 2020, from Need a Secured Loan? Here's a Guide to Understanding Collateral: https://due.com/blog/guide-to-understanding-collateral/

ECFA History. (2020, January 17). Retrieved from www.ecfa.org: https://www.ecfa.org/Content/GeneralBackground

Edney, H. E. (2013). Black Bankers President warns Churches: Change the Way You Do Business. *Wire News.* Washington, D.C. Retrieved June 3, 2019, from http://triceedneywire.com/index.php?option=com_content&view=article&id=1767:black-bankers-president-warns-churches-change-the-way-you-do-business-&catid=54&Itemid=208

FDIC Law, Regulations, Related Acts - Part 323 - Appraisals. (n.d.). Retrieved December 20, 2019, from Federal Deposit Insurance Corporation: https://www.fdic.gov/regulations/laws/rules/2000-4300.html

Federal Deposit Insurance Corporation. (2007, January 22). *FDIC's Supervisory Policy on Predatory Lending.* Retrieved February 29, 2020, from www.fdic.gov: https://www.fdic.gov/news/news/financial/2007/fil07006.pdf

Federal Fair Lending Regulations and Statutes. (n.d.). Fair Housing Act. Retrieved January 29, 2020, from https://www.federalreserve.gov/boarddocs/supmanual/cch/fair_lend_fhact.pdf

Flitter, E. (2019, December 11). This is What Racism Sounds Like in the Banking Industry. *The New York Times.* Retrieved December 16, 2019, from https://www.nytimes.com/2019/12/11/business/jpmorgan-banking-racism.html?smid=nytcore-ios-share

Garnet Capital Advisors. (2019, May 15). *Church Foreclosures Are on the Rise - Here's What Lenders Need to Know.* Retrieved March 1, 2020, from Garnet Capital Advisors Blog: https://www.garnetcapital.com/news/article/Church-Foreclosures-Are-on-the-Rise----Heres-What/40062757

Glantz, A., & Martinez, E. (2018, February 17). Modern-day redlining: How Banks Block People of Color From Homeownership. *Chicago Tribune.* Retrieved November 7, 2019, from https://www.chicagotribune.com/business/ct-biz-modern-day-redlining-20180215-story.html

Good News Bible. (1994). Bible Societies/HarperCollins Publishers Ltd UK.

International Standard Version Bible. (1996). The ISV Foundation.

Jamieson, J. T., & Jamieson, P. D. (2009). *Ministry and Money: A Practical Guide for Pastors.* Louisville, Kentucky: Westminster John Knox Press.

Johnson, B. (n.d.). *The Sinking of RMS Titanic.* Retrieved February 29, 2020, from HIstoric UK: The History and Heritage Accommodation Guide: https://www.historic-uk.com/HistoryUK/HistoryofBritain/RMS-Titanic-the-unsinkable-ship/

King James Version of the Holy Bible. (1611).

Laskow, S. (2018, September 19). A Highway in Cape Town Has Been Left Half-Finished for 40 Years. *Atlas Obscura.* Retrieved December 20, 2019, from https://www.atlasobscura.com/articles/cape-town-unfinished-freeway

Leubsdorf, B. (2014, December 4). Decline in Church-Building Reflects Changed Tastes and Times. *The Wall Street Journal.* Retrieved September 24, 2019, from https://www.wsj.com/articles/decline-in-church-building-reflects-changed-tastes-and-times-1417714642

Maps & Trends: New Cases of COVID-19 in World Countries. (2020, May 8). Retrieved May 9, 2020, from Johns Hopkins University & Medicine Coronavirus Resource Center: https://coronavirus.jhu.edu/data/new-cases

Merriam-Webster's Unabridged Dictionary. (n.d.). Retrieved June 27, 2019, from https://www.merriam-webster.com/dictionary/finance

Merritt, J. (2018, November 25). America's Epidemic of Empty Churches. *The Atlantic.* Retrieved September 24, 2019, from https://www.theatlantic.com/ideas/archive/2018/11/what-should-america-do-its-empty-church-buildings/576592/

New American Standard Bible. (1995). La Habra: The Lockman Foundation.

Newport, F. (2017, July 18). More U.S. Protestants Have No Specific Denominational Identity. *Gallup.* Retrieved January 28, 2020, from https://news.gallup.com/poll/214208/protestants-no-specific-denominational-iden-tity.aspx

Newport, F. (2018, September 7). Church Leaders and Declining Religious Service Attendance. *Polling Matters.* Retrieved September 23, 2019, from https://news.gallup.com/opinion/polling-matters/242015/church-lead-ers-declining-religious-service-attendance.aspx

Ortiz, A. (2019, December 13). JPMorgan Chase C.E.O. Says It Needs to Do More to Tackle Racism. *The New York Times*. Retrieved December 16, 2019, from https://www.nytimes.com/2019/12/13/business/Jamie-Dimon-racism-chase. html?action=click&module=RelatedLinks&pgtype=Article

Pew Research Center: Religion & Public Life. (2009, March 12). Is a Bad Economy Good for Church Attendance? Retrieved September 21, 2019, from https://www.pewforum.org/2009/03/12/ is-a-bad-economy-good-for-church-attendance/

Pew Research Center: Religion & Public Life. (2018, June 13). The Age Gap in Religion Around the World. Retrieved September 21, 2019, from https://www. pewforum.org/2018/06/13/the-age-gap-in-religion-around-the-world/

Phaneuf, A. (2019, August 26). *Here is a List of the Largest Banks in the United States by Assets in 2020*. Retrieved December 16, 2019, from Business Insider: https://www.businessinsider.com/largest-banks-us-list

Porter, M. E. (1985). *Competitive Advantage: Crating and Sustaining Superior Performance*. New York, NY: The Free Press.

Radcliff Pastor Resigns as Gloryland Harvest Faces Foreclosure. (2014, March 25). Retrieved from WDRB.com: https://www.wdrb.com/news/radcliff-pas-tor-resigns-as-gloryland-harvest-faces-foreclosure-still-running/article_ 76f3a709-9693-5d36-aeee-056320e74e4e.html

Rainer, A. (2018, July 13). Should Churches Go Into Debt? *Lifeway*, p. 1. Retrieved August 6, 2019, from https://factsandtrends.net/2018/07/13/ should-churches-go-into-debt/

Rainer, T. S. (2014). *Autopsy of a Deceased Church: 12 Ways to Keep Yours Alive*. Nashville, TN: B&H Publishing Group.

Reid, T. (2012, March 8). Banks Foreclosing on Churches in Record Numbers. *Reuters*. (J. Weber, & M. Perry, Eds.) Los Angeles, CA. Retrieved June 1, 2019, from https://www.reuters.com/article/us-usa-housing-churches/banks-fore-closing-on-churches-in-record-numbers-idUSBRE82803120120309

Rolling Updates on Coronavirus Disease (COVID-19). (2020, May 7). Retrieved May 9, 2020, from World Health Organization: https://www.who.int/ emergencies/diseases/novel-coronavirus-2019/events-as-they-happen

Rothstein, R. (2017). *The Color of Law: A Forgotten Hisotry of How Our Government Segregated America*. New York, NY: Liveright Publishing Corporation.

Schneider, C. (2011, February 2). Foreclosure Crisis Hitting Some Metro Churches. *The Atlanta Journal-Constitution*. Retrieved September 17, 2019, from https://www.ajc.com/business/foreclosure-crisis-hitting-some-metro-churches/73kmzappmPRlavfWD41aaM/

Shusman, B. (2017, January 13). American Dream of Home Ownership Changing. *Voice of America*. Retrieved August 6, 2019, from https://www.voanews.com/usa/american-dream-home-ownership-changing

Society, A. B. (1966, 1967, 1970, 1971, 1976, 1979). *Good News Translation*. United States: HaperCollins.

Son, H. (2019, December 13). Jamie Dimon Says He's 'Disgusted by Racism' and Progress is Needed at JP Morgan After Report. *The New York Times*. Retrieved December 13, 2019, from https://www.cnbc.com/2019/12/13/jamie-dimon-says-hes-disgusted-by-racism-and-progress-is-needed-at-jp-morgan-after-report.html

Sorensen, M. (2020, May 11). *PPP Loan Developments: Only $120 Billion Left, Favorable Forgiveness Guidance from SBA and IRS Tax Pitfall*. Retrieved May 18, 2020, from Entrepreneur: https://www.entrepreneur.com/article/350444

Stack Exchange. (n.d.). Retrieved February 24, 2020, from Stack Exchange: https://english.stackexchange.com/search?q=skin+in+the+game

State COVID-19 Data by Race. (2020, May 7). Retrieved May 8, 2020, from Johns Hopkins University & Medicine: https://coronavirus.jhu.edu/data/racial-data-transparency

Story, L. (2008, December 26). Foreclosures Don't Spare the House of God. *New York Times*. Retrieved February 27, 2020, from https://www.nytimes.com/2008/12/27/business/27church.html

The Holy Bible, English Standard Version* (ESV*). (2001). Wheaton, IL: Crossway Bibles.

The Holy Bible, New International Version. (2011). Grand Rapids: Zondervan.

U.S. Small Business Administration Office of Advocacy. (2018, August). Frequently Asked Questions About Small Business. Retrieved January 26, 2020, from https://cdn.advocacy.sba.gov/wp-content/uploads/2017/08/04125711/Frequently-Asked-Questions-Small-Business-2018.pdf

Understanding Employee vs. Contractor Designation. (2017, July 20). Retrieved May 8, 2020, from Internal Revenue Service: Understanding Employee vs. Contractor Designation," Internal Revenue Service, July 20, 2017, online: https://www.irs.gov/newsroom/understanding-employee-vs-contractor-designation.

Vanderbloemen, W., & Bird, W. (2014). *Next: Pastoral Succession That Works.* Grand Rapids, MI: Baker Books.

Washington, K. A. (Ed.). (2006). *NIV Aspire: The New Women of Color Study Bible.* Grand Rapids, MI: Zondervan.

What is USPAP? (n.d.). Retrieved December 20, 2019, from The Appraisal Foundation: https://www.appraisalfoundation.org/imis/TAF/Standards/Appraisal_Standards/Uniform_Standards_of_Professional_Appraisal_Practice/TAF/USPAP.aspx?hkey=a6420a67-dbfa-41b3-9878-fac35923d2af

Williams, V. (2020, May 6). Disproportionately Black Counties Account for Over Half of Coronavirus Cases in the U.S. and nearly 60% of Deaths, Studies Find. *Washington Post.* Retrieved May 8, 2020, from https://www.washingtonpost.com/nation/2020/05/06/study-finds-that-disproportionately-black-counties-account-more-than-half-covid-19-cases-us-nearly-60-percent-deaths/

INDEX OF KEY TERMS AND TOPICS

Amortization Schedule 45
Appraisals 99,100,101,104,151,152,261
Attorney 194,195,281,282

Balance Sheet 24,25,43,262,266
Balloon Note 46,179,180,181,182,184
Boiler Plate Documents 152,153

Capital xiii,83,84,88,98,108,109,110,.
115,141,228,264,275
Capital Campaign 83,84,85,86,88,89,.
172,275
Cash Flow 72,83,84,85,86,87,88,89,.
90,91,108,110,116,145,147,149,174,.
215,271,277,279
Cash Flow Statement 25,26,268
Character 72,73,75,76,80,81,84,188
Collateral 92,93,95,97,99,105,108,151,.
264
Commitment Fee 49,50
Commitment Letter 149,150,151
Conditions 117,119,120,130,224
Construction Loans 167,175
Contingency Costs 173
Covenants 148,149,150,162,195,283,284
Credit Reports 77,78

Debt Financing 43
Debt Schedule 261,263
Debt Service Coverage 88,140,141,148,.
193,269,270,271,274
Debt-to-Equity Ratio 112,113
Deed in Lieu of Foreclosure 201
Demographics 56,128
Discrimination 2,53,56,57,58,60,65,.
124
Diversification of Donations 138

Environmental Risks 105,106,262
Equity Financing 43

Financial Reporting Requirements 161
Financial Statement Quality 27
Five C's of Credit 72
Fixed Interest Rates 47
Floating Interest Rates 47
Forbearance Agreement 198
Formal Underwriting 147
Fund Accounting 28

Giving Unit 134
Ground-Up Construction Projects 167

Income Statement 25,26,28,262,266,
    267,274,277
Interest Expense 5

Key Person Life Insurance 65,127

Lawyer. *See* Attorney
Leverage 110,111,112,113
Loan Closing 153
Loan-to-Value 97,115,138

Maximum Debt Per Giving Unit 137
Maximum Debt Service to Annual
    Unrestricted Tithes and Offerings
    136
Maximum Debt to Annual Unrestricted
    Tithes and Offerings 136
Mechanics' Lien 173
Minimum Age of Church 134
Minimum Church Size 134
Minimum Contribution Per Giving
    Unit 137
Minimum Liquidity 139
Minimum Tenure of Senior Pastor 135
Modification Agreement 197

Non-Denominational Churches 135
No Oral Agreements Clause 52

Opportunity Costs 8
Origination Fee. *See* Commitment Fee

Paycheck Protection Program 207
Personal Guaranty 107
Predatory Lending xiv,xv
Prepayment Penalty 48

Racism. *See* Discrimination
Raw Land 105
Redlining x,58,59,60,66
Renovation Construction Projects 168

Seven Standards of Responsible
    StewardshipTM 223
Sexism. *See* Discrimination
Statement of Activities. *See* Income
    Statement
Statement of Cash Flows. *See* Cash
    Flow Statement
Statement of Financial Position. *See*
    Balance Sheet
Succession Planning 119,127,128,136
Survey 152
Sustainable Competitive Advantage 129

Technical Default 148,162,190,193,197,
    202
Tenant Income 90
Term of Loan 45
Term Sheet 146,147,149,150
Title Company 152
Types of Commercial Loans 50

CPSIA information can be obtained
at www.ICGtesting.com
Printed in the USA
LVHW021158280720
661632LV00020B/310

9 781735 028200